# Dark Smiles

# Dark Smiles

## RACE AND DESIRE IN GEORGE ELIOT

### Alicia Carroll

OHIO UNIVERSITY PRESS

ATHENS

Earlier versions of material in this book originally appeared in the journals cited below. All material is reprinted by permission and with thanks
to the editors of *Novel* and to the trustees of Brown University and to the
editors of *Journal of English and German Philology* and the trustees of the
University of Illinois.

"The *Giaour*'s Campaign: Desire and the Other in *Felix Holt: The
Radical*," *Novel: A Forum on Fiction* 30 (winter 1997): 237–58.

"Arabian Nights: Make-Believe, Exoticism, and Desire in *Daniel
Deronda*," *Journal of English and German Philology* (April 1999): 219–38.

Cover art credit: *The Greek Slave*, Hiram Powers, 1846, marble statue, 65 x
19 $^{1}/_{2}$ in. In the collection of the Corcoran Gallery of Art, Washington,
D.C., gift of William Wilson Corcoran.

Ohio University Press, Athens, Ohio 45701

09 08 07 06 05 04 03      5 4 3 2 1

*Library of Congress Cataloging-in-Publication Data*
Carroll, Alicia, 1960-
    Dark smiles : race and desire in George Eliot / Alicia Carroll.
       p. cm.
    Includes bibliographical references and index.
    ISBN 0-8214-1441-0 (alk. paper)
       1. Eliot, George, 1819-1880—Criticism and interpretation. 2. Eliot,
George, 1819-1880—Views on race. 3. Difference (Psychology) in literature. 4. Ethnicity in literature. 5. Exoticism in literature. 6. Desire in literature. 7. Race in literature. 8. Sex in literature. I. Title.

PR4692.R25 C37 2002
823'.8—dc21
                                                           2002016928

*For Rob and Alexandra*

# Contents

# Illustrations

Following page 60

**PLATE 1:**
Hiram Powers's *The Greek Slave*.

**PLATE 2:**
Henriette Browne's *A Greek Captive*.

**PLATE 3:**
Julia Margaret Cameron's *The Shunamite Woman and Her Dead Son*.

**PLATE 4:**
William Harvey's *Queen Budoor in Captivity*.

# Acknowledgments

I COULD NOT have completed this book without the friendship, collegiality, and good sense of many people. First, I am grateful to my teacher and advisor Fred Kaplan, who has listened, read, and responded to my work on Eliot from the beginning. To N. John Hall and Anne Humpherys, I am also indebted for their generous reading of my work on Eliot during my student years at the Graduate Center of the City University of New York. David Sanders and my anonymous readers at Ohio University Press have patiently provided encouragement and insight during this project's evolution from manuscript to book. My early teacher, Tom Lewis, has been consistently good-humored, a critical reader and good friend over the years. David Auerbach, Christina Boufis, Carol Johnson, Jacqueline Lautin, Hope Parisi, and Jay Prosser are linked in my mind with all the particularly excellent qualities of learning to become a scholar in New York City. In my current position at Auburn, many new colleagues have been instrumental in the completion of this project. I would like to thank Paula Backscheider and Constance Relihan in particular for reading and responding to my work. They know how valuable their contributions have been. Ruth Crocker, Jacqueline Foertsch, Peter Logan, and Hilary Wyss have been indispensable sources of scholarly inspiration and academic community here in Alabama. My students at Auburn have tolerated my enthusiasm for George Eliot with grace; in the classroom they have listened, talked, and written back. I thank them for what they have taught me. Nancy Armstrong and Achsah Guibbory of *Novel* and *The Journal of English and Germanic Philology*, respectively, deserve my thanks for their interest in and suggestions for earlier versions of the third and fifth chapters here. I am grateful to the J. Paul Getty Museum, the Tate Gallery, and the Corcoran for permission to reproduce the artwork that appears in this book. Auburn University supported my work with a Competitive Research Grant, a Humanities Development Fund Grant, and a College of Liberal Arts Grant. All were instrumental in the completion of this project.

But my largest debts are personal ones. My parents Davis Carroll and Valera Carroll gave me much. I hope that all they taught me is evident here. I am grateful to my husband's parents, Jan Kulick and the late Richard Kulick, for their help and their confidence in this project. My uncle and aunt W. L. Smith and Judy Smith helped materially at the beginning when I needed it most. During the writing process, Becca Bridges, my sister Elizabeth Carroll, Jill Lewis, Susan Varisco, Mary and Phil Warbase, Rhoda Weyr, and Claire Wilson often provided encouragement. Finally, it is to Rob and Alexandra that I am most indebted. They know what a book costs and have paid it; so to them all that is good here is dedicated. The mistakes are exclusively my own.

# Introduction

IN 1851, at the Crystal Palace in London, the American artist Hiram Powers exhibited *The Greek Slave* (1846) (plate 1), his life-size sculpture of a slim, idealized female nude. Wrought of the whitest marble, the sculpture is a powerfully iconographic representation of race and desire. The statue's head is shamefully, gracefully, inclined, her eyes averted from the Turkish marketplace in which she stands for sale. A paradigm of modest, sexually vulnerable "innocent white womanhood," the image of the Greek slave was used to raise sympathy and money for the defense of Greece against the Ottoman Turks.[1] The Greek woman sold into the slavery of the Turkish harem was a metaphor for the sacking of classical values; her sexual violation by the "bestial" Turks represented the ultimate desecration of Western civilization itself.[2] Powers's image of the Greek slave was used to raise money for the abolitionist cause in England and in America. There, ironically, the image was also used in Confederate states to raise money for Greek independence.

Those moved by the statue found the perversity of slavery especially dramatized in the figure because she was white. Her degradation and violation seemed the more pernicious to Frederick Douglass, for example, because her master was imagined as a Turk or "Mussulman," an "infidel" who was profoundly Other to Westerners.[3] Indeed, the nude statue itself, so idealized as to be literally smoothed of the marks of adult sexuality, is not erotic, but prim, chaste, and childlike in her marble purity. But although the slave is not herself a desirous subject, her viewer is. Desire belongs to her buyer and in the act of looking, the viewer mimics his "cruel" role. Approaching the statue, then, one simultaneously steps into a representation of the Turkish marketplace and into the boundaries of Victorian sex roles. Chastity and nondesirous innocence are powerfully represented as white, Christian, and female; sexual experience and desire are as powerfully represented in the mind's eye of the viewer as dark, "infidel," and male, the subject position which the viewer shares.[4] The tragedy of the Greek slave lies not just in her violation by the "Turk," but also in her future captivity in a buyer's harem where she might become one among many of her master/husband's sexual partners: Powers's "*Greek Slave* pauses on the threshold of a momentous change in her life; her future in the harem is the great unstated drama that gives the sculpture its poignancy."[5] Painted almost obsessively by Delacroix, Gérôme, Ingres, Renoir, Matisse, and others as a variation on the Orientalist theme of the odalisque, the nude, white captive highlights a veritable phobia of the nineteenth century: the violation of an exposed or partially veiled white woman captive whose whiteness is exaggerated in contrast to the body of a "dark" attendant of the harem or amongst the bodies of many dark women.[6] Such representations in nineteenth-century Western art act, Meyda Yeğenoğlu writes, to indict the "cultural practices and religious customs of Oriental societies which are shown to be monstrously oppressing women. Hence the barbarity of the Orient is evidenced in the way cultural traditions shape the life of its women."[7] The statue, like many nineteenth-century Orientalist representations, made human desire publicly visible, allowing "viewers" to "confront their own erotic impulses," while "the device of the imaginary Turkish captors enabled [Hiram Powers's] audience to participate in the gaze of sensuality and to distance themselves from it simultaneously."[8] Envisioning the captive woman on the "threshold" of her sexual violation then indicts the "barbarism" of the Other and reifies the "purity" of the white subject, reclaiming and racializing her innocence or her violation as white.[9]

Accompanied by John Chapman, a man with whom she had shared some degree of intimacy, Mary Ann Evans visited the Great Exhibition where *The Greek Slave* was prominently displayed. The visit articulates the vast abyss between Victorian representations and Victorian realities. Having ended the intimacy which had provoked much unhappiness between Chapman, his wife, his mistress, and Evans herself, the two met at the exhibition on new terms and neutral ground.[10] For the postcolonial critic, it is tantalizing to wonder what Mary Ann Evans made of the statue if she encountered it that day; certainly, its celebrity made *The Greek Slave* difficult to avoid.[11] As George Eliot would later write in *Felix Holt: The Radical* (1866), of an "Oriental" Englishman who had purchased his own Greek slave for a wife, it is tempting to speculate. Of course, Eliot's frequent visits to galleries, exhibitions, and museums in London and Europe would have made the popular genre of the Turkish slave market and its "human wares" very familiar to her (*JGE*, 47). However, the impression of the statue, if indeed Eliot ever recorded one, is gone, ephemeral as the cut leaves of Chapman's diary wherein he recorded the details of his "love" for three women with whom he shared a large house in London.[12] Still, the irony of the moment resonates. So far from the statue's image of girlish white innocence and darkened male desire, the lives of these Victorians speak to the subtext of sexual transgression which was very much alive under the rigorously drawn morality of their day. For all the recent interest in the statue as an icon of Victorian sexual and racial politics, *The Greek Slave's* insistent naïveté contrasts almost crudely with the sophisticated complexities of two such actual people as Mary Ann Evans and John Chapman.

Powerful representations of an Other's "desire" for chaste "white" femininity through such commodities as *The Greek Slave* become crucially important to understanding Victorian fashionings of "desire" and their impact on forms like the novel as well as on the culture as a whole. In this book I will make the assumption, with materialist feminists and cultural historians, that sexual "desire" or erotic longing is shaped and developed by social experience, particularly through heteronormative encounters such as "the individual's encounter with the nuclear family and with the symbolic systems" which saturate "social arrangements." Representations of such encounters in Eliot's fictions seem an important record of what we "need to know" about "how women have come to be who they are though history" and particularly through heteronormative courtship narratives.[13] Indeed, as Nancy Armstrong argues, in such narratives the representation of sex "determines what one knows to be sex, the particular form sex assumes in one age as opposed to another, and the political interests these various forms may have served."[14] Clearly, Eliot's representations of desire represent a process through which Western women have fashioned their sexuality or have had their sexuality fashioned for them as a category opposing the "desirous," acquisitive sexuality of Other peoples.

Negotiating the conservative mainstream in her fiction, as she had in life, George Eliot became deeply engaged in representations of desire which often question and subvert the *status quo* of white innocence and dark desire as it is represented in the most conventional nineteenth-century images of racial and ethnic otherness like *The Greek Slave* or other Orientalist visions of the harem. Eliot's interest in representing the "captivity" of both women's and men's desire has long been remarked upon; however, the intersections of race and gender in her work remain a rich field of investigation.[15] Eliot's narratives often refuse the clarity of her contemporaries' representations of Otherness. "Dark" desire in her work may subsume representations of white innocence, constructing multiple discourses of resistance within the "borders" that bind her poetry, fiction, and essays.[16] Eliot's dark-haired, black-eyed heroines, like the "Gypsies" Maggie Tulliver of *The Mill on the Floss* (1860) or Fedalma of *The Spanish Gypsy* (1868), are "dark," "rough" questions posed to the smooth assumptions of Victorian images of chaste whiteness like *The Greek Slave*.[17] Indeed, like her contemporaries, the painter Henriette Browne (1829–1901) or the photographer Julia Margaret Cameron (1815–1879), who used the school of Orientalism to explore, respectively, the education of girls and the experience of maternity, George Eliot's use of Orientalism and racial Otherness often explores themes absent from the odalisques of male artists like Powers. Reading Eliot's work against the work of other women artists of her time can reveal the extent to which she too may be revising the extant traditions of Othering to address her own concerns about female agency.

The questions I will explore in this study similarly challenge many of our own postcolonial assumptions about the imperialist agenda of the Victorian novel. In her consistent narrative attraction to the ethnic or racial other, the novelist of the Midlands questions not just stereotypes of white innocence and dark desire but also the stereotype of the British novelist as a wholeheartedly committed participant in the national project of empire. Eliot's Others reveal just how conflicted such participation can be. If the emphasis of much recent work is to argue for or against the novelist as an agent of empire, my goal is not to rehabilitate Eliot as a resistor to that project, for I agree that "[b]y contemporary standards, all Victorians would stand accused."[18] Rather, I want to begin to unfold the multiple discourses and epistemologies Eliot constructs within her representations of the desirous English self and the racial or ethnic other.

Studying Victorian notions of race necessitates an explanation of my own use of the term "Other." The dangers of the trope of the "Other," as Henry Louis Gates Jr. argues, are still too much with us. For that reason, it is essential to note that the terms "race," "blood," "exotic," "Gypsy," and "Oriental" are always used here with the knowledge that they are particular constructs. In studying their particularities, George Eliot's particularities, and those of her contemporaries, I, as Gates urged in 1985, demarcate these terms with quotation marks when their cultural constructedness is not otherwise overtly stated. I am assuming that since the publication of Gates's landmark *"Race," Writing, and Difference* (1986), I am addressing a community that is also aware of the socially, culturally, and historically constructed aspects of these terms.

In my use of the terms "cultural Other" and "Other," I write from a perspective which recognizes Otherness as an invention of a dominant culture, here the culture of Victorian England. I capitalize the first initial of "Other" in order to suggest its constructedness. Indeed, in using this term I wish to invoke and emphasize, not share, the sense of distance and strangeness with which Victorians viewed non-English peoples. In my use of this word, as in my use of the terms "race" and "blood" I demarcate their socially constructed quality with quotation marks when their quality as cultural constructions is otherwise unclear. Since the publications of Edward Said's *Orientalism* and *Culture and Imperialism,* the very denotations of these words have changed to include an awareness of the racial stereotypes and false assumptions that the British and Westerners have applied to people of other cultures and races.

Finally, even as George Eliot practices reverse Orientalism or reverse discrimination where value is ultimately placed on the Other over the English, she takes liberties with those Others themselves, appropriating their stories for her own purposes. She is, perhaps like all of us, self-interested. While she considered herself "a foreigner on the earth," she remained indisputably English in the details of her social-realist landscapes (*GEL,* 1:335). Her career-long interest in Otherness, and her championing of the Other, however, often seek less to reinscribe than to reinvent the rigid boundaries, the cultural prisons, which bind us all.

# Abbreviations

# ONE

# *Eroticizing the Other*

TO SPEAK OF the erotic in her novels, George Eliot habitually writes of something else. Infamous for the power of her silences, Eliot is as famous for a desirous subtext that avoids representations of the body only to pervade the very landscapes of her Midlands settings.[1] The middle-class or gentle English body, female or male, demanded modesty in narration, and, writing around that constraint, George Eliot, paradoxically the quintessential novelist of "English life," often renders the erotic through the presence of a racial or ethnic Other who enters her poetry, short fiction, and novels or essays through allusions to or representations of the Gypsy, Jew, "Oriental," or African.[2] The "novelist of the Midlands" constructs her experience of home by alluding consistently, in a career-long pattern, to the lives of racial and ethnic Others, many of whom she knew only in books. In English and European sources, the Others whom Eliot studied rarely spoke for themselves; their voices were mediated, appropriated, and translated through fictional, theatrical, scientific, political, and historical narratives of discovery, definition, and classification. Clearly opposing the contemporary construction of a nondesirous English subjectivity, Eliot yet insists that an eroticized Other speak what the English subject may not, and as she does so she protests her own confinement over Other bodies. A recurrent engagement with racial difference in George Eliot's works may, optimistically, "seek to control," to end "the authority by which 'printed books' construct paradigms that nurture racial hatred."[3] When her narratives of women's lives, however, rely upon the eroticized Other to oppose home culture's compulsory erotic silence, the phenomenon of "racial desire"

1

becomes a central problem.[4] Eliot's Others provide perhaps the most provocative Victorian movement "backwards and forwards" between contemporary discourses of race that comply with and resist the binary division of self and Other that we associate with nineteenth-century racist discourse.[5]

In Eliot's work, the desire for an Other body is palpable, disruptive, and ultimately unresolved in moments of acute erotic longing or "primal" identification.[6] Such desires construct a familiar paradigm; the privileged white author, Barbara Smith writes, falls prey to the "seductions of reading her own experience as normative and fetishiz[es] the experience of the Other."[7] In fetishizing what is not perceived as English, however, Eliot seems again and again to indict her own cultural categories and to identify the "normative" idea of white women's sexual innocence as punitive.[8] George Eliot's writings then avoid "that Victorian 'writing the nation'" which Deirdre David describes as "produced by women and which is about women as resonant symbols of sacrifice for civilizing the 'native' and women as emblems of correct colonial governance."[9] Her representations of the desirous Other anxiously resist authoritative or official definitions established in the nineteenth century primarily by masculinist responses to cultural icons of racial desire. Representations such as Leila of George Gordon Byron's poem, *The Giaour* (1813), or the odalisque and her "black" attendant in Edouard Manet's painting *Olympia* (1863), assume racial difference to be a sign of the sexual availability of women to European men. Implicit to such depictions is the "commonplace that the primitive was associated with unbridled sexuality."[10] Eliot's conflicting desires to represent and discipline Other and domestic sexualities create anxious narratives that complicate the voyeurism we associate with the odalisques of Manet and Byron. That Eliot allows Maggie Tulliver, for example, a "primitive" childhood, but insists upon an egregiously chaste adult womanhood for her heroine reflects the complex anxieties of Eliot's appropriations.[11] Indeed, careful narrative exhibitions and displays of the disciplining of "racial desire," often with tragic consequences, contradict Eliot's attempts to purge her texts of the same.

As I shall argue in the chapters to come, Eliot's appropriations of Greek and Arabian captivity, Gypsy travelers, proto-Zionism, and native uprisings raise moral questions for the contemporary postcolonial feminist critic. Even as Eliot's representations of Otherness and her racialized discourses of desire often avoid the "civilizing responsibility" that inspired Victorian feminists to envision "the agent of civilization [as] woman herself" and "their sex as the vessel of a better—which was to say, more civilized—society," her images of racial darkness engage an entrenched nineteenth-century habit of racist voyeurism.[12] As desire is figured through images of darkness and ethnic Otherness throughout Eliot's canon, her writings may anticipate the colonialist literature that will succeed her, the "explosion of romantic images of Western women in the empire" in "late nineteenth- and early twentieth-century" British literature.[13] As in those plots, in Eliot's narratives the assumption of the "marginality" of racial difference risks "mask[ing] 'complicity' [with imperialism] on one hand or authoritarianism on the other."[14] Many of the recent postcolonial readings of George Eliot then have been engaged either with celebrating her work, on Judaism, for example, as progressive and enlightened, or chiding the same as essentially reifying a colonizing, hegemonic authority.[15] It strikes me that absent from these debates is an investigation of how Eliot's eroticized Others elide those margins to the right and left of the centers of hegemonic colonialist discourses; what is most remarkable about Eliot's representations is their instability. Other than their obvious recurrence, no single pattern defines or marks Eliot's representations of Otherness. Particularly in the shifting of their gendering, Eliot's Others resist "stable" or static meanings. Within the same novel, they may be represented as threatening erotic outsiders who must be "purged" from the text, as unwilling captive queens, or as competent Radicals who marry into British society and attempt to resist assimilation or conversion.[16] Eliot's concessions to and divergences from conventional stereotypes of desirous Others are essential to her negotiation of novel writing itself.

IF WE VIEW "racial desire" from the heart of English writing, its most familiar erotic paradigm situates it as a British man's "temp[tation]" to "embrace" a phobia by "immersing [him]self in— or, more appropriately, 'penetrating'—the Other." We read racial desire in the British novel as a white man's potential lapse, "most commonly manifested in the form of an erotic relation with a native woman." In this model the colonizer's "fantasy of erotic domination, the sexual relation with the native woman appeals to [his] imagination because it combines erotic desire with the desire for mastery." Ali Behdad suggests that in the most mainstream literary vision of this sexual fantasy, the fiction of Rudyard Kipling, the British seek the "Oriental passion and impulsiveness" of the "old *Arabian Nights*" (from Kipling's 1888 *Plain Tales from the Hills*, 127, 131) in contemporary India. "In contrast to the sexually inhibited women of the club, the native woman is represented as a sexualized figure incapable of resisting her master's desire; the racial difference makes her powerless."[17] Western women writers, Meyda Yeğenoğlu suggests, often "supplement" this masculinist colonial gaze and its "epistemic violence" as they take upon themselves the role of penetrator and voyeur, particularly in narratives of the harem, a space Western men could not enter. For example, even though she is there alone in her narratives of the Turkish harem, Lady Mary Wortley Montagu, in her *Travel Letters* (1763), imagines a male presence penetrating the women's quarters she visits. "To tell you the truth," she writes, "I had wickedness enough to wish secretly that Mr. Gervase [eighteenth-century Orientalist painter] could have been there invisible. I fancy it would have much improved his art to see so many fine Women naked in different postures." Montagu's "look," Yeğenoğlu argues, "then turns into a masculine gaze. She takes up the masculine, phallic position and employs his *frame* in enjoyment, 'wickedly.'"[18]

Perhaps the most difficult aspect of reading Eliot on race and desire is her dual reliance upon and rejection of masculinist hegemonic discourses like these. Even as she turns an Other's story into a "self-reflexive" or "narcissistic" one about English women, she consistently alters the gendering of her representations to subvert the power discourses of the masculinist-colonial model as it appears above. Within that model "the transgressive desire for the native woman and the desire for colonial power reproduce each other . . . in a spiral relation that engenders only alienation and discontent," the serial adulteries of Kipling's officers and the violence of their occupation of India, for example.[19] In Eliot's writings, the enclosed spiral of such literary sexual and political exploitations is disrupted when its grossest forms—like British participation in the slave trade in Turkey—are made visible, at "home," under the "pale English sunshine" of her domestic settings (*FH,* 582).

If phallocentric contemporary culture sought to penetrate the veil in representations of the harem, Eliot's Others, particularly her celibate women heroines, seem as likely to appropriate the veil themselves. It is no surprise that George Eliot admired the work of the painter Henriette Browne, who painted primarily two subjects: the

Christian cloister and the harem. Fond of veiling or draping female figures in her literature, Eliot too often places female characters in iconic or representative poses that are similar to nineteenth-century visual representations of "white captivity" such as those painted by Browne. Her *Greek Captive* (1863) is a small girl (plate 2), clearly not pubescent, and not naked like Hiram Powers's statue of the same subject, but wearing a Turkish costume that suggests a veil. Unlike the "white thunder" of the marble statue, Browne's painter's palette is dark: rose, brown, and black, and the Greek child's very dark hair and eyes contest the idea of difference itself. The child's straightforward, overtly nonerotic positioning in Turkish costume tells a different story from the masculinist odalisques. Browne's *Greek Captive* looks directly at her audience. Her contemplative look and liminal age suggest that she looks into her destiny, a future of captivity, but Browne's child rewrites the problem of captivity as one held in common in Eastern and Western women's lives. Although I am not suggesting an implicit or explicit connection between Eliot's work and Barbary Coast "captivity narratives," her work does share with them an attraction to the problem of captivity "as a fictional source" for articulating a crisis in the politics of "race and gender" in the nineteenth century.[20] The colonial nature and melodramatic quality of such images seem inappropriate in the fiction of the greatest nineteenth-century social realist novelist, but Eliot finds them profitable, importing captivity into the text through a slave-owning empire builder, through a child's comic escape to a Gypsy camp, through one daughter's drudgery and another's flight from prostitution. Unlike Hiram Powers's *Greek Slave* or Lady Montagu's harem narratives, which clearly speak of their subject's penetrability and their own "incapacity" to resist the penetrating gaze, Eliot's women and some of her men are literally or metaphorically impenetrable sexually. They are less "incapable of resisting" than incapable of giving in, often self-made as "powerless," chaste captives like Maggie Tulliver, Esther Lyon, Daniel Deronda, and Fedalma of the epic poem *The Spanish Gypsy* (1868). "The sexually inhibited women" and men of Eliot's "club" are likely to be racially different in some way, but the pain of their sexual "powerlessness" problematizes what their appropriation, in the phallocentric model, should mimic. Half the equation is missing; that is the performative sexual desire that should be mimicked by the "desire for mastery." The "fantasy of erotic domination" in Eliot becomes an act of will over bodies that signify the loss of sexual experience dramatically. Erotic domination and fantasies of "mastery" are present in Eliot's work, particularly in her many constructions of "queenly" women and "princely" men; however, the phallocentric model of reading these figures as either clearly penetrated or as penetrator is subverted.

Indeed, it is important to this project to distinguish Eliot's approach to race from those of her contemporaries, some of whom were markedly engaged in the "forward" pushes of racist imperialist discourses.[21] Representative texts like Charles Dickens's *Oliver Twist* (1837), William Thackeray's *Vanity Fair* (1847), Emily Brontë's *Wuthering Heights* (1847), Charlotte Brontë's *Jane Eyre* (1848), Lord Byron's "Oriental" tales, *The Giaour, The Corsair,* and *Lara* (1813–1814), Sir Walter Scott's *Ivanhoe* (1819), E.W. Lane's translations of *The Thousand and One Nights* (1838), George Borrow's *The Zincali; or, An Account of the Gypsies of Spain* (1841), J.W. Goethe's *Parliaments of East and West* (1819), and G.A. Rossini's *Otello* (1816) shaped a vision of Other peoples that was highly mythologized and irrevocably linked to the realms of metaphor and imaginative representation. In many of the texts mentioned above, for example, burgeoning ethnologies and their precursors idealized, ennobled, and desexualized the white European body while they made Other bodies and their perceived differences accessible as subjects. A discourse of perceived difference soon became discourses of "perversions" and entire catalogs of sexual perversities of race that were studied *ad infinitum,* in the name of science, by Victorian social scientists, many of whom, like Herbert Spencer, George Eliot knew and read carefully.[22]

The discourses of race that proliferated in the nineteenth century are tautological, constructing an "ideological circle" or cycle that was important to the way in which Victorians constructed themselves as "white" and British.[23] Seemingly disconnected to Other races through their binary opposites, then, "the nineteenth-century discourse on bourgeois sexuality may better be understood as a recuperation of a protracted discourse on race, for the discourse on sexuality contains many of the latter's most salient elements." The dominant Victorian "discourse on sexuality . . . always pitt[ed] that middle-class respectable sexuality as a defense against an internal and external Other that was at once essentially different but uncomfortably the same. The contaminating and contagious tropes of nineteenth-century sexual discourse were not new: they recalled and recuperated a discourse that riveted on defensive techniques for 'constant purification."'[24] Eliot's canon seems drawn to just these issues: bodily purification, contrastive characters and plots, and troubled representations of "middle-class respectable sexuality." Eliot is also drawn to both internalizing and externalizing images of Otherness, creating characters who are both "Oriental" and English, both European and Gypsy, both experienced adult and innocent or primitive child, both English gentry and exotic Other, both "captive" and "free," and even both male and female.[25] Indeed, Eliot's work has been identified as perhaps the high-Victorian captivity narrative *par excellence* since Sandra Gilbert and Susan Gubar's reading of her representation of women's "entrapment" in the fifth part of their *Madwoman in the Attic: The Woman Writer and the Nineteenth-Century Literary Imagination,* entitled "Captivity and Consciousness in George Eliot's Fiction."[26] Often implicitly, often quite explicitly, racial and ethnic Otherness becomes a way to articulate that entrapment;[27] and racial "fusion" becomes a threat to the hegemonic voices of her fictional provincial communities.

Placing Eliot within the discourses of nineteenth-century imperialism or racism is piqued by the complex interpretive experience of reading Eliot's narrative voice itself. Otherness is a compelling embodiment of the many "distances" that mark George Eliot's characteristic mode of self-expression.[28] Constructing the English subject in dialogue with an imagined racial or ethnic Other, Eliot further complicates a fictive narrative voice that is often in "dialogue" with a variety of fictive "readers." Eliot's "we," as Rosemarie Bodenheimer points out, is characterized by its sense of "shared distance" from those many organic communities she creates in her novels and essays. Arch, punitive, or chastening, narrative intrusion in the novels and essays often addresses a morally inferior reader who is a "child" compared with the Eliot narrator.[29] A typical Eliot statement on empire, then, engages multiple fictive audiences, and it becomes extremely difficult to discern narratorial authority. Eliot's views on race also evolved over time, becoming more sophisticated as she left a provincial town in the Midlands for Europe and London. When we look for George Eliot to speak directly for Mary Ann Evans, we engage a complex identity politics that involves the presence of several voices and several audiences in an evolving dialogue that takes place over thirty years, in both personal and "private" writings and accounts. Querying her letters, it is clear that in her early twenties, when her "conservative" attachment to England and to Englishness was pronounced, Evans was also interested in an idea of the "fusion" of races through mutual attraction and intermarriage. In the early letters, she appears half-resentful, half-admiring of Disraeli's exploitation and glamorization of his own "Oriental" heritage, and she used his "theory of races" as a platform for her own.[30] She also, in an early letter to John Sibree, reveals her ability to speak like a chillingly dispassionate ethnographer: "Extermination up to a certain point seems to be the law for the inferior races—for the rest, fusion both for physical and moral ends. It appears to me that the law by which privileged classes degenerate from continued intermarriage must act on a larger scale in deteriorating whole races. The nations have always been kept apart until they have sufficiently developed their idiosyncrasies and then some great revolutionary force has been called into action by which the genius of a particular nation becomes a common mind of humanity." The twenty-eight-year-old Mary Ann Evans's candid letter blithely classifies races into levels of fitness even while it speaks frankly about the role racial "fusion," or intermarriage, plays in building a "common mind of humanity." Exterminated, diluted, or inbred, the "races" are dispassionately discussed here on a pseudoscientific level that reappears in Eliot's fiction. Early letters also reveal the erotic attraction to Otherness that reappears in later fiction: "Looking at the matter aesthetically, our ideal of beauty is never formed on the characteristics of a single race. I confess the types of the 'pure races,' however handsome, always impress me disagreeably" (*GEL*, 1:246).

In the Sibree letter, Eliot imagines racial "impurity" as beautiful and desirable. In *Tancred*, she writes, the illustrations of "Oriental" attire struck her as "beautiful" in comparison to "ours [which] are execrable." But such concessions seem to provoke a great deal of anxiety as well. She denounces Disraeli's "exult[ation]" over the idea of a "fellowship of race." Using decidedly anti-Semitic language, she argues against exclusive racial claims to "superiority." Much that is culturally Jewish, she suggests, "seems to have been borrowed from the other Oriental tribes. Everything specifically Jewish is of a low grade" (*GEL*, 1:246, 247). In youth, the "Gentile nature" of Mary Ann Evans "kicks most resolutely against any assumption of superiority in the Jews" (246). Her belief in a salutary interbreeding and "dilution" of the races collides with her own fear of difference, which in this writing is voiced in the language of ethnic prejudice. Her struggle for a "common mind of humanity," the desire to repeal racial exclusivity, is qualified by Eliot's own nationalism and her still aggressive Christian bias as well as by a desire to protect the "genius" of English culture from the process of intrusion and exclusion which must accompany racial "fusion."

Disparaging both anti-Semitism and British imperialism in *The Impressions of Theophrastus Such* (1879), her late "fable about authorship, origination, and community,"[31] Eliot complains "though we are a small number of an alien race profiting by the territory and produce of these prejudiced people [the colonized], they are unable to turn us out; at least when they tried we showed them their mistake. We are a colonizing people, and it is we who have punished others." The former sentence is sharply critical of Britain's imperialist acquisitiveness as well as archly aware that, ironically, the British believe the colonized to be "prejudiced" against them. But the same arch narrative irony is unsettling, at once disparaging and dismissive toward the colonized themselves. Eliot's remark, "At least when they tried [to turn the British out] we showed them their mistake," is discomfortingly glib. Although throughout *The Impressions of Theophrastus Such,* the narrator attempts to separate himself from an audience comprised of a nation of Philistines who understand neither Christianity, nor Judaism, nor "Shakespere," nor any other site of learning and culture (78), Eliot's "internal dialogue" and "alternations between the invocation of a sympathetic and an oppositional reader" in such a text can obscure or obviate her political perspectives, particularly when their imagined audience is not accounted for.[32]

Eliot's last published work is "The Modern Hep! Hep! Hep!" which is the final chapter of *The Impressions of Theophrastus Such,* a chapter often read as Eliot's representative discussion on race and nation. My discussion of that essay will, I hope, clarify—and complicate—a reading of Eliot on race by highlighting the work's complex dialogues between a distanced narrative voice and its often estranged fictive audiences. In "The Modern Hep! Hep! Hep!" Eliot's "ostensible" defense of the Jews, the narrator Theophrastus Such has been perceived as a "crusty old gentleman" and "an enabling mouthpiece" for Eliot's "more ruthless political impulses," a nationalism that is to culminate in the solidifying of national boundaries and the "removal" of the Jewish people from England in what Susan Meyer defines as "Proto-Zionism." For Meyer this is a "disturbing image of national defense against alien intrusion."[33] Meyer's position troubles both readers with Zionist sympathies and those who believe in the possibility of a national identity that is not potentially fascistic.[34] Equally problematic, however, is Meyer's assumption that Eliot's Theophrastus, or any Eliot narrator, may be so simply perceived as a "mouthpiece" for Marian Evans herself.[35]

From the beginning of his essay, Theophrastus Such seeks either to indict his own reliability or to defy the very integrity of self-representation. In the first chapter, ironically titled, "Looking Inward," he begins: "It is my habit to give an account to myself of the characters I meet with: can I give any true account of my own?" (7). After discussing the folly of self-knowledge, Such envisions the process of speaking for oneself as a grotesque dance, contorted both by public misperception and self-deceit; he then wonders aloud: "What sort of hornpipe am I dancing now?" Such seeks to avoid accusations of "evil speaking" from a provincial, ignorant audience—an audience of intellectual children. He claims the sting of his critique will be assuaged by an act of self-implication: "Thus if I laugh at you, O fellow-men! If I trace with curious interest your labyrinthine self-delusions, note the inconsistencies in your zealous adhesions, and smile at your helpless endeavors in a rashly chosen part, it is not that I feel myself aloof from you: the more intimately I seem to discern your weaknesses, the stronger to me is the proof that I share them" (4). But the only thing that is clear about Such as a narrator is that he is actively engaged in distancing himself from the sin of "evilspeaking," disguising ownership of his own critique by claiming fellowship with the people whom he is renouncing as self-deluded, zealous, rash, and weak. The contempt of the narrative voice for a national audience that is sometimes literally bovine, and often violently anti-intellectual, jingoistic, and materialist rings through Such's disguise nonetheless. To avoid "evil-speaking," Such often speaks sentimentally to an English audience whose "affectionate joy in our native landscape . . . one deep root of our national life," mingles "certain conservative prepossessions" with the influences of "our midland scenery" (25). Such's ruminations place sentiment in the past where it is joined by "our historic rapacity and arrogant notions of our own superiority" (136). The bargain that Such makes as a narrator does not rob the text of its bite, but it marks the fault lines in Eliot's indictment of English ignorance and insularity (8).

How Marian Evans uses Such to voice her own political opinions is a problematic question even when one turns outside of the text itself to possibly corroborate her statements there, researching Evans's private and public dealings with the imperial project. Theophrastus Such discusses the attempts of the colonized to "turn out" the occupying British. It seems likely that Eliot is referring to the two most important examples of nineteenth-century colonial rebellion, the Jamaican Uprising of 1865, murderously quelled by the infamous Governor Eyre, or the drastic measures on the part of the British following the Indian Mutiny.[36] In "The Governor Eyre Case," we know that George Eliot was not one of the many writers who supported Eyre's bloody retaliation against former slaves who had attempted to oust the British government.[37] In *Orientalism,* Edward Said lists George Eliot among those "liberal cultural heroes like John Stuart Mill, Arnold, Carlyle, Newman, Macaulay, Ruskin," and "even Dickens," who had "definite views on race and imperialism, which are quite easily to be found at work in their writing. So even a [modern Victorian] specialist must deal with the knowledge that Mill, for example, made it clear in *On Liberty* and *Representative Government* that his views there could not be applied to India (he was an India Office functionary for a good deal of his life, after all) because the Indians were civilizationally, if not racially, inferior." Said's representation of the authors above creates a powerful phalanx of "liberal" white male Victorian racists. Rhetorically, his list links each individual named to Mill's hypocrisy. Although Said's *Orientalism* was, of course revolutionary, part of its impact results in a monolithic clarity of vision that I would like to challenge. Unlike many of the authors Said names, "even Dickens," for example, George Eliot did not sign the petition in support of Eyre when he was tried for war crimes against freed slaves in Jamaica. The "definite views on race and imperialism . . . easily to be found at work in their writing" is markedly less definite, as well, in Eliot's writing than in the work of many of her contemporaries.[38]

But Nancy Henry's recent research into Mary Ann Evans's finances reveals her significant investments in colonial India, South Africa, and the western United States.[39] It is tempting to make such investments themselves a "mouthpiece" for George Eliot, but here too, authority and agency are vexed. George Henry Lewes handled all of Marian Evans's money. "Bank account, investments, and property were all in George Henry Lewes's name. Though 'Mary Ann Evans, spinster' was the sole executrix of his will, several legal maneuvers were necessary before she came into possession" of the money she had earned throughout her career. Only in her diary of 1879 does she begin to keep thorough account of her money, all of which had been handled by Lewes.[40] Earlier, Evans sporadically notes that her investments in the Anglo-Indian Railway were profitable; she was clearly informed that her money had been invested in colonial projects. However, evaluating the investments' politics is, as Henry argues, "trickier" in "retrospective moral terms than it would initially appear." The political

> strategy of "divestment," emerging from Vietnam War resistance and succeeding Vietnam as the central issue among students protesting Apartheid in South Africa in the 1980s, has grown into the phenomenon of ethical, or "socially responsible investing" (SRI). If we were to apply this late twentieth-century sensibility to Eliot's colonial investments, we would assume that she was capable of making a blanket critique of imperialism comparable to that made by American students in the 1980s about Apartheid, the very result of colonial conditions in South Africa that Eliot helped to create when she invested in the Cape Town Rail, or when she provided money for her stepsons' farm in South Africa. Such an assumption on our part, however, would be anachronistic.[41]

Eliot's colonial investments are certainly problematic. It seems clear that she had some discomfort with her own role in the colonial projects of Lewes's children, Thornton and Bertie. As Henry notes, with her earnings and returns on investments, Evans had supported Lewes; his estranged wife, Agnes; her children with Thornton Hunt; his three children with Agnes; and his two grandchildren and their mother, Eliza Harrison Lewes, after the death of his son, Bertie. Bertie and Thornton were sent to Natal in South Africa to farm, an enterprise that ended in failure and their early deaths. In an 1875 letter to John Cross, Evans seems chastened about these sons' colonial endeavors. She wrote that "we felt ten years ago that a colony with a fine climate, like Natal, offered [Bertie Lewes] the only fair prospect within his reach. What can we do more than try to arrive at the best conclusion from the conditions as they are known to us?" (*GEL*, 6:165). Evans seems cognizant that she and Lewes sent his sons off to an uncertain future in a distant place they knew little about. She seems to suggest that "conditions" in the colonies were misrepresented to them. However, Evans and Lewes's concern over his children's very limited "prospects" makes clear the extent to which both of them found it difficult to negotiate within entrenched social systems that offered little opportunity outside their boundaries. The most ironic aspect of Marian Evans's "personal" colonial investments and their twenty-year history (including Lewes's investments of her money in the farm in Natal) is that they were legally not her own. She distanced herself from her money and its management, giving George Henry Lewes full control for reasons upon which we can only speculate. The question of her financial agency remains ultimately elusive, even as it reveals a great deal about the inculcation of an "average" well-to-do British family in the material progress of empire.[42]

Shortly before the death of Lewes and Bertie, Eliot was finishing *The Impressions of Theophrastus Such;* Nancy Henry writes that Eliot expresses there "a newly self-conscious and moral, if ironic, attitude toward colonialism. Only *Impressions of Theophrastus Such* unites Eliot's broad concerns about economics, the colonies and English national identity. Crucially this synthesis takes place through an experimental work investigating the privileges and responsibilities of authorship."[43] The conservative "prepossessions" of youth are viewed from a distance. From that perspective, the narrator "checks" his nostalgia. He is well aware that "this England of my affections is half-visionary—a dream in which things are connected according to my well-fed, lazy mood, and not at all by the multitudinous links of graver, sadder fact, such as belong everywhere to the story of human labor." The "sober harmonies" of the English landscape reflect sometimes grimly sober truths. "My father's England," that "elder England" before the reform process began in earnest, possessed meadows unsullied by the locomotive, but it also possessed "frankly saleable boroughs," prisons without water, "bloated, idle charities," and, "a blank ignorance" of its own legacy, "of what we, its posterity, should be thinking of it" (*ITS,* 26).Purportedly acting as editor of *The Impressions of Theophrastus Such,* "George Eliot" is unmistakably present. Her narrative voice's distance from its subject is caught between its own nationalism and its frustration with the process and fruits of reform. Nostalgic for its own Midlands identity, the narrative voice is also problematically removed from the ramifications of national identity itself.

Although Theophrastus "cherish[es his] childish loves—the memory" of home—the adult narrative voice is freed in the act of exile: "I have learned to care for foreign countries, for literatures foreign and ancient, for the life of Continental towns dozing round old cathedrals, for the life of London, half sleepless with eager thought

and strife, with indigestion or with hunger; and now my consciousness is chiefly of the busy, anxious metropolitan sort. . . . I belong to
the Nation of London" (26). In this position of "voluntary exile"
within the very hub of the British empire itself, Theophrastus acts as
both outsider and insider, identifying with those who have been persecuted. The voice's collective "we" is self-critical, and the "glories" of
empire are represented as crimes. Moreover, the essay celebrates "di-
versity" amidst "general sameness," condemning ethnic prejudice as
"that grosser mental sloth" which makes people prefer things because "of their likeness" (142). With a remarkably clear-eyed, unsenti-
mental acumen, Eliot extends the British preference for sameness to
its propensity for colonization. Valuing its own national heritage,
England has not "recogniz[ed] a corresponding attachment to na-
tionality as legitimate in every other people, and [does not] understand that its absence is a privation of the greatest good" (147).
Theophrastus Such seeks to reconcile both British and Other nationalisms, while the latter's intrinsic connection to projects of empire is
left unsaid, a problem that, Amanda Anderson suggests, marks
Eliot's commitment to "radical cosmopolitanism."[44]

Indeed, Theophrastus's ruminations on nation become most
problematic when he discusses "a feeling of race, a sense of corporate
existence, unique in its intensity" (150). In her fiction and poetry as
well, Eliot engages what Henry Louis Gates Jr. calls the "dangerous
trope" of ethnic difference in the passionate intensity of her Gypsy
characters; the strength of her dark women, and the spirituality of
her Jewish figures are emphatically outlined as "natural attributes" of
"racial character."[45] The average Victorian's reading in Borrow's *The
Zincali; or An Account of the Gypsies in Spain,* Byron's *Oriental Tales,* and
Lane's translation of *The Thousand and One Nights* was a powerful con-
veyance of cultural information that captured the imagination and
formed popular opinion. It created a deeply entrenched popular belief that Theophrastus quotes: "'[A] people with Oriental sunlight in
their veins'" were bound to feel differently and act differently than
Northern Europeans (*ITS,* 157).[46] Although Theophrastus's quotation is out of the people's mouth, not his own, it is often "blood," a
fluid, powerful presence that prompts Eliot's cultural Others to discover and claim their heritage. The "mark" of blood and its biological
element is undeniable in Eliot's canon (*DD,* 215).

Indeed, as in *Daniel Deronda,* a "natural rank" of the Jewish people
is discussed in *Theophrastus* where it is envisioned as having developed

alongside a history of persecution: "After being subject to this process [of persecution and discrimination] the [Jewish people] have come out of it . . . rivaling the nations of all European countries in healthiness and beauty of physique, in practical ability, in scientific and artistic aptitude, and in some forms of ethical value. A significant indication of their natural rank is seen in the fact that at this moment, the leader of the Liberal party in Germany is a Jew, the leader of the Republican party in France is a Jew, and the head of the Conservative ministry in England is a Jew" (157). Eliot's "praise" of the Jewish people, establishing them in a "natural rank" of physical and intellectual superiority suggests her tendency to call upon hierarchical racialist discourses as well as nationalist ones, both of which are at odds with an Enlightenment discourse of a common humanity. These are perhaps the major stresses in her representations of erotic Otherness in which intermarriage raises both the specter of assimilation and alienation.[47] Marriage between the English and ethnic Others seems eternally "premature": "Let it be admitted that it is a great calamity to the English, as to any other great historic people, to undergo a premature fusion with immigrants of alien blood; that its distinctive national characteristics should be in danger of obliteration by the predominating quality of foreign settlers. I not only admit this, I am ready to unite in groaning over the threatened danger" (*ITS*, 158). It is perhaps this "threatened danger" that creates a stress in Eliot's fiction, a conflict between dual allegiances to a culture once valued, a "great historic people," but now, to Eliot, rapidly becoming a nation of Philistines. The "danger" is inherent in Eliot's careful avoidance of the "dilution" of Englishness through sexual liaisons between characters of "alien blood" and different classes. Although the prophet Theophrastus groaned over the danger of "premature fusion," he accepted that such fusion was an inevitable stage in the evolutionary process. For "the tendency of things is toward quicker or slower fusion of races. It is impossible to arrest this tendency: all we can do is to moderate its course so as to hinder it from degrading the moral status of societies by a too rapid effacement of those national traditions and customs which are the language of the national genius" (160).

The only hope or recourse for the preservation of national culture is in the "striving after fuller national excellence . . . the moulding of more excellent individual natives" (160). Attracted to the ideal of "fusion," Eliot also seems simultaneously to stall it and mourn its difficulty as she nurtures both a "romantic nationalism" and an Enlightenment fantasy of a "common humanity."[48] These conflicting agendas are clear in the sexual stalemate drawn between Daniel Deronda and Gwendolen Harleth and in the remarkably unconflicted narrative in the same novel of the marriage between Catherine Arrowpoint and Herr Klesmer. Paradoxically, in Eliot's canon, it is the sexual attraction between Others and the English or European that drives narrative forward, engaging problematically with discourses of classification, separation, and identity.

DANIEL DERONDA'S RIGOROUS preference for "the beauty of the closed lips," like the Gypsy queen Fedalma's vow of chastity and Maggie Tulliver's refusal to elope with Stephen Guest, are each in a sense captive to a sexual threat imagined in the Other's "dark smile" ("B&S" [1869], 4.14). Insisting that the contained eroticism within such figures drives narrative, Eliot is able to address the disruptive presence of desire through the terms of race and ethnicity. Clearly aware of trends in natural history, Eliot knew that the dominant culture perceived Gypsies, Jews, Orientals, and Africans as sexualized in sharp contrast to the English of a certain "club."[49] As such, racial and ethnic Others might possess a heightened access to "sense, instinct, and passion,"[50] and heavily mythologized perceptions of the English self created an ideal, highly "evolved" English woman who was politically and sexually passive and, above all, domesticated. Her equally evolved male counterpart was warned to fight his own "natural" inclinations toward the lower appetites and to devote himself to chastity, virtue, progress, industry, and empire. Disrupting that progress with images of darkness and difference, Eliot allows them to pull away from those traditional values of the Victorian text. "Diluting" her English characters' blood allows her to dilute the stranglehold of sexual frigidity, but rarely the compulsory sexual virtue which then grasped literature itself.

Like the visual tradition of Orientalism which Eliot knew, the literary tradition of representing women in slavery or captivity allowed the terms by which they could be eroticized. As the East in particular became "an encyclopedia of exotic display and a playground for" English and European scrutiny,[51] Orientalists such as Edward Lane, the translator of Eliot's edition of *The Thousand and One Nights,* viewed themselves as moral and Christian in opposition to the "barbaric" or "licentious" Others they represented. Walter Scott's *Ivanhoe,* with its many visions of captive women who are importantly linked by ethnicity, the dual pairing of the Jewish Rebecca and the ultra-Anglo Rowena, became an important book on the subject of "the conflict of races" for George Eliot, and there the Jewish woman is Orientalized and heavily eroticized.[52] Paradoxically a collection of Eastern or Oriental stereotypes, Rebecca, the "lovely Jewess," is described with a visual abandon that is in sharp contrast to Scott's representation of the cool Anglo Rowena:

> Her form was exquisitely symmetrical, and was shown to advantage by a sort of Eastern dress, which she wore according to the fashion of the females of her nation. Her turban of yellow silk suited well with the darkness of her complexion. The brilliancy of her eyes, and the profusion of her sable tresses, which, each arranged in its own little spiral of twisted curls, fell down upon as much of a lovely neck and bosom as a *simarre* of the richest Persian silk . . . permitted to be visible. It is true, that of the golden and pearl-studded clasps which closed her vest from the throat to the waist, the three uppermost were left unfastened on account of the heat, which something enlarged the prospect to which we allude.[53]

In her Persian veil and turban, Rebecca is a representative of an East imagined as warm and alluring; she brings its heat and perceived sensuality to cold England.

Behind this sexual mythology of difference which Victorians created and institutionalized in both fiction and science lies a wealth of information, confusion, and fear about English sexuality itself. Both Eliot's attraction to "miscegenation" and her wariness of it are based on Victorian concerns about the sexuality of her own people and the people of other cultures and races. Versed in contemporary anthropological "discoveries" about the bodies and sexual practices of Other peoples, convinced of the then-common belief that ethnicity could be linked to body type, character, and morality, Eliot's use of the cultural Other reflects contemporary anthropological and medical texts where Others serve as a basis for comparison to English bodies and, ultimately, English culture. That comparison inevitably reflects the "civilized" self-containment and harnessed productivity of English men and both the absence of sexual desire (a destructive, nonproductive energy) and the presence of fecundity (a positive, reproductive energy) in English women. Constructing a medical mythology that supported such beliefs, the English medical profession often created paradigms of nondesirous women and desirous men. Pat Jalland writes that William Acton, a mid-Victorian surgeon, embodied contemporary advocacy for "the absence of sexuality in women: 'The majority of women (happily for them) [Acton wrote] are not very much troubled with sexual feeling of any kind. What men are habitually, women are only exceptionally.' This was moral prescription rather than physical description."[54] Although Acton's quotation has become a cliché in literary studies, and James Kincaid, in particular, has argued against the weight attributed to it, it cannot be denied that even if there is not a Victorian "block of official views on 'sexuality,'" there is nonetheless an official record, in fiction, of the extraordinary difficulty in owning desirous female subjectivity in Victorian culture while there is a concomitantly enormous pressure to convert desire to productive domesticity there.[55] Nancy Armstrong has proven the ruthlessness of this pressure in her landmark study, *Desire and Domestic Fiction: A Political History of the Novel*, while Anita Levy's *Other Women: The Writing of Class, Race, and Gender, 1832–1898* has envisioned representations of Otherness in the British novel as a threat to that domesticity or to "civilization" itself which is pictured as white and English.

Novels which were important to Eliot were likely to keep Englishness and Otherness entirely separate. This is clear in *Ivanhoe*'s binary representation of Rebecca and Rowena, a representation that epitomizes the double victimization of English women and other women. If the Jewish Rebecca is depicted as overtly erotic, her English counterpart is modeled on Dr. Acton's frigid ideal. A "Saxon beauty," she is even the more striking to the returning crusaders because she "differs" from "the Eastern sultanas." Like Rebecca's, Rowena's beauty exists in direct relation to her ethnicity and class status. "Exquisitely fair" and blue-eyed, her English, aristocratic body is largely unmentionable and inaccessible, linked to Rebecca by her veil. Like alabaster in her whiteness, she is as cold to the touch. Dressed, as Gwendolen Harleth will also be, in "pale sea-green," Rowena, with her bare arms and flaxen hair, is made of water or ice, not fire. Her bedchamber, richly decorated with tapestry and white ivory, is frigid. Its "rich hangings [shake] to the night blast" while the "torches stream sideways" from the cold air that permeates the castle.[56] The lady Rowena, for all her status, is clearly imprisoned by her own cultural category. The blonde, blue-eyed Ivanhoe is equally chaste, cool, and, most importantly, sexually disciplined. In the backlash of exoticism, so clearly if simplistically delineated by Scott's frigid and overtly sensual characters, both the victimized and the victimizing cultures are punished. Imperialism, as it categorizes sexualities, seeks to discipline its own women as it disciplines the outlander or native subject. The empire constructs an idealized chastity while it eradicates desirous female subjectivity. It is this ideal of English women, who are rather unproblematically reinscribed as "the sexually inhibited women of the club," which Eliot resists, disrupts, and subverts.[57]

WITH HER PARTNER, George Henry Lewes, Eliot shared a suspicion of "generalisations current about" Other cultures as they were represented by "harsh and ungenerous" ethnographers like the self-styled "Oriental" and government agent, Captain Sir Richard Francis Burton.[58] The high scholarly seriousness which we associate with George Eliot, however, is often absent from her notes on, for example, Travelers, a group of peoples whom contemporary British writers named "Gypsies," a separate race. Dotting her notes for *The Spanish Gypsy* with exclamation marks, the sybilline George Eliot seems remarkably touristic as she travels to Africa from her desk in the Priory.[59] The search for Otherness, and the satisfaction in its discovery, is clear in these notes which ring with curiosity and even literary opportunism. The pursuit of Others through research serves Eliot's writing projects where conflict between races is perceived as the most dramatic material of representation, "witness *Ivanhoe*" (*SE*, 380). The thrill of her chases contradicts the solemnity and chasteness of discourse which makes George Eliot "Queen George," commander of a "masculine authority" over the realist novel itself and over the "range of her intellectual, philosophical, and scientific interests" which "placed her in the role of the father" to a generation of novelists.[60] Eliot's research into the racial heritage of the Gypsies is less authoritative than experiential: she and Lewes followed a Gypsy musician to his home in Granada, Spain, where they sought a private performance.

Indeed, in researching Otherness, Eliot is also researching other plots. Gillian Beer, in *Darwin's Plots: Evolutionary Narrative in Darwin, George Eliot, and Nineteenth-Century Fiction,* has argued that Eliot, like Zola, seeks "to track and uncover natural laws. This pursuit is the deepest level of plot in [her] fictions."[61] Eliot's research into Other races leads her, similarly, to other plots of fiction and epic that do not affirm the values of home culture. It seems a very different thing to "sacrifice" Other characters and expunge them from Brontë's or

Dickens's novels, than to place them in Midland scenery, "pale English sunshine," to which they wish they had never returned (*FH*, 582).[62] A complex series of images developed from the "Gypsy changeling" of Eliot's first short stories to the "cursed alien"—Will Ladislaw—of her greatest novel, Eliot's representations of an eroticized Otherness allow her to create plots that subvert and question the narrative tendency to oppose "the rhetorical dimension of the obsession with sexual purity" in Victorian literature.[63] Indeed, establishing a kinship and identification with cultural Others through an imagined captivity within their ranks, or through the "tragedy" of thwarted miscegenation allows Eliot's narrator to articulate what an English character cannot: the loss of the unmentionable experiences of sexual desire and pleasure (*SE*, 417). Transposing elements of the Orient or Moorish Spain into English narratives and literally into the "blood" of English characters allows Eliot to attempt to resist, sometimes successfully, sometimes unsuccessfully, a pervasive "cultural frigidity" which affects the representation of both men's and women's experiences of desire and sexual pleasure in the English novel.[64]

Earlier, I appropriated the image of the "club" from Ali Behdad. It is perhaps as well a useful metaphor for our own monolithic image of that phalanx of Victorian "liberal cultural heroes," linked as Edward Said's litany of colonizing literary "men": "John Stuart Mill, Arnold, Carlyle, Newman, Macaulay, Ruskin, George Eliot, and even Dickens"[65] The club of empire is a problematic structure, we now find, in many ways. The relation of disenfranchised European women to their enfranchised male counterparts is extraordinarily complex. Some women writers may indeed "supplement" the projects of men or participate in "writing the nation," but in each case, politics of gender and race should be carefully examined. More subtle in this regard than those of the Brontës, Dickens, Thackeray, or Disraeli, Eliot's representations of Otherness complicate what students of nineteenth-century multiculturalism or imperialism have come to see as the Victorian *status quo*. Eliot's technique presents a complex challenge to the readings of Edward Said and Gayatri Chakravorty Spivak, both of whom see the fiction of the Victorian period, especially the period of imperialist domination during which Eliot wrote, as unreflectingly supportive of the values of empire. Expunging the text of the deviant and foreign Other Fagin, for example, allows the middle-class Englishness of Oliver Twist to replace "the

Jew's" monstrous Otherness and so reestablishes the value of the home culture. Patrick Brantlinger excludes *Daniel Deronda*'s "reverse Orientalism" from this pattern in Victorian fiction, recognizing that the novel's "romantic nationalism" works "against a host of what might be called provincial nationalisms, including the simple nationalist/racist proposition that it is better to be an Englishman than a Jew."[66] To Brantlinger, Said, and Spivak, Eliot's earlier novels make no such propositions. Aside from Deronda, the exotic figures who intrude on Eliot's earlier texts are discounted. Indeed, their presence is overshadowed by an entrenched critical perception of Eliot as a novelist of the English Midlands and private, domestic life.

Both Kate Millet and Elaine Showalter have discussed the "internal colonization" imposed on all women by patriarchy; Showalter has even described the literature of women as the "literature of the colonized,"[67] as in colonial writing the image of woman is often a trope for the image of Otherness. Brantlinger, perhaps unwittingly, demonstrates this conflation in his *Rule of Darkness: British Literature and Imperialism, 1830–1914:* "In British literature from about 1830 to the 1870's, white heroes rarely doubt their ability to tame various geopolitical mistresses—Africa, the sea, the world—and to bring civilized order out of the chaos of savage life."[68] Equating Africa, the sea, and the world beyond England with the "chaos of savage life," Brantlinger also genders that "savage" element as female. The primary Other of the "white hero" is woman. Otherness, like Africa, or India, is a "mistress" which must be "tamed" or domesticated. Undomesticated, those entities were a threat to culture itself.

Indeed, if the English viewed themselves as "superior" to Other peoples, the essence of their superiority, it was popularly believed, lay in their domestic *status quo.*[69] In Victorian anthropology, the ideal cultural family structure was arranged in a hierarchy ruled by a patriarch who ventured out into the social world to provide for his wife and child. Marriage was to be exclusively monogamous, a legal institution that sanctioned sexual relations. Studying Other "primitive" cultures led the Victorians to refute earlier notions that the patriarchal family was, as had been argued in the seventeenth and eighteenth centuries, a product of "natural law." In their many case studies of Other cultures, Victorians discovered, and named, the existence of exogamy, endogamy, promiscuity, and incest. These practices were "natural" as well as "primitive." The political organizations of such cultures, often matriarchal or matrilineal, might also be natural. In contrast, the domestic and political arrangements of Victorian England were clearly the result of "a long and painful evolutionary struggle away" from nature. Casting aside Rousseau's noble savage, the Victorians envisioned themselves as "the final culmination, the glorious end-product of man's whole social, sexual, and moral evolution from savagery to civilization."[70]

The particular mark of that moral evolution was the domestication of women. Throughout his *Principles of Sociology* (1876–96), Herbert Spencer argues that the absence of women from social and political life is the hallmark of a civilized culture. Women in primitive cultures were treated with neither dignity nor respect. "Forced" to work alongside men, they were not ladies. Spencer tallies the evidence. His sources record that in primitive societies women have been observed "fishing, carrying and pitching tents, digging up roots, planting, plowing, and reaping, building houses, climbing trees for small animals, and even hunting and going to war." In his own culture it was clear that "women's status" was improved "by limitation of their labors to the lighter kinds." Middle- or upper-class European culture had reached "the pinnacle of female evolution.[71] As Fee writes:

> Women had ascended the pedestal to become "the angels of the home"; no longer sexually or economically exploited, the women were safe in their drawing rooms, far removed from the frightful realities of "natural" life. Men, of course, were firmly in control. Though the demands of marital fidelity might sometimes conflict with their own "natural" passions, they too felt far removed from the savage state. And the rewards of civilized life compensated for any lingering sympathy for the primitive freedoms.[72]

The pseudoscientific ideology that Elizabeth Fee critiques also invaded Victorian studies of Others who might not be actual primitives but who might be closer to primitivism than middle-class or upper-class Victorians thought themselves to be, for example the working and nonworking poor, the Irish, the Gypsy, the Jew, and the Oriental. Living with less "definite, coherent, order" both socially and domestically, they were "anthropological survivals of an earlier stage. Like the savages, the lower classes had simply not advanced very far in evolutionary terms."[73] To the Victorian sociologist, the working-class hovel looked similar to the African hut or the Indian teepee. As the savage instinct flourished in both those domiciles, so might it flourish at home in England.

Certainly, Eliot's fiction "shows her continuing skepticism about Spencer's glib readings of Nature's syntax." And although Eliot may have agreed with both Spencer and Darwin's theories of evolution, she, particularly in *The Mill on the Floss* (1860), "demystifies" gender ideals as the construction not of nature, but of culture. "In contrast to Spencer," Eliot "saw sex differences not only as determined by biological function but also as constructed by profoundly misogynistic cultural traditions and ideologies." Moreover, as Eliot encountered representations of Otherness through contemporary scientific writings, she engages what Gillian Beer in *Darwin's Plots* has termed a conflict between her "vehement fascination with individuality" and the plots of what she perceived as "natural laws."[74]

Eliot writes against a tradition then in which an eroticized Other subverts the precariously balanced construction of the plot of domesticated woman, signifier of an advanced state of evolution. Within that scale, the identifying protagonist risks becoming an anthropological "deviant" or evolutionary throwback; she might possess "primitive sexual impulses that threaten to disrupt the order of things." Linking female disruption to "primitive" sexuality, Victorian pathologists conducted numerous comparisons between "savage and working-class women," and particularly between "savage" women and English prostitutes. Their dissections confirmed their suspicions; the two were anatomically similar. "The oversexed prostitute and the improperly gendered African female seemed to be at the same stage of genital evolution." In this sense, the savage herself could be as nearby as the next neighborhood. As Anita Levy argues, all disruptive or desirous English women risk comparison to those "improperly gendered" women of different cultures. All women may have "primitive sexual impulses that threaten to disrupt the order of things. The female nature of the woman's body is her link to these 'Other' women and thus it authorizes and shares their subjection."[75]

Allowing the "oversexed" qualities of cultural Others into her texts presents Eliot with a number of narrative and political problems and opportunities. Unleashed in a Victorian narrative, sexual desire is a disruptive force that threatens the desirous figure's commitment to community. These conflicts are clear in *The Mill on the Floss, The Spanish Gypsy, Felix Holt: The Radical,* and *Daniel Deronda,* in all of which the desire of or for the cultural Other causes or threatens the disruption of the novel's moral value system. Maggie Tulliver, Gwendolen Harleth, Fedalma, and Esther Lyon, in particular, all recognize that "desire is a regressive force in women's lives"; they "sublimate women's sexual pleasure to meet a passionless and rational ideal."[76] Whether that ideal involves the narrative commitment to class, family, race, or community, Eliot's characters are caught between their desire to experience sexual pleasure and their fear of moral compromise. The threat that they will become "the slave" to another's "voice and touch," losing their rational ideals and values, is the ever-present dark side of sexual pleasure in Eliot's canon, and often Eliot's desirous figures employ a language of white captivity to articulate their dual allegiance.[77] If, as in "the official scientific discourses of Otherness, fiction relocates sexual desire within the female,"[78] Eliot seems drawn to cloaking that desire with a dignifying and ennobling veil of Other queenliness, not the least of which is the one Showalter identifies, her own.

Although Eliot's "Other" women clearly inherit stereotypes reserved for women of Other races and classes, the narrative voice of George Eliot does not sanction that subjection but attempts to release women from the narrow plots of domestic fiction. Embracing the dark, the "savage," and the wild over the fair, the civilized, and the domestic, Eliot's narrators disrupt contemporary Victorian standards of "pink and white" beauty and feminine passivity. From the darkly smiling Gypsy woman of "Brother and Sister" to the luxuriously veiled and draped Fedalma, Eliot uses the trope of the beautiful, threatening Other to bring sensuality, aggression, and disruption into the English novel as she brings a tribe of Gypsies into her epic poem: "tall maidens" who lead "a busy, bright-eyed sportive life," wearing clothes which expose "the living curves, the shoulder's smoothness parting the torrent strong of ebon hair."[79] The eroticism of Eliot's Others disrupts the binary divisions held sacred in most Victorian texts—the separation of the domesticated and public selves, the dominant race and the minority, the colonizer and the colonized. The disciplined chastity of each of these Othered women, thrown into relief by the overt eroticism of their representation, becomes a disturbing presence in Eliot's canon.

So powerful is Eliot's link between the desirous female self and Otherness that in her two final novels, in which the primary Other figures are male, their maleness is washed over with an androgynous femininity. The resident alien of *Middlemarch*, Will Ladislaw, is possessed of a "queer genealogy" which spills over into his gendered representation as well. His face seems always "in preparation for metamorphosis." Indeed, as Dorothea contemplates the portrait of

Ladislaw's grandmother, "the colours deep[en], the lips and chin [seem] to get larger . . . the face [becomes] masculine."[80] Ladislaw's androgynous beauty, "his frequent blushes, and his transparent girl-ish complexion" have disturbed some critics.[81] Yet these elements emphasize his ability to slip in and out of genders as he slips in and out of a variety of ethnic and class identities. First introduced through the portrait of his rebellious grandmother, Ladislaw and his queerness of gender and ethnicity cement Eliot's alliance between the imprisoned sexual self and the victimized ethnic self. As both a beau-tiful, "girl"[ish] man and the object of Dorothea's girlish desire, Ladislaw, and Dorothea's attraction to him, act as a conspiracy against the silencing of desire in the Victorian novel.

Daniel Deronda, too, seems described in "the language of hero-ines," as he is "a soft, lovely creature whose clothes enhance his attractiveness."[82] My chapter on Eliot's last novel discusses her com-parison of him to Prince Camaralzaman of *The Thousand and One Nights* who is the androgynous twin of his lover Queen Budoor. Mak-ing the strangely foreign Ladislaw and Deronda both cultural Others and objects of desire is a subversion of contemporary anthropologi-cal "discoveries" about the bodies and gendering of Other peoples. Each figure suggests, through contrast and paradox, the denial of sexual desire in English novels. In leaving the boundaries of those narratives and entering Other cultures, Other races, and even Other bodies and genders, Eliot ultimately expresses a troubled resistance to Victorian family values and contemporary illustrations of racial difference.

In *Black Looks: Race and Representation,* bell hooks asserts that black women "have always known that the socially constructed image of innocent white womanhood relies on the continued production of the racist/sexist sexual myth that black women are not innocent and never can be."[83] George Eliot relies on just this constructed image of darkness to "wash" her English or European characters free of a com-pulsory sexual innocence. The weight of the construct of "white womanhood" is so heavy, and so despised, in Eliot's fiction that it is often expressed in images of drowning and chains. Clasping her blue-eyed brother, the dark Maggie Tulliver becomes a "little mulatter" again as she drowns on an impassable river to nowhere, pulled under the flood at the novel's end by a suicidal need to prove her sexual in-nocence to her very white brother and "master." Stretching her arms over her head as if she were, in fact, throwing off manacles, Gwendolen Harleth also feels the weight of her own masquerade as a sexual innocent.[84] Bell hooks's statement addresses the absurdity of binary conceptions of racial difference. It also, because hooks refers to contemporary American media, chillingly reminds us of how little distance separates us from the early-nineteenth-century divides between Scott's dark, sensual Rebecca and his blonde, frigid Rowena. From the Other side of the racial construct of difference, hooks's frustration speaks to the same issues as shown in Eliot's fiction. But it also inscribes an assumption that the "socially constructed image of white womanhood" itself is not as pernicious a "racist/sexual myth" as the one that refuses the sexual innocence of black women. Eliot's canon asserts that, indeed, both constructs deny the full experience of desirous subjectivity.

Eliot's refusal of white womanhood needs to be discussed and evaluated in order to achieve an understanding of the insidious and complex workings of British imperialism on both its "own" and Other women and men. As Spivak urges in her landmark essay on *Jane Eyre:* "It should not be possible to read nineteenth-century British literature without remembering that imperialism, understood as England's social mission, was a crucial part of the cultural representation of England to the English. The role of literature in the production of cultural representation should not be ignored. These two obvious 'facts' continue to be disregarded in the reading of nineteenth-century British literature. This itself attests to the continuing success of the imperialist project, displaced and dispersed into more modern forms." Implicit in Spivak's critique is that the author under discussion above, Charlotte Brontë, represents a monolithically imperialist England to a monolithically imperialist English population. Spivak owns a "degree of rage" for the "imperialist narrativization of history" that "produces so abject a script" for writers like Charlotte Brontë.[85] Edward Said, too, sees the centrality of English perceptions of its own racial superiority, its own right to rule, constructing the plots of the nineteenth-century English novel: "Jane Austen sees the legitimacy of Sir Thomas Bertram's overseas properties as a natural extension of the calm, the order, the beauties of Mansfield Park, one central estate validating the economically supportive role of the peripheral other. And even where colonies are not insistently or even perceptibly in evidence, the narrative sanctions a spatial moral order, whether in the communal restoration of the town of Middlemarch centrally important during a period of national turbulence, or in the outlying spaces of deviation and uncertainty seen by Dickens in London's underworld, or in the Brontës' stormy heights."[86]

The sweeping political generalizations of Said's *Culture and Imperialism* join equally sweeping formalist generalizations of D. A. Miller to arrive at a reading of Eliot and of *Middlemarch* as "no substantial challenge to the way things are" in the English novel.[87] Eliot, like Austen, Dickens, and the Brontës, concludes her novels by "confirm[ing] and highlight[ing] an underlying hierarchy of family, property, [and] nation" as well as imparting "a very strong spatial *hereness* to the hierarchy."[88] As, according to Miller, the "mere monogamy" of the end of *Middlemarch* makes marriage the center of narrative interest,[89] so does the "spatial moral order" of the novel, according to Said, make Middlemarch the center of stability in the universe.[90]

The disruptive presence, in George Eliot's works, of an outsider whose presence, for some within the novel, fractures the very concept of "communal restoration," however, often throws settings far off the very "spatial *hereness*" which rankles Said and Miller. If Dorothea Brooke leaves Middlemarch with Ladislaw, whose blood is "frightfully mixed," the narrative is not sanctioning but violating the "spatial moral order" established by Austen, Dickens, and the Brontës. If the Gypsies, who reappear in Eliot's "Brother and Sister Sonnets," *Scenes of Clerical Life,* and *The Mill on the Floss,* ultimately culminate in Eliot's creation of a Gypsy heroine in *The Spanish Gypsy* who rejects a European life for a nomadic, tribal "home," that too is a violation of what Said sees as the English novel's comprehensive validation of Englishness. The spatial counterpoint of Englishness, and its "positive ideas of home, of a nation and its language, of proper order, good behavior, moral values," is more often, in Eliot's England, a sham.[91] Although I agree with Said that "even George Eliot (in whose *Daniel Deronda* the Orient has plans made for it) [is a] writer . . . for whom the Orient was defined by material possession, by a material imagination," I cannot align Deronda's troubling possessiveness with any "positive ideas of home" or nation.[92] In Eliot's fiction, the two do not go hand in hand.

For example, what satisfaction does the new Mrs. Grandcourt feel "as they approached the gates, and . . . her husband said, 'Here we are at home!' and for the first time kissed her on the lips"? Gwendolen "fell silent . . . a numbness had come over her personality" (*DD*, 405).

With her fair-haired, white-handed husband only pages earlier taking the part of Governor Eyre, Gwendolen, like Deronda, identifies with the colonized, not the colonizer. I have "always felt a little with Caliban," remarks Deronda during the discussion of the rebellion in Jamaica (376). Although the rendering of Deronda's actions may affirm the vicious circle Brantlinger describes as "nationalism-imperialism-racism," the representation of Gwendolen Harleth's captivity both in her marriage and to Deronda's "vocation" remains a profound critique. Never studied comprehensively, Eliot's trope of Otherness suggests that the critique of empire and Englishness, and the struggle to express desire, begins far earlier in the history of the British novel than was once thought.

Interrupting and often fragmenting her novels of vocation, Eliot's exotic subtexts challenge the absence of pleasure and desire in English domestic fiction. Gwendolen Harleth and the Jew Daniel Deronda, like Esther Lyons and the "giaour" Harold Transome, act out roles that evoke stereotypes older than Shakespeare's *Othello* as willing links of miscegenation are created between a desirous white woman and a threatening, sexual Other. As in Shakespeare's play, in Eliot's novels, "femininity is not opposed to blackness and monstrosity, as white to black, but identified with the monstrous, an identification that makes miscegenation doubly fearful" and, in Eliot's texts, doubly intriguing.[93] Often attracted to the dark Other, the monstrous white figure in this Victorian writer's canon is far more conflicted than readers like Said or Spivak conclude. Indeed, through her characters who possess not one but several ethnic and cultural allegiances, Eliot challenges our assumptions about English domestic fiction which, as Said suggests, is expected to worship a national and personal construct of "home." It is appropriate to begin this study of Otherness and eroticism, then, with George Eliot's would-be Gypsy queens, Caterina Sarti, Maggie Tulliver, and Fedalma of *The Spanish Gypsy,* all of whom struggle to feel at home in domestic settings that seem anathema to them.

## TWO

# *"Dark Smiles"*

## *George Eliot and "Gypsydom"*

IN GEORGE ELIOT'S "Brother and Sister Sonnets," a little English girl wanders into a "copse, where wild things rushed unseen." She suddenly stumbles upon a Gypsy woman. Frightened, the child meets the woman's "dark smile" and is soon connected to "the fear, the love, the primal, passionate store which makes mankind whole."[1] This moment of recognition and primal identification between English girl and Gypsy woman is one of several in Eliot's works where encounters occur between an English or European subject and a "Gypsy" of a purportedly "wild" or "savage" culture.[2] Often depicted as children or child women, these images of Gypsies are neat reversals of her chaste "little sister[s]" ("B & S," 11.14). These truant girls eventually evolve in Eliot's canon into a fantasy of exiled queenliness embodied by the powerfully erotic "virgin majesty," Fedalma, of Eliot's epic poem, *The Spanish Gypsy* (1868–69).[3] Her story ends in a fleeting, dramatic gesture of the royal "laying on of hands" between Gypsy queen and a child subject, a pose that may replace the colonialist discourse of "penetration" with an equally problematic erotics of maternal pleasure located within the nexus of dominion and racial desire.[4] Indeed, as Eliot's representations of Gypsies link queenly fantasies to plots of abduction and captivity, they engage powerful contemporary discourses of gender and race, critiquing the domestic settings that contrast unfavorably to the imagined "refuge" of "Gypsydom."[5]

Kimberly VanEsveld Adams and Carol Mavor have recently seen the image of queenliness, particularly through representations of the

Madonna and classical or historical queens, as a response to both Victoria's passivity and contemporary cultural pressure to limit women's experience to the home. In the works of Victorian women writers like George Eliot, Anna Jameson, and Margaret Fuller, and in the visual works of photographers such as Julia Margaret Cameron, or Reina Lewis has argued, in the works of the painter Henriette Browne, placing women within the context of vocational nobility, as queens, nuns, or Madonnas, allowed an artist to represent "women and their work with dignity and stature."[6] Eliot participates in this type of negotiation in *The Mill on the Floss* and *The Spanish Gypsy* through her troubled representations of the "noble" heroines Maggie Tulliver and Fedalma, queen of the Zíncali Gypsies (*TMF*, 490). In Eliot's novel, Maggie's childhood confusion of escape to the Gypsies for abduction by them foreshadows her botched elopement with Stephen Guest, indicting the absence of her agency through her paradoxical nobility of moral purpose. Later, in the epic poem, Fedalma's legitimate "claim" over her people as their queen is the logical result of her innate "majesty" early in the poem. The escape or "abduction" of each heroine strives to release her from a hegemonic, gendered "captivity" within European culture. Historically, the Gypsies were associated with child abduction and pastoral freedom as well as with a mythology of their own "primitive" royal hierarchy, and they could be appropriated as a fluid site within which Eliot might narrate the experience of European women whom she figures as prisoners at home.

Anthropological and philological work of the late eighteenth and early to mid-nineteenth century had identified "Gypsydom" as "Eastern," tribal, and "ancient." Easily Orientalized because of their imagined origin in India or Egypt, Gypsies were often represented in literature as the subjects of fierce tribal hierarchies.[7] It is perhaps because the male Eastern ruler was so easily represented as a "despot" or "tyrant," who oppressed women in Victorian and Romantic literature, that Gypsy leaders were very often imagined as queens who could be romanticized because of their rebellious independence and the intense familial loyalty they were thought to inspire from their tribes.[8] The Gypsy queen could then be appropriated as having at her core the same female values espoused in maternalist iconography which represented Victoria herself.[9] Indeed, as Sharon Aronofsky Weltman has argued, "a metaphorical queen occupies a more real imaginative space for subjects of Victoria than the equally metaphorical but avowedly supernatural angel." In literature like John Ruskin's "Of Queens' Gardens," Queen Victoria's image is invoked only to be easily subsumed by "pagan imagery which mythically elevates woman into a colossal nature goddess, holding dominion over flora and fauna, controlling darkness and light."[10] This figure becomes capable of containing a different kind of "woman worship," a "mythopoesis" of womanly authority and competence.[11]

Ruskin's queens rule over "a sacred place, a vestal temple, a temple of the hearth. . . . [I]t vindicates the name, and fulfils the praise, of Home." But Ruskin is nonetheless capable of romanticizing female resourcefulness in "homelessness" or vagrancy as an effective signifier of woman's essential domesticity; his perception of the appropriately gendered woman's ability to contain and create home as a moral space stretches far beyond the house: "[T]he stars only may be over [a woman's] head; the glowworm in the night-cold grass may be the only fire at her foot; but home is yet wherever she is; and for a noble woman it stretches far round her, better than ceiled with cedar or painted with vermilion, shedding its quiet light far, for those who else were homeless."[12] From her position as a near-goddess of moral insight, Ruskin's noble vagrant may have "feminist appeal" for, despite her association with domesticity, she critiques the highly visible passivity of Victoria, "merging political and mythic images of queenship" and "trans[forming] the patronizing ideal of [Coventry Patmore's] 'woman worship' into an empowering model for material action" beyond women's home "gardens."[13] Ruskin must work his rhetoric hard to conflate both woman's wifely submission and her moral capacity to "praise" or condemn those in public or private life around her. He relies upon a popular Victorian discourse of white slavery to throw his notion of queenliness into relief, promoting "the idea that woman is only the shadow and attendant image of her lord, owing him a thoughtless and servile obedience, and supported altogether in her weakness by the pre-eminence of his fortitude. This, I say, is the most foolish of all errors respecting her who was made to be the helpmate of man. As if he could be helped effectively by a shadow, or worthily by a slave!"[14] Ruskin's image of white women's slavery in England allows him to critique masculinist desire even as he creates his own problematic counterimage of female agency. A similar construct which pushes the confines of woman's traditional role within domestic ideology is clearly engaged in Eliot's Gypsy queens, the last of whom is nearly exactly contemporary with Ruskin's essay written during a high pitch of cultural awareness and anxiety over Victoria as woman, widowed wife, and queen. However, the flights of Eliot's would-be Gypsy queens engage two cultural discourses, one of every English woman's potential nobility, the other of every Gypsy's potential sensuality.

Indeed, when Eliot's girls get alone with the Gypsies, their escape plans can easily be read as threatened abductions. In camp with their imagined Other tribes, they face the most problematic aspect of Eliot's Gypsy narratives, the representation of the Gypsy woman's eroticized body. Traveling with Gypsy men, in Victorian literature, in contrast, the reader often encounters a body potentially revivifying in its wildness:

> Confronted with what seemed to be the enfeeblement of a tough, independent peasantry, the city-based lovers of country life turned to that last bastion of rural resourcefulness, Gypsydom. By looks as well as temperament a foreign people, the Gypsies would not do as models of English racial virtue. But they could serve as representatives of the hardy competence associated with "true" country folk. Once mid-Victorian cultural critics began insisting that prosperity had been won at the cost of physical languor and a slavish regard for the norms of polite society, Gypsy waywardness could be seen as a virtue rather than a vice.[15]

But the competence of only the Gypsy *man*'s body is clear in many nineteenth-century narratives of life amongst them, narratives like Walter Scott's *Guy Mannering* or Matthew Arnold's "The Scholar Gipsy," in which abduction by Gypsies or truancy in their camp provides sanctuary with a people who still existed in the state "rude nature had formed them."[16]

It is through the presence of Gypsy men, in George Borrow's classic *Lavenegro*, that England can contain within it a "wild" country that Borrow wants to experience and claim; as ethnographer and philologist in search of Gypsy "lore," Borrow charts the "fluid, tangled pathways of an England that never quite unfolds into a map of home."[17] The closer he comes to the Gypsy people at home, the more a stable Englishness is disrupted until "Borrow's Britain is less a geography, a set of fixed and knowable places, than a topology: a shifting patchwork of wild and outlaw spaces, a reticulation of paths traversed by outcasts and wandering tribes."[18] Borrow's gendered access to both easy movement and training as a "Gypsy lorist" and linguist allows him to "pass" amongst them, and like the accomplished spy/translator/explorer/ethnographer/linguist Sir Richard Francis Burton in the Middle East, to come and go from their nomadic campsites at will.

Escape from civilization, however, is a gendered experience. For men such sojourns pose no challenge to an entrenched system of domestic ideology. An image of sylvan escape from "what wears out the life of mortal men," "this strange disease of modern life, with its sick hurry, its divided aims, its head o'ertaxed, its palsied hearts," Gypsy life might be embraced by a "truant boy" seeking a muscular faith now gone from Victorian England.[19] But in the books of "gypsy-lore" which Eliot owned and annotated, George Borrow's *The Zincali, or, An Account of the Gypsies of Spain* (1841) and H. M. G. Grellmann's *Dissertation on the Gipsies* (1787), the transient Gypsy culture, where women often worked alongside men, is represented as an earlier, older anthropological model that is as potentially dangerous for women as it is liberating for adult men. The disciplined path of English sexual mores—premarital chastity, sentimental courtship, marriage, and the proper education and rearing of children—seemed glaringly absent from Gypsy life. Marked by the darkness of their skin, hair, and eyes, Gypsies could embody multiple European fears and fantasies of racial contamination and sexual debauchery. Conflated within anthropological accounts of Gypsy women, those fears reveal a wealth of information about cultural perceptions of woman herself.

If, in the primitivist scheme, the Gypsy woman is quintessentially female, remaining in the state which "rude nature" had originally formed her, as such she was primarily a contaminant, an eroticized threat to the moral virtue of European men. In Grellmann's *Dissertation on the Gipsies,* he describes the Gypsy woman's "unclean" skin and loose morals; she might seek to seduce and exploit light-skinned European men, contaminating them in the process. The exotic Gypsy woman in the same work is alternately "beautiful" and "disgusting." Although mitigated by "black skin," her "white teeth, long black hair . . . lively, black rolling eyes, are, without dispute, properties which must be ranked among the list of beauties even by the modern civilized European world." But Grellmann's description of the male Gypsy body as fit and lean from his Spartan outdoor existence contrasts sharply with his vision of the female Gypsy body. Living the same active life as her male counterpart, the Gypsy woman strikes lorists as overtly sensual, earthy, and sexually corrupt. Her perceived heightened awareness of her body translates into a dangerous and threatening exploitation of its charms. This is clearest in his description of another business in which Gypsy women engage, dancing for profit, which is described as "another means they have of getting something" from "men in the streets." It too is aligned with prostitution:

> Their dances are the most disgusting that can be conceived, always ending with fulsome grimaces, or the most lascivious attitudes and gestures, uncovering those parts which the rudest and most uncultivated people carefully conceal; nor is this indecency confined to the married women only, but is rather more practiced by young girls ... who ... for a trifling acknowledgment, exhibit their dexterity to anybody, who is pleased with these unseemly dances. They are trained up to this impudence from their earliest years, never suffering a passenger to pass their parents' hut without trying to get something by striking about naked before him.[20]

Like Grellmann's Hottentot, the Gypsy woman was perceived as sexually promiscuous, nondiscriminatory, immodest, "rude," and "uncultivated." Unlike the Hottentot, however, she often lived in England or Europe where her "disgusting sight" might be glimpsed firsthand. "Let me only ask," reminds Grellmann, "if as children we have not at some time or other run affrighted from a Gipsey?"[21] Encounters between travelers and English people became a part of social mythology, for, "unlike the colonial subject who remained a remote and wholly foreign figure," the Gypsy was "a visible but socially peripheral character."[22] Sighting the Gypsy woman's "dark smile," perhaps in a rural "Gipsey Lane" as John Cross says Marian Evans had as a child, was a not uncommon experience fraught with a variety of implications.[23] "Persistent" rumors of gypsy abduction were mythologized in the nursery "by mothers and nurses who wanted to keep their children from wandering."[24] The Gypsy was a highly visible scapegoat, breaking laws not just of town and country but of culture and gender as well, and Gypsies found a special place as kidnappers within the burgeoning Victorian cult of the child and within a "novelistic tradition of foundling or bastard plots" through which "an English child might end up in the Gypsy world or a Gypsy child in the English."[25] As Gypsy children themselves could not be trusted, having been raised up to sexual and moral "impudence" from their infancy, they provided an effective backdrop against which white, British children could be contrasted as virtuous and innocent.

In addition to its portrayal in literature that includes Walter Scott's *Guy Mannering* and Matthew Arnold's "Scholar Gipsy," Gypsy culture was made accessible, by experts, to the public through the dissemination of Gypsy "lore," a special kind of scholarship that mimics the techniques of Orientalist texts. Gypsy lorists also appropriated and reconstituted information from each other, circulating the same falsehoods as facts. Although Orientalists presented their materials as "Indology" or "Oriental" ethnography, the Gypsy ethnographer or philologist represented his or her information as a particular type of knowledgeable discourse: "Gypsy lore." Even recent work on the nineteenth-century vogue for "Gypsy lore" sometimes uses the phrase innocently.[26] But the term "lore" is an important signifier of a particular epistemology that encompasses "the body of traditional facts, anecdotes, or beliefs relating to some particular subject; chiefly with attributive substantive, as animal, bird, fairy, plant lore."[27] In Victorian writings, the term is specific to the study of Gypsies as a people; it is not, that I can see, used to refer to the study of real people of other racial or ethnic identities. The term implies the possession of a master body of knowledge that is accomplished, total, and even mystical, extending to an understanding of the "beliefs" of a particular people. As "lore" is a word Eliot herself and many other Victorians often use to describe their own knowledge of nature, the term applied to the Gypsy places her almost in the same category, as a subject of nature rather than of civilization ("B & S," 5.1). Used also to describe imaginary subjects such as fairies, "lore" places its knowledge within the realm of the imagination rather than of reason or intellect. To know "deepest lore" in Eliot's "Brother and Sister Sonnets" is to place oneself within a tradition of nature "rambling" that provides special knowledge of oneself and one's connection to the natural world as well as to an Enlightenment construct of the "human family" and its sameness. In her notes from Gypsy lorists like George Borrow, Eliot follows their construction of the mythological origins of the Spanish Gypsies to Africa with great excitement, participating in a search for their origin that was clearly meaningful to her.[28] As Deborah Epstein Nord suggests, for Eliot as for the Brontës "Gypsy figures mark not only cultural difference but a deep sense of unconventional, indeed aberrant, femininity, experienced by these women writers." In "their own anomalousness and their deviance from acceptable modes of feminine thought, behavior, and appearance . . . they found in the Gypsy an image that would express in a self-consciously literary way their feelings of an almost racial separateness."[29] My interest here is in the extent to which an access to that racial separateness is troubled by gendered images of power and racial desire.

In Eliot's "Brother and Sister Sonnets," the sighting of a Gypsy woman articulates the price of the child's desire to escape the "trodden way" of convention. The woman's "lurk[ing]" otherness clearly signals the chasm between the child's desire for escape and her desire to be enclosed, safe within the "benediction of her [mother's] gaze" and her brother's handclasp (3). Walking away from brother and mother, both authority figures, the girl momentarily quits her own destiny to try on another. "Rambling" with her brother, she evokes Wordsworth's nature poetry, "roam[ing]" amidst a pastoral "wonder" land where the natural world "seem[s] all to speak with eyes of souls that dumbly heard and knew," a "deep tone chant from life unknown to me," a "happy strange solemnity." The girl's trust in her brother is signaled by her willingness to learn from him there, and his excellent woodsmanship is naturalized in what seems like an imitation of Wordsworth's youthful ramblings. But the moment of primal identification between brother and sister is disrupted, "darkened" by the entrance of the homeless, vagrant Gypsy woman and the dramatic sign of her transience, the "black-scathed grass" left by her fire (4.10). This moment of encounter may be linked to other Gypsy scenes in Eliot, scenes in which girls assess the cost of their own wandering away from convention.

In her landmark essay on Eliot and Wordsworth, Margaret Homans links Eliot's representations of rural wandering from *The Mill on the Floss*'s "Maggie and the little sister in the sonnets" to the sisters "instructed" by the Wordsworthian narrator in his rambles. Homans notes that Eliot's siblings in novel and poem "live in a fallen, gendered world in which they can never escape for very long the pain produced by their social condition." In both texts, Eliot's narrator speaks lovingly of a "reciprocity" that is never explicit in plots which make the separate, unequal realities of boys', and girls', lives clear: "Our basket held a store baked for us only, and I thought with joy that I should have my share, though he had more, because he was the elder and a boy" ("B & S," 2.5–8). Roaming the woods lost in "vagrant thoughts," the sonnet's little sister is like Maggie and Wordsworth's sister "protected" from receiving not just her share of bread, but her share of "enlarging transgressions" which are necessary, in Wordsworth's nature poetry, to "the boy's moral and imaginative education."[30] When Eliot's little sister steps away from a fleeting glimpse of a "startling" sight, a nomadic woman, her "play" in the footsteps of her brother is disrupted by a transgressive paradigm which is female and Other. The moment flirts with "lorist" images of the Gypsy's "mystic" appearance, and disappearance, in the forest setting, and with the child's accidental penetration of an Other woman's hidden life in nature. That solitary moment in the poem, when the girl seems to have penetrated or entered into an Other plot, possibly into the literary tradition of Gypsy abduction, quickly retreats into one of human community and "whole[ness]" with her brother and all the world of nature. The instability of that vision seems confirmed by the rift between brother and sister at the poem's end. Linking poem and novel, these vagrant sisters are indeed returned home to "fallen, gendered" plots that are bodied forth by Other women, rather than by the brother's discipline and the mother's complicity in the girl's privation, the restriction of her "share."

The sighting of the Gypsy in Eliot's poem can be read as a moment of crossing over between plots and racial scripts that seems less to link the sister to her brother than to prefigure the "blot" in this overtly autobiographical narrative of Eliot's sexual transgression. Her alienation from her brother in the poem is permanent: "the dire years whose awful name is Change had grasped our souls still yearning in divorce, and pitiless shaped them in two forms that range two elements which sever their life's course" (11). The encounter with the Gypsy foreshadows the final "blot" of sexual experience; however, it avoids the phallocentric gaze which supplements masculinist colonial visions of racial desire. In careful language Eliot suggests the nomadic Gypsy woman provides a window into a primitive willfulness and embodied sexuality that was both romantic and liberating, terrible and frightening, when encountered by young, disenfranchised girls. Ultimately, Gypsydom promises its pleasures to Eliot's girl heroines, but those pleasures are so heady that they must be negotiated and disciplined by an "intoxicating" rhetoric of queenliness, one of the few languages available to Eliot in which she might envision a way out of women's domestic captivity. [31]

VIOLENT RAGES AND impulses mark Eliot's first flirtation with the image of the Gypsy in fiction, Caterina Sarti in "Mr. Gilfil's Love

Story," the second of the *Scenes of Clerical Life*. Sarti is of Italian descent, not an ethnic Gypsy like those in *The Mill on the Floss*, *The Spanish Gypsy*, and the sonnets. However, her interesting juxtaposition with Heathcliff and Catherine of *Wuthering Heights* and her constant description in the language of exotic Victorian darkness as a "Gypsy changeling," a "tigress," a "little black-eyed monkey," suggest that a symbolic ethnic and racial presence is central to her character.[32] The story importantly establishes an ethnic context for woman's political and sexual rebellion in Eliot's later works, initiating questions on domesticity, maternity, desirous sexuality, and the desire for self-rule, which are elaborated upon in later texts. Through Caterina, Eliot seems to reject the anthropological model of the evolved British family, led by its profoundly domesticated and non-desirous woman, the hallmark of Victorian social evolution. Her Caterina produces, at the end, no abbreviated, gentle, and maternal "Cathy." Instead, as Eliot ends the Cheverel family dynasty, she creates a paradox of domesticated sterility. Against the background of their racial desire and their racial prejudice, Caterina is represented not as a queenly but as an impotent white "Other," a captive first of seduction, then of marriage, and finally of maternity.

As with Catherine in Brontë's novel, the reader first meets Caterina Sarti after her death. Her room is preserved, never entered by anyone besides her widower, Mr. Gilfil, and old Martha the housekeeper (129). This "locked-up chamber" in Mr. Gilfil's house is "a sort of visible symbol of the secret chamber in his heart, where he had long turned the key on early hopes and early sorrows, shutting up forever all the passion and the poetry of his life" (130). The isolated room, with its disintegrating, half-finished infant clothes, preserved for thirty years like empty talismans, underscores the barren quality of the story's infertile ruling family and their class. The familiar narrative proceeds in the voice of the "communicative old lady," Mrs. Patten, but is soon interrupted by Eliot's narrator who offers to "carry your imagination back to the latter end of the last century" to tell of Caterina's childhood, her unhappy love affair, her marriage, and her early death in childbirth (132).[33]

Rescued from starvation by the British aristocrats, Sir Christopher and Lady Cheverel, Caterina is brought from her native Italy to England where she soon takes on the role of resident outsider (147). Growing up almost wild, "very much like the primroses which the gardener is not sorry to see within his enclosure, but takes no pains to cultivate," Caterina bonds with nature, and, in keeping with Victorian stereotypes of ethnic difference, becomes a passionate adolescent, a desirous child-woman who has begun a liaison with an adult man (159). But Caterina's Otherness prevents her from marrying the object of her desire, Sir Christopher's nephew and heir, Anthony. A social-realist retort to the Earnshaws, the Cheverels never "had any idea of adopting her as their daughter, and giving her their own rank in life. They were much too English and aristocratic to think of anything so romantic." Caterina might become a "protege, to be ultimately useful" (152). Set in 1788, on the advent of revolution in France, Caterina's story is a microcosm of that class revolt which is here played out in the domestic realm. As the "great nation of France was agitated by conflicting thoughts and passions," so does she experience "terrible struggles" of will and desire. In her passion for Anthony she "dashes" herself against "the hard iron bars of the inevitable," the deep-seated British fear of exogamy (147).

In this story, the issues of color and race, Britishness and foreignness, are consistently gendered as Caterina's sexual desire and her woman's body itself are made to seem strange, even monstrous in their foreignness. Against a background "all of creamy white," Caterina seems "yellowish" (134). The difference is most emphatic when she and Anthony are together "in all the striking contrast of their coloring—he with his exquisite outline and rounded fairness, like an Olympian god; she dark and tiny, like a Gypsy changeling" (146). In contrast to her petite stature, Caterina experiences violent, demonic currents of jealousy and desire which cause her to "set her teeth against the window-frame" in her "mad passion" for Anthony (177).

Audrey Carr Shields has explored the imagined emotional "intensity" of Gypsy people in Victorian fiction. Passion, in literature, can lead "Gypsy women in Victorian melodramatic fiction to mental instability, actual insanity, aggressive behavior, and suicide." Indeed, combining stereotypes of "gender and race," the Gypsy woman who is wronged in love often behaves with complete abandon in literature, as, in the popular mind, she always does in matters of the heart.[34] Like the heroines of William Harrison Ainsworth's *Rookwood* or Hannah Maria Jones's *The Gipsey Girl*, Caterina plans to stab her lover before the degenerate aristocrat is struck down by a highly symbolic heart attack. But although violent Gypsy women in the popular literature are carefully "distanc[ed] on racial grounds" from "more controlled and civilized Victorian womanhood," Caterina violently disrupts the Victorian cult of womanly virtue. Her rage may have an ethnic mask, but its source is clearly based in domestic ideology.[35]

Eliot is utterly explicit on the agenda of the English people who surround Caterina in her illness after Anthony's death. "If she were domesticated for a time with [Mr. Gilfil's] mild, gentle sister, who had a peaceful home and a prattling little boy, Tina might attach herself anew to life and recover" (237). Yet, what Gilfil desires, along with attaching Caterina anew to life, is that she attach and adapt herself to the tradition of nondesirous femininity and self-sacrificing maternity. As she is "domesticated," Caterina is held captive even within her own body. Pregnant, she shrinks to prepubescent size. "She looked younger than she really was, like a little girl of twelve who was being taken away from coming instead of past sorrow" (233). The passionate "tigress" who would have stabbed the faithless Anthony in a fit of sexual jealousy is firmly returned to childhood, becoming a pathetic figure: the "utmost improvement in Tina had not gone beyond passiveness and acquiescence" (239).

Newly acquiescent, in her nondesirous body, Tina marries the curate, Mr. Gilfil, and is expected to blot out her memories of her past desire by producing "a new 'little black-eyed monkey'" (242–43). But that element of herself, her ethnicity and its intrinsic link to her sexuality, has been permanently quelled. Deirdre David has briefly argued that "Mr. Gilfil's Love Story," with its focus on an impassioned, uncontrollable Italian woman, foreshadows the rebellious female challenge presented in *Daniel Deronda*.[36] I agree, but I think that the story has further significance for Eliot's Gypsy narratives and for *Middlemarch* which continues to portray the erotic through Otherness. Caterina's refusal of maternity without sexual pleasure, moreover, links her to Fedalma of Eliot's epic poem, another Gypsy woman who refuses biological maternity. The "rebellious female challenge" which the Gypsy woman presented to domestic ideology and her binary opposite of "white innocence" becomes even less metaphoric in Eliot's *Mill on the Floss* where discourses of race, both whiteness and blackness, clarify Maggie Tulliver's struggle with women's compulsory innocence.

MAGGIE TULLIVER IMAGINES herself to be a Gypsy and attempts to escape to them, her "unknown kindred," in the chapter titled "Maggie Tries to Run Away from Her Shadow" (*TMF*, 168). Once there, she hopes to displace their home rule and become their leader. Indeed, after a harrowing afternoon with her tyrannical "master" Tom and her meek cousin Lucy, Maggie seems interested in replacing not just her race but also in exchanging the law of the father for that of the queen: "My father is Mr. Tulliver. But we musn't let him know where I am, else he'll fetch me home again. Where does the queen of the Gypsies live?" Maggie's desire to rule is clear: "I'm only thinking that if [the queen of the Gypsy tribe] isn't a very good queen you might be glad when she died, and you could choose another. If I was a queen, I'd be a very good queen, and kind to everybody" (174). Maggie's comic presentation of herself as the next queen of this particular group of Gypsies is usually read as a temporary fantasy while Maggie herself has been seen as "incomprehensibly foreign."[37] She "abandons" her escape or "fails." However, Maggie's early desire to rule is linked to her moral nobility later in the novel. As an adult, her moral and physical "superiority" will provide the novel with its tragic conflict between will and desire. Indeed, Maggie's model of queenly behavior recalls other Victorian images of queens whose power, like Ruskin's queens, is strictly disciplinary—chaste, maternalist, and nondesirous. Maggie's desire to be queen of the Gypsies, to teach them of Columbus and good hygiene, expresses as much her lure to a moral "queen's garden" as to "eccentricity" and "rebellion." Paradoxically, Maggie's representation as a white captive links her to a popular nineteenth-century "rhetoric of freedom" that informs her earliest incarnation as a Gypsy.[38]

Nina Auerbach has linked Maggie's attraction to the Gypsies with her demonic and witchlike qualities, both of which are "entangled in her pull toward the smoky, nocturnal underworld of the Gypsies."[39] Certainly, early in the novel, from the safety zone of childhood, Maggie is potentially able to replace the Victorian script of feminine reticence with desirous action. But as Maggie grows, her life options contract, and Eliot begins to use race and a subtle Orientalism as a metaphor for her "bondage" (*TMF*, 559). Eventually, Maggie's "queenly" "nobility" and "uncommon" dignity become the overseers of her own captivity (388). If the first half of the novel represents Maggie's "eccentricity" as a "mark of race" made visible in a corporeal darkness that requires allusions to Gypsies and mulattoes, her captivity in the second half of the novel requires a discourse of race that operates by the same logic.[40] What remains in her adulthood after Maggie's childhood blackness has fallen away is the logical result, an expropriation or image of queenly white slavery that, like Hiram Powers's *Greek Slave* or Henriette Browne's *Greek Captive*, dispenses with slavery's black historicity.[41]

A chaos of dark images pervades the earliest representation of

Maggie Tulliver. She is a mulatto and "Jael" before Eliot settles on Gypsydom as an accessible localized site for Maggie's racial difference. Susan Fraiman has read Maggie's flight to the Gypsy camp as Eliot's flirtation with and then abandonment of the male, colonial *bildungsroman* plot.[42] But the free, indirect discourse that narrates Maggie's thoughts is divided on the colonialist project of her escape. She is as interested in "civilizing" the Gypsies as she is in finding with them "a refuge from all the blighting obloquy that had pursued her in civilised life" (*TMF*, 168). Like Caterina and Fedalma, Maggie experiences the "civilized" world as a constant obstruction of her most elemental desires even as she experiences her own desires as intolerable and unacceptable or "savage"—a word that is repeated many times in the second half of her story. Maggie's fantasy of kinship and queenship tells a disturbing story of coming of age and sexual initiation that owes much to colonialist thinking throughout the novel.

Deborah Epstein Nord has already argued the serious nature of Maggie's biological identification with the Gypsies within the context of women and the Freudian family romance. Locating the competing tones of irony and tragedy in Eliot's narration of the scene, Nord suggests that the "urgency of Maggie's desire to find 'unknown kindred' ceases to remain merely comic when she glimpses the tall figure she takes to be 'the Gypsy-mother.' . . . Maggie imagines—and suddenly sees—a mother who reflects back at her and thereby affirms what her own mother rejects."[43] If Eliot does "lampoon" the colonial *bildungsroman* "narrative of self-definition through domination" in *The Mill on the Floss* she takes the same narrative quite seriously in her epic poem and, I believe, in the novel as Maggie comes to establish there, despite her near vagrancy and shabbiness, a "queenly" dominion over its moral world (*TMF*, 388). Susan Meyer has discussed the failures of both Maggie Tulliver and Fedalma "to solve the problem of [their] secondary status as wom[e]n by joining the community of an alternate race," and Eliot's appropriations of Gypsy Otherness have been discussed as an attempt to employ Victorian stereotypes of Gypsy "willfulness" to signal female political rebellion.[44] Maggie's "incomprehensible foreignness" has been seen as part of the novel's "planlessness, riddles, and impropriety—the enigmas, accidents, and incorrectness of language" in the text which Margaret Homans suggests are "at odds with the closures of plot (here the plot of incestuous reunion) and with interpretation itself."[45] I would like to suggest that the problem of exile to another race and Eliot's expropriation of the image actually share the same logic constructed by Victorian discourses on race and gender, discourses that directly engage the conflict of reunion between Maggie and her blue-eyed brother, Tom.

Like Victorian minstrelsy in which white male actors took the guises of black men and women, Maggie's trying on of a Gypsy identity becomes "a sure way to discover . . . or at least to attempt to define through negation" what she "might be" and what new plots she might invent for herself.[46] Her encounter with the Gypsies is best explored in the context of her childhood desire to escape the rigidly antisensual aspects of adult English society and in her concomitant bodily fear of what a new plot might bring. Indeed, as in the "Brother and Sister Sonnets," Maggie's encounter with the Gypsy camp constitutes a journey from the heart of encultured domesticity to a wild, free place populated by "half-savage" cultural Others. Once there, Maggie imagines that she will be devoured, either in a Gypsy stew or as their captive bride. The politics of race and gender converge in the escapade to ensure that Maggie, unlike Arnold's escapee, is not a wild queen but a disciplinary one who holds the desirous self captive. Written only a few years after the Indian Mutiny of 1857, which Jenny Sharpe convincingly argues initiated fictional representations of "interracial rape," the Gypsy episode does not just lampoon the colonial plot; it also lampoons representations of sexualized colonialist hysteria.[47]

The day that Maggie runs away "had begun ill," with elaborate "civilized" rituals of domestic ideology, all of which involve the taming, control, and enclosure of her body (*TMF*, 145). After Maggie and her "wild" hair are subjected to the contempt of Mr. Rappit, the town hairdresser, she is dressed uncomfortably in the clothes of adult womanhood for her visit to Aunt Pullet's equally uncomfortable home. Once there, the men and women divide, and the latter participate in the elaborate revelation of Aunt Pullet's house: deep within a domestic heart of darkness is Aunt Pullet's closet, the comic center of her domestic empire. Soon Maggie finds herself in the parlor with her aunt, uncle, mother, and cousins. There, she and the children are instructed to hold carefully "tempting" pieces of smooth, brown cake in their hands, not eating them until the maid brings a tray and plates. Eliot gracefully alludes to Homer to underscore both the antisensuality of the scene and Maggie's estrangement from her family. While holding her piece of cake, the nine-year-old girl becomes "fascinated" by a print of Odysseus and Nausicaa. She is, of course, looking at a picture of Nausicaa who is standing in the water and gazing at Odysseus, who is nearly naked. The sexual politics of the moment from Homer are important:

> So was Odysseus about to mingle with the fair-braided girls,
> Although he was naked. For need had come upon him.
> Frightfully begrimed with brine did he appear to them.
> One ran one way, one another, on the jutting shores.
> The daughter of Alcinoos alone stayed; Athene
> Had put courage in her mind and taken fear from her limbs.
> She stood in one place facing him.[48]

Looking at Nausicaa, Maggie privately views a revelation of a different sort, a stately and graceful celebration of a royal princess's fearless viewing of a male nude. It is particularly important that Nausicaa's vision of Odysseus takes place under the sanction and guidance of the virgin goddess figure, Athene. Maggie drops her cake to the floor and is soon brought to a state of "conscious disgrace" (154); she has made a mess on Aunt Pullet's spotless floor. Her shame is compounded when next, in pleasure over Uncle Pullet's music box, Maggie throws her arm around Tom's neck and spills his wine. Maggie's pleasure is "too rough," undemure, unladylike, for this civilized gathering. She is placed in direct contrast to the vigorous and athletic Nausicaa, who is favorably compared with the "arrow-shooting Artemis" and who is engaged in a vigorous game of ball when her shouts arouse the sleeping Odysseus.[49] But Maggie is not entitled to such physical pleasure; nor is she entitled to embrace the blue-eyed brother whom she fiercely loves.

Moving from inside to outside, Maggie and her cousins are then asked to leave the house and to play in the garden, an extension of the house. But "in so prim a garden where they were not to go off the paved walks there was not a great choice of sport" (162). Tom leads Lucy out the garden gate to the pond in the meadow while the estranged Maggie follows. There a Victorian version of the encounter between Odysseus and Nausicaa is ironically reenacted. Rather than the rigorous games on the beach, where Nausicaa and her maidens rush in and out of the water, the English children's play is marked by stillness and silence as they approach the shore. Lucy is particularly fearful as she approaches the mud-ringed pond, careful not to soil her clothes. Unable to forgive Maggie for spilling his wine, Tom excludes her from play as he sights not a naked man but a highly erotic substitute, "a golden arrow-head darting through the water. It was a water-snake" (163).

Eliot's play on Homer is subtle and ironic. Her changes reflect the gendered sexual politics of her own day in which gods and goddesses are eschewed for one celibate male God, who with a cloistered Queen of Heaven, expressed in the image of the Madonna, rather than vital goddesses or princesses, sets sexual boundaries. Tom, the juvenile patriarch, who is also very much the object of his little sister's "incestuous" desire, sets the boundaries.[50] He decides that the timid, fair, still Lucy, whom he later idealizes as an unattainable lover, is alone to be permitted to see the snake. She comes to the water "carefully, as she was bidden" by him (163). He defines what she sees. "It was a water-snake, Tom told her, and Lucy at last could see the serpentine wave of its body, very much wondering that a snake could swim." Maggie is literally marginalized, told to "get away. . . . There's no room for you on the grass here. Nobody asked you to come." The dignified moment of discovery, the sensuous pleasure and stately physical grace that had fascinated her in Aunt Pullet's parlor, is wiped away. The scene moves from the epic to the mock heroic: "There were passions at war in Maggie at that moment to have made a tragedy, if tragedies were made by passion only, but the essential τι μέγεθος which was present in the passion, was wanting to the action; the utmost Maggie could do, with a fierce thrust of her small brown arm, was to push poor little pink-and-white Lucy into the cow-trodden mud" (164).

It is this action of brown on pink-and-white violence that precipitates Maggie's decision to run away to the Gypsies whom she is convinced will accept and embrace her as their ruler and queen. After this moment at the pond, which contrasts so sharply with Nausicaa's vision of the male body, it becomes clear to Maggie that she is an outsider and that there is "no room" for her. As a queen she might remake herself as a leader and respected authority figure. But as a child, unlike the young Nausicaa, Maggie lives in a world that does not perceive any outward signs of her innate right to rule. As she leaves her English self and kin to take up with what she imagines to be her true family, she encounters her vulnerability to men for the first time. In the road, she is immediately frightened by two men, "formidable strangers . . . shabby-looking . . . with flushed faces," Suddenly, she feels naked. She realizes that "she had no sleeves on— only a cape and a bonnet." The men, smiling and winking at each other when she gives them a sixpence, are "less respectful" than she would like. She walks on past them "hurriedly" but "was aware that the two men were standing still, probably to look after her and she

presently heard them laughing loudly" (169). It is a "humiliating encounter" which drives her off the high road to the hedgerows where
she experiences "a delightful sense of privacy in creeping along"
(170). Like Dickens's Little Nell, this unprotected, wandering girl is
dangerously vulnerable to an exploitation that has specifically sexual
overtones. Her escape seems potentially to be rewritten as abduction
at any moment.

Maggie's encounter with the Gypsies epitomizes her sense of Otherness. Beginning her "adventure of seeking her unknown kindred,
the Gypsies" (171), she brings with her the cultural assumptions so
well expressed by Grellmann and Borrow. As Anita Levy convincingly
argues, the base of anthropological prejudice against "Other" women
expresses cultural anxieties about the sex itself. As earlier evolutionary models, Gypsy women embody the origin of woman herself, in all
her perceived depravity. As soon as she acts on her desire to be a
Gypsy, Maggie immediately, and for the first time, feels herself to be
a woman and a sexual target. Walking down this "strange lane" of
sexual self-discovery she "hardly dared look on one side of her, lest
she should see the diabolical blacksmith in his leathern apron grin-
ning at her with arms akimbo" (171). Her journey to the Gypsies then
becomes fraught with unwanted sexual opportunities. Making her
desire to escape her position in her own culture a reality, Maggie receives in return the punishment that her society doles out to female
deviants. Eliot makes clear that the resulting sexual threat has its
source in the cultural baggage Maggie brings to her escape. When she
finally arrives at the Gypsies' camp, she is so disoriented that, like a
Gypsy "lorist," she does not even recognize these others as human
rather than as animal or plant, "a small pair of bare legs sticking up,
feet uppermost, by the side of a hillock . . . seemed something
hideously preternatural—a diabolical kind of fungus." ("[S]he was
much too agitated at the first glance to see the ragged clothes and the
dark shaggy head attached to them. It was a boy asleep . . . it did not
occur to her that he was one of her friends the Gypsies, who in all
probability would have very genial manners [171].)

This exposure of the body contrasts sharply with the graceful moment between Odysseus and Nausicaa. This scene of the sleeping
boy's "bare legs sticking up," like the viewing of the water snake, has
none of the natural grace of Homer's scene of awakening and encounter. Contrasted with the boy's unselfconscious, abandoned
sleep, Maggie carries with her a deeply internalized fear of the body.

Her vision of male "bareness" is disrupted, compromised by threats to her sense of security and safety. Unlike the "daughter of Alcinoos" who calmly "stood in one place facing" the awakened Odysseus, Maggie fearfully runs "along faster and more lightly lest she should wake him." With no protective Athene, Maggie is very much alone and vulnerable. She is accompanied instead by terrible disciplinary or outlaw men, characters from her Bible and *Pilgrim's Progress*, who are jumbled with secular images of threatening male criminals and freaks in one hallucinogenic stream. Apollyon walks with a "highway man with a pistol, and a blinking dwarf in yellow with a mouth from ear to ear." The devil himself watches her in the shape of a "diabolical blacksmith" (171). Things seem to improve at first when Maggie meets the Gypsy women: "This face with the bright dark eyes and the long hair was really something like what she used to see in the glass before she cut her hair off." She is "reassured by the thought that her aunt Pullet and the rest were right when they called her a Gypsy." The tall, young Gypsy mother is the only woman Maggie physically identifies with throughout the novel. The Gypsies are the first characters in the novel, moreover, to refer to her as a "pretty lady" (172).

Reversing the popular myth that Gypsies kidnapped white children and the equally prevalent belief that they sought to entrap white girl children to exploit them as prostitutes, Eliot's Gypsies only hope to be compensated for their good deed when they return Maggie to her home. The narrator then creates a clear division between the true nature of the Gypsies and Maggie's nearly hysterical perception of them. Although Eliot's narrator reveals the band of Gypsies as merely hungry and tired, Maggie's vision of Gypsy culture is a nightmarish glimpse into the shadows within herself, particularly her sexual self. She perceives the Gypsy camp as a terrifying, sexualized place. In contrast to the high domestication of Aunt Pullet's home, the camp seems topsy-turvy. The Gypsies are described through Maggie's eyes as the old woman, the young female with a baby, the tall girl, the older man, and the younger man. Maggie is unable to identify the Gypsy "family" within this group. Indeed, Eliot points out that Maggie's perspective here, as in so many other episodes in the novel, is compromised by her poor education. "Her thoughts generally were the oddest mixture of clear-eyed acumen and blind dreams." But, the narrator adds, Maggie does know the meaning of the word "polygamy." Ironically, the anomalous family setting turns threatening as the Gypsies' clear intent *not* to adopt Maggie finally becomes evident. Now "her ideas about Gypsies undergo a rapid modification" (177). In her comic panic when she realizes that the Gypsies do not perceive her as their "queen," Maggie enacts Jenny Sharpe's understanding of colonialist sexual terror: "[T]he European fear of interracial rape does not exist so long as there is a belief that colonial structures of power are firmly in place."[51] Without her imagined dominion, Maggie perceives her vulnerability at once and fears that the Gypsies see her as a body. She believes they may be cannibals; they might "kill her as soon as it was dark, and cut up her body for gradual cooking." She dislikes the earthy smell of their stew and fears that the older Gypsy "was in fact the devil" who might be able to read her thoughts (177).

Ironically, Maggie's nightmare of colonial encounter becomes most lurid when the Gypsies determine to return her to her parents and to her "true" identity and ethnicity. Indeed, "no nightmare had ever seemed to her more horrible" than riding home on the Gypsies' donkey behind the younger man. "I wish you'd go with me too," Maggie says to the Gypsy mother. "She thought anything was better than going with one of the dreadful men alone" (178). The sexual fear Maggie experiences is made explicit through Eliot's allusion to G. A. Burger's *Leonore,* "a powerful, lively, and gruesome work about a bride taken on a long ride by her dead lover."[52] Eliot compares Maggie's terror to Leonore's "with her phantom lover." Not even she "was more terrified than poor Maggie in this entirely natural ride on a short-paced donkey, with a Gypsy behind her who considered that he was earning half-a-crown" (179).

Maggie's inability to protect herself sexually is endemic to her political position. Alone on the high road, she knows that she is perceived, as Grellmann and Borrow perceive Gypsy women, as sexually available, unprotected by an "organized" coherent family system. In her adult life, Maggie will confront the accusation that she is "unnatural" as well as sexually corrupt or morally loose because she chooses to forego male protection. For Maggie, to acknowledge her sexuality is to be seen as she, through her distorted, hallucinogenic vision, sees the Gypsies. It is the fear of being perceived by her family and society as Grellmann and Borrow perceive the Gypsies which prevents her from experiencing sexual pleasure; that experience carries heavy burdens in the novel. Try as she might, Maggie will never be able to escape the disciplinary "shadow" of the sexual disapproval that she herself has internalized. Her desire to escape civilization is written over an internal text that shames her for experiencing that desire. Her attempted flight to the Gypsies poignantly illustrates that double bind that becomes the crux of the novel and the source of Maggie's painful stasis. While Nina Auerbach has illustrated the psychological aspects of Maggie's static role, it is clear that Maggie's psychological stasis is located in a culturally constructed system that defines and limits the behavior of women by placing them in a rigid anthropological standard of "civilization" that insists upon their sequestration under male agency.

Eliot's representation of the absurdity of Maggie's vision of the Gypsies' desire to eat or rape her suggests the many, many Victorian representations of the colonial encounter as the rape of white women who were in turn represented as "illustration[s] of courage in adversity, of spiritual power arising from temporal powerlessness."[53] Maggie's *fear* in adversity, her panic on the way home to her family, foreshadows her outrage at Stephen Guest who also fails to recognize her nobility, taking advantage of her body rather than envisioning her as a "war-goddess" in the battle of sexual "renunciation."[54] Again when Maggie allows herself to float downriver with Stephen Guest she imagines herself robbed of her agency and accuses him of abducting her against her will. Initially, Maggie's attempted escapes seem to fulfill her paradoxical double fantasy of wild domestic dominion and refuge from civilization. As there is an entrenched Victorian discourse of identification through racial expropriation operating in Maggie's Gypsy escapade, the "trying on" of Gypsydom returns Maggie to a whiteness that is continually disrupted by other presences.[55]

Throughout the last books of *The Mill on the Floss,* Maggie Tulliver continues to be haunted by racial desire, but it is no longer her own desire for difference that she experiences or represents. The gendering of desirous Otherness shifts as she becomes an object of desire in the marriage market which Eliot, like so many Victorian artists, represents as a slave market. The "Bazaar" or open market of "Charity in Full Dress" in which Maggie is viewed by the men of St. Oggs, for example, is marked by a subtle Orientalism. It seems the point of the scene is to make her visible, to "penetrate" her own desire for privacy, and to contrast her refinement with the vulgarity or physical flaws of the women around her, as if she were indeed one of the "commodities" on sale. Maggie's "simple noble beauty, clad in a white muslin of some soft-floating kind . . . appeared with marked distinction among the more adorned and conventional women around her" (547). Like the central white captive figure in an Orientalist harem or Bazaar painting, Maggie becomes the "object of such general attention and inquiry and excited so troublesome a curiosity as . . . to make her post a very conspicuous one." In contrast to Maggie, who is, like the many Victorian representations of white captives on the "threshold" of a major change in her life, Stephen Guest's male luxury and vanity are epitomized by his wearing of a "scarlet Fez" at the Bazaar (548). As the gendering of racial desire in the novel reverses, Maggie becomes both more white and more queenly. She takes up the exacting, low-paid textile work of "plain sewing," acquiring a subtle association with another popular nineteenth-century representation of captivity, the white slavery of nineteenth-century textile workers.[56] Eliot's appropriation of race becomes expropriation, adopting the subject position of the Other while subsuming racial difference into Maggie's whiteness. The logic of Eliot's positioning Maggie within this particular rhetoric of freedom recalls Maggie's early Otherness, linking it irrevocably to her subject position in the later stages of the novel.

It is all too easy to fail to conflate the child and adult versions of Maggie Tulliver; the contrast seems "incomprehensible." Philip Wakem has to explain to his father of the portraits he has painted of Maggie, as a girl and a woman: that "they are the same person . . . at different ages" (540). But there is a unity in the novel from Maggie's excursion to Gypsydom to her near-vagrancy as an adult; her moves from Lucy's home, to her Aunt Gritty's, on the canal and aboard ship with Stephen Guest, to Bob Jakin's rooming house, and finally home to a house that is under water. Because of her homelessness, Maggie begins more seriously to embody a vision of tragic rather than comic queenliness, like "Marie Antoinette" looking "all the grander when her gown was darned" or like "a fallen princess serving behind a counter" (440, 550). Maggie's "queenly head, noble" bearing, and constant crown or "coronet" of hair mark her as the novel's queen who seeks to but cannot transcend the open market in which she finds herself. "I knew well enough what she'd be, before now—it's nothing new to me," says Mr. Tulliver. "But it's a pity she isn't made of commoner stuff—she'll be thrown away, I doubt" (388). Maggie's ideals seem to prefigure Ruskin's desire for a female nobility which is transcendently homeless, a "queen of the air" defying material constraints, exploding categories of "private and public." The Victorian period's gendered discourse of women's essential queenliness reified a "notion of queenship that offers women under the reign of Queen Victoria a powerful political and mythological model for the broadening of their scope of action, thereby redefining the traditionally domestic arena to include a broad range of philanthropy and social activism."[57] But like Maggie's nobility, the Victorian everywoman's queenliness often foundered on its antithesis, her near-"slavery." Both discourses can be fashioned around narratives of vagrancy, abduction, nobility, and the problem of embodied "freedom" in Eliot's epic, *The Spanish Gypsy*.

THE DISTURBING ENDING of *The Spanish Gypsy* (1868–69) has struck critics as failing to fulfill the definition of tragedy itself.[58] Its ending is "horrifying" because its heroine's decision to lead the Zincali people to a permanent homeland seems doomed to fail.[59] Fedalma's rejection of personal happiness, in the shape of marriage to her Spanish lover, Don Silva, seems then, nearly perverse, willfully self-abnegating. Moreover, as Kimberly Adams writes, the poem doesn't seem to work as tragedy, which, by Eliot's definition, involves a choice between two morally good options. To go with the Zincali people seems less a virtuous sacrifice than a guarantee of vocational failure. Much of the critical interest in Eliot's epic poem has shaped itself around this problem, without considering how Victorian understandings of Fedalma's pleasures as "mother" to her people might possibly inform a reading of the poem. Indeed, an awareness of the rising cultural interest in the representation of maternal subjectivity in the 1860s helps contextualize Eliot's representation of Fedalma's complex, figurative maternity. Epitomized in the contemporary photographs of sensuous and even erotic Madonnas by Julia Margaret Cameron, and in the nurse/nun paintings of Henriette Browne, it is clear that some women artists were pushing the cultural limits placed upon representing maternity. However, as Victorian women artists seek to represent a previously forbidden experience, two phenomena result: first the vocabulary of empire permits their speech while the legacy of the odalisque permits their images; second, Orientalist representations of maternal pleasure as unproductive or destructive are placed as binary opposites against productive Christian maternalism. In response to high-Victorian culture which increasingly demanded the erosion of maternal subjectivity in favor of the ascendancy of the child subject, representing the story of the mother is a new enterprise that often looks to the past for authentication—

to Titian's Mary in the *Annunciation* which inspired *The Spanish Gypsy*, or to Old Testament women like the "Shunamite Woman" in Julia Margaret Cameron's photograph of the same title (plate 3). Eliot's many thematic and representational turns and reversals in *The Spanish Gypsy* may very well reflect her difficulties in experimenting with ways to represent motherhood that actually include the pains and pleasures of the mother herself; *The Spanish Gypsy* may indeed be "horrifying," not just for its exigencies of form, but also for its difficulties in locating a plot beyond those offered by maternalist culture.

Abducted from her Gypsy home, raised by Spanish nobility, and then forced to leave that adoptive home or face torture under the Inquisition, Eliot's epic heroine is caught between two narratives of captivity, becoming a "subject under siege" like other subjects of British captivity narratives. Her experience as an Other within both Western and Eastern or African cultures locates the female self as in possession of a potentially "divided, corruptible, transgressive identity." Her destabilizing experience of captivity then can be considered as a process which, rather than "enshrin[ing] an aggressive colonialism. . . . register[s], and pose[s] in its turn, fundamental problems in national identity and character."[60] As the fundamental problem Fedalma most points to is the problem of maternal subjectivity, becoming "goddess," queen, and virgin mother of her people (*TSG*, 456), the poem's narratives of colonial sexual exploitation avoid colonialist tendencies to "penetrate" or violate the Other. Rather, the poem is disturbing for its tendency to Orientalize another type of touch: the mother's touch, her caress, and her embrace of a dependent tribe.

When Eliot conceived her poem, she imagined a young woman like the Mary of Titian's *Annunciation*: "Suddenly" she has "announced to her that she is chosen to fulfill a great destiny, entailing a terribly different experience from that of ordinary womanhood" (*SE*, 416). Like the Catholic Madonna, Fedalma will "sacrifice" her personal happiness to become a living icon to her people. Those people may play the role of figurative Christ child as well; their anticipated search for a homeland is sure to fail at great cost to them. In choosing between Spain and the Zincali, Fedalma will face, Henry James says, "a struggle between nature and culture, between education and the instinct of race."[61] But as the poem displaces Fedalma's racial identities, it also displaces her conventional gendering and the representation of her body and its pleasures. At the end of the poem as the heavily robed and bejeweled virgin Fedalma touches a Gypsy child, she represents a technically chaste maternal sexuality that nonetheless resonates with erotic meaning.

Fedalma enters the text as a dancer; her performance links her body to the body of the community and establishes their common humanity. The many visual images of Fedalma dancing frame her as an object of worship, and even as an image of divine femininity itself. Eliot invests her with the dynamic quality of a Renaissance Madonna like Titian's and with the sense of movement and touch that drapery and flowing hair imparted to Julia Margaret Cameron's photographs of Madonnas. Moving in a "dance religious" (326), "swayed by impulse passionate" (327), Fedalma dances "in slow curves, voluminous, gradual, feeling and action flowing into one" (326). "Sweet community informs her limbs" as "words" are "impregnate with the master's thought" (327). Tendrils of her black hair stray and her clothes cling to her body as Fedalma's sensuous dance veers near the gypsy dances described by the scandalized Grellmann and Borrow. But Eliot subverts those entirely. Fedalma's body is made to seem a place unto itself over which she herself is "majesty" and "master." As her dance is described as "religious," it attempts to enter into the poem's religious discourses. Such a role for women is particularly absent from the Protestantism Eliot knew, for it, as Julia Kristeva notes, suffers "a *lack* . . . with respect to the Maternal" in its rejection of the Madonna, an image we know was very important to Eliot.[62]

In her work on the Madonna in George Eliot, Adams notes that in the poem, the sexuality of the image is divided along racial lines, for "the Christians worship her as Virgin, while the Zincali see *their* goddess as Queen and Mother." The Madonna is then culturally specific, "an indigenous figure . . . expressing their ideals, beliefs, and sense of their identity as a people." The Zincali violently oppose the Christian Madonna as "Our Lady of Pain," whose "defenders persecute and kill those of other faiths."[63] The feminist tenor of the poem's spiritual discourse is piqued by its contrast with traditional Christianity, here represented by no less a performance of aggressive, colonizing power than the Inquisition. Eliot had brilliantly expressed the radical role of the sexual body in spirituality in her translation of Ludwig Feuerbach's *The Essence of Christianity* (1841). In *The Spanish Gypsy* that concept informs Eliot's heroine's epic battle against medieval repudiations of the body. In Eliot's translation, Feuerbach argues that "a personal being apart from Nature is nothing else than a being without sex. . . . Nature is said to be predicated of God. . . . Repudiate then, before all, thy own horror for the distinction of sex. If God is not polluted by

Nature, neither is he polluted by being associated with the idea of sex. . . . A moral God apart from nature is without basis." Fedalma's eroticized dancing literally embodies Feuerbach's stress on the morality of "corporeality," for Nature is "nothing without" it; the body links one to the moral life, for "flesh and blood is life, and life alone is corporeal reality."[64] Punishing the sexualized body through its institutionalized policies of chastity and torture, the prior and chief inquisitor, Isidore, embodies medieval Spain's organized ecclesiastical racism and misogyny. Uncle and confessor to Silva, Fedalma's betrothed, Isidore values that "blue-eyed" Goth as a white "flower of Christian knighthood" and insists that his nephew follow his order's now-defunct vow of chastity (366). Having danced in public, Fedalma has convinced the prior that she is a "harlot," a "bride of Satan in a robe of flames" (337). On her body "she bears the marks of races unbaptised, that never bowed before the holy signs, were never moved by stirring of the sacramental gifts" (337).

The prior "reads" Fedalma's "skin" like a text and asserts that her "blood is as unchristian as the leopard's." In her public dancing, "she has profaned herself," "flaunting her beauties grossly" (339). Silva also reflects this ideology in his rhetoric, chastising Fedalma for shrinking "no more from gazing men than from the gazing flowers that, dreaming sunshine, open as you pass" (345). Fedalma, however, perceives her dance as a transcendent experience through which her body "seemed new-waked to life in unison with a multitude" (344). Eliot's language is steeped in Feuerbach at this point. But the Feuerbachian content is rife with pointed feminist commentary. Fedalma asserts that she "should like the world to look at me with eyes of love that make a second day"; her audience's eyes are "a little heaven" (345). Fedalma's ecstatic dance signifies her embodied ecstasy as the only heaven she can know.

In contrast, the "Holy Inquisition's discipline" acquires new energy and commits its worst sin, misrepresenting the Madonna as a vengeful goddess of destruction, the "Immaculate Mother, Virgin mild" who "shalt see and smile, while the black filthy souls sink with foul weight to their eternal place" (368).[65] Medieval Catholicism, represented here solely through the Inquisition, is painted as a cruel religion whose "love must needs make hatred." Punishment of the body, the "shuddering, bleeding, thirsting, dying God . . . scourged and bruised and torn" (367), is the central emphasis of the Inquisition's Christ. His image is contrasted with images of bodily purging that flood the prior's rhetoric. In accepting her Gypsy identity, Fedalma rejects a Catholicism that has been particularly indicted for its misogyny, male hierarchy, and its particular focus on the value of the soul over the depraved body. As the Spanish stole Fedalma from her Gypsy tribe, upon her return she reclaims and reconstitutes their image of the Madonna, importing it into her rule as queen.

The Gypsy faith which Fedalma will come to lead in the poem certainly increases our understanding of the role of the gendered body in Eliot's religion of humanity. The Zincali possess "a faith taught by no priest, but by their beating hearts" (375). Their religion lies in "fidelity" between people. It believes in no heaven; its sole metaphysical element lies in the transmigration of souls. Having no "prophet," the religion exalts "fellowship" over hierarchy. Its "Holy Place" is not a church but "the hearth that binds us in one family" (376). Rather than forsaking the body as profane, Eliot's version of Gypsy religion finds its source there, "in the silent bodily presence feel the mystic stirring of a common life which makes the many one" (375).

Because of its sympathetic representation of Gypsy faith, Eliot's treatment of the Zincalis in her poem has been seen as politically progressive. Adams notes: "It is unexpected to have peoples usually treated as the Other by nineteenth-century writers given voice and subjectivity. Eliot's dialogic text asserts the value of every religion, as a cultural and racial inheritance, and uses the scenes of religious bloodshed to show the need for sympathy and tolerance." When Fedalma is accused of biological heresy, having "unchristian blood" as a Gypsy, Adams notes, her lover defends her by reminding the prior that "Mary is not a Christian at the time of the Annunciation—the Gospels characterize her as a Jewish maiden—and Fedalma, responding to *her* father's call to be exceptional among women, remains where the Prior has situated her, outside the Church." Eliot's poem, Adams continues, "seems designed to unsettle the Christians among her readers in several ways. She suggests the Annunciation might be paralleled among other peoples and cultures, she redefines the event as a tragedy, and (at a time when faith is threatened by science) she explains religion in evolutionary terms."[66] The narrative of pain that Adams identifies with the Catholic Madonna of the Spanish Inquisition in the poem is contrasted with the narrative of pleasure associated with the poem's "multiple perspectives" of the Madonna/goddess apparent in the poem's representations of land as mother, the Virgin Mary, and Fedalma as the "goddess" of the Zincali (456).

In Eliot's epic poem, the Gypsy body which was so fearful when seen through little Maggie Tulliver's English eyes is allowed to encompass both the reverent and the sensuous as Fedalma's body does at the poem's opening. This Other body can access the "mystic" essence, "which makes the many one," as the dark smile of the Gypsy woman in Eliot's sonnets can access the "primal, passionate store which makes mankind whole." The poem seeks to release the body, particularly the female body, from orthodox notions of its profanity. Fedalma's decampment with the Gypsies, in what seems to be a capture by her father who climbs through her window to take her "home," rescues her from what British culture perceived as the Western world's most heinous form of captivity, imprisonment and torture by Spanish Roman Catholic Inquisitors.[67] Once actually with the Gypsies, Fedalma is surrounded by pagans who find no shame in the female body, only beauty. The physical "unrest" which is present in heroines from Dinah Morris to Gwendolen Harleth is replaced with stillness and composure.[68] Moreover, as Eliot writes of the Gypsy woman's body, she treats it explicitly, using language that she retreats from in her novels.

As Fedalma joins the Gypsy camp in book 3 of the poem, she finds them in a liminal position between the old world of Europe and the new world of Africa, the destination of their new nation. Establishing Africa and the East as the source of the primeval family of humanity, Eliot's narrator, who spans all generations, compares the Gypsies' journey with that of her own European predecessors who came "westward past the Caucasus." Camping in tents, like those ancient predecessors, the tribe leads a "busy, bright-eyed, sportive life." True to the anthropological accounts, the women work. "Tall maidens" are shepherds, their legs exposed. "Above the living curves" of their bodies, "the shoulder's smoothness part[s] the torrent strong of ebon hair." Men and women contribute equally to the sustenance of the camp and to the physical life of the tribe. Eliot provides one of her extremely rare images of embodied maternity in her vision of the Gypsy camp:

Most like an earth-born race bred by the Sun
On some rich tropic soil, the father's light
Flashing in coal-black eyes, the mother's blood
With bounteous elements feeding their young limbs. (425)

The Gypsies have bodies, "knees," and "naked limbs," which "with beauteous ease bend, lift, and throw, or raise high signaling hands" (492). Fedalma herself is finally pictured as a "steadfast form" among her tribe (494). Her return to this setting seems to answer the call begun in a version of the poem's opening when Spain is represented as "broad breasted . . . A calm earth-goddess crowned with corn and vines."[69]

As she once asked her father to protect the rights of the women of her tribe, Queen Fedalma is presented as a protector of young women herself. "Sent to guard her people and to be the strength of some rock-citadel," she is described as an Athene or protective "goddess." Mourning for her lover and her father at the poem's end, she sits in black robes with a "slim, mischievous" Gypsy girl, Hilda. "Happy" and "bedecked with rows of berries," the girl flirts with an admirer who "clad in skins seemed the Boy-prophet of the wilderness escaped from tasks prophetic." Turning from the boy, the girl seeks Fedalma's blessing, fondles her feet and lifts her head to Fedalma's hand, "hoping to feel the gently pressing palm which touched the deeper sense." Fedalma responds with her touch, and "from out her black robe she stretched her speaking hand and shared the girl's content." As Fedalma touches the child, Hilda squirms with pleasure and bends "to fondle her Queen's feet," making "myriads of little joys, that ripen sweet and soothe the sorrowful spirit of the world, Groaning and travailing with the painful birth of slow redemption"(494). Fedalma's moment of pleasure in touching the Gypsy girl's head mirrors contemporary representations of queenly women and their children, in particular those of Julia Margaret Cameron. The pose between women and their children in the work of these women artists seems to be a reenvisioning of the Orientalist theme of the odalisque and represent an erotics of maternal touch rather than phallocentric penetration.

Despite the notoriety of Titian's *Annunciation* as the inspiration behind *The Spanish Gypsy,* the poem's representation of maternity itself has until recently been neglected, as has Eliot's keen interest in representations of the Madonna. Eliot's 1868 "virgin majesty" seems to participate in an important cultural conversation on the Queen of Heaven and even resembles other transgressive images of her, such as the carefully constructed photographs by Cameron of the same subject: the draped Madonna who is more sensuous and human than she is spiritual and divine. Cameron's Madonna photographs, begun in 1864, the same year Eliot began her epic poem and Ruskin wrote his essay "Of Queens' Gardens," also "alter" the representation of human "maternality" as the image of Victoria as wife, mother, and reclusive queen had begun to grow stale in the public imagination. Like Fedalma, Cameron's Madonnas touch children and are "focused on the ways in which women touch. Cameron further dramatizes this touching and what it feels like to be touched by featuring appealing folds of drapery in the Madonna pictures. [She] recorded women touching their babies, with their fingertips and even with their lips." Her work, Carol Mavor suggests, "feels particularly subversive when one considers how Victorian women 'lacked' their own narratives of difference, biological or otherwise."[70]

Fedalma's hand on Hilda's head recalls Eliot's "favorite" erotic trope, of two children "holding hands."[71] But in her black robe, Fedalma performs, like Cameron's Madonnas, both "loss" and a queenly, maternal "pleasure." Her pose also "embodies death and negates it." For if her contemporary reader knows that Fedalma's project has failed, the Gypsies do not have a homeland, she also knows that their tribe survives into Eliot's own day where it is popularly believed that they are led by women and have survived, like the Jewish people, with a living faith separate from nation and homeland. Indeed, comparing Eliot's Gypsy mother with contemporary Victorian images of women and children reveals that letting the mother's subjectivity into the frame is often a subversive, feminist act. In a representation that also expropriates an Other woman, Cameron's *Fresh Water* or *The Shunamite Woman and Her Dead Son* (see plate 3), it is clear that Victorian images that purport to resonate with maternal tenderness and apparent sacrifice may also tell a story of women's pleasure as well. In *The Shunamite Woman and Her Dead Son,* a woman sits watching a sleeping child model. In the Old Testament story, the child will be revivified. Cameron's infant model lies naked, sleeping like a white odalisque upon velvet cushions while his veiled mother gazes past him, lost in thought; our gaze lingers on the pair less as a representation of the maternalist dyad than as a subjectivity at once linked and separate. "The woman and the baby share lines of sensual erasure where the mother's arm sinks into the belly and thighs of her child." The intense eroticism of *The Shunamite Woman and Her Dead Son,* however, also enlists her difference as a Jewish, Old Testament mother rather than as a Christian Madonna. Her hair, Mavor writes, "an overdetermined sign in the Victorian sexual imagination, slips beyond her madonnaesque veil and hints at Magdalene eroticism." The "dead" baby, who (the viewer is aware) is actually sleeping, enjoys, like Eliot's Gypsy children, a degree of disheveled nudity that Cameron evidently found unacceptable for her Christ children. In *The Shunamite Woman and Her Dead Son,* Cameron "let mother into the picture" in contrast to those contemporaries, like Mary Cassatt, who "whisk[ed] the mother's individuality and human characteristics out of the picture" in order "to 'focus' on the child."[72] Often, Mavor argues, in Cameron's photographs of women and children, the subject of focus is the woman rather than the child. This is clear in *The Shunamite Woman and Her Dead Son,* as the woman's eyes refuse to focus on the infant's naked body. Deep in thought, the mother establishes herself as a subject independent of the child as well as bonded to him or her through the casual pressure of his arm on her hip. Although Eliot's Fedalma presses the head of the child and that child fondles her feet, she is represented as lost in thought, "yearning, resolving, conquering; though she seemed still." Eliot, like Cameron, represents Fedalma's experience of maternal "joys, that ripen sweet," but she does so without erasing representations of Fedalma's consciousness or subjectivity itself (494). Fedalma appears, like Cameron's Shunamite woman, as intensely erotic, intensely tactile with her "people"; yet in the value system of the poem, she is represented as a subjectivity entirely focused on her own "struggling life" (494).

As a mother, Fedalma rewrites the masculinist model of the colonizer's "fantasy of erotic domination" in which "the native woman appeals to [his] imagination because it combines erotic desire with the desire for mastery."[73] Eliot's fantasy of a Victorian heroine's racial identification with Gypsydom and her gendering of colonial desire as female alters both the home culture's perception of its own women, "the sexually inhibited women of the club," and "the native woman" as "a sexualized figure incapable of resisting her master's desire; the racial difference makes her powerless."[74] It is possible that Eliot simply places her queen mother in the master's place, so performing the Western woman writer's "supplementation" of the masculinist colonial gaze and reenacting its "epistemic violence."[75] Fedalma's watching of her subjects' bodies and her laying on of hands may be perceived as a kinder, gentler model of colonial penetration and domination. However, such acts of erotic violence are also acutely disciplined in the poem.

If Ruskin's challenge that women "be no more housewives, but queens" may be read as a protofeminist argument, Eliot's Gypsy heroine takes up that challenge, rejecting marriage and "love" for a political and spiritual vocation. It seems ironic that her plot has received so much criticism in past and recent scholarship, where Fedalma's rejection of marriage is located as a failure or loss as well as the sole potential source of her erotic pleasure. In light of Fedalma's critique of marriage as a "prison house" in the poem, her vocation as "mother" of her tribe seems an alternative to hegemonic structures. But even more importantly, the poem's colonialist narrative needs to be read for its subtleties, elisions, and its critique of popular colonialist representations of the erotic encounter. Rape and mutiny are rejected for an impenetrable, sensuous vision of "shared content," that Madonna-like image of Fedalma pressing her hand upon the head of the Gypsy child. Originally conceived as a play, *The Spanish Gypsy* is highly theatrical and even melodramatic. As Victorian "acting was highly gestural: it made a particular point by striking an illustrative pose," so Fedalma's final "black-robed" bejeweled pose with her people resonates as an icon of both her sacrifice and her capacity for pleasure.

At its end, the poem's language maternalizes the qualities of human evolution: "the birth of thoughts" seep along in an evolutionary "ocean measureless" which "groans and travails with the painful birth of slow redemption" (494–95). I don't find this ending either "deflating" or "ennervating," as Nord does. She writes that "Fedalma sails to Africa in search of a homeland, conscious of the futility of her quest and yet pledging herself the 'temple' of her father's trust, ready to die alone, a 'hoary woman on the altar-step.' She declares her love for Silva to have been 'subdued . . . [by] the larger life.'" What began as a "vision," in the poem "ends as a burden," and the heroine is "bereft of father, lover, and passion."[76] However, what Fedalma loses in "father, lover" is their definition of her extraordinarily narrow subjectivity, one she envisioned as a "prison" of inactivity, sexual inactivity even, as is suggested by the disembodied orgasmic image of the marital gift of rubies which desire to burst and flood their settings with "glory." Eliot's Gypsy queen rewrites Orientalist images of penetration and mastery to produce a plot of maternal pleasure which, while problematic in itself, subverts the phallocentric plots of both colonialism and domestic ideology.

PLATE 1: *The Greek Slave,* Hiram Powers, 1846, marble, 65 x 19 ¹/₂ in. The Corcoran Gallery of Art, Washington, D.C. Museum Purchase, Gallery Fund. Photo © Corcoran Gallery of Art.

PLATE 2: *A Greek Captive,* Henriette Browne, 1863, oil on canvas, 92.1 x 73 cm. Tate Gallery, London/Art Resource, NY.

PLATE 3: *The Shunamite Woman and Her Dead Son,* Julia Margaret Cameron, 1865, black and white photograph, 10 ⁵/₈ x 8 ³/₈ in. The J. Paul Getty Museum, Los Angeles.

PLATE 4: *Queen Budoor in Captivity*. Woodcut by William Harvey
from *The Thousand and One Nights,* translated by Edward William
Lane. London: Charles Knight & Co., 1839–1840.

## THREE

# The Giaour's Campaign

## Seduction and the Other in *Felix Holt: The Radical*

"SOMEONE IS EXPECTED" from the East on the first page of *Felix Holt: The Radical.*[1] A child of the text's sexual secrets, prince and heir to its decidedly unstable political and sexual underworld, Harold Transome, the Radical candidate who opposes Felix Holt, is an exoticized outsider. In Smyrna, Transome made a fortune and bought a Greek captive as his wife. Returning to England on the eve of a political crisis, Transome brings with him a baby, living proof of his participation in the slave trade. A *"Giaour,"* or an "Oriental, you know," he is not just a Radical politician but also a radical critique of the Western construct of Orientalism (*FH*, 541, 194). He is represented as holding an unstable place in Romantic Orientalist texts, particularly as such categories of *Giaour* and *Hassan* were constructed by Lord Byron in his Oriental poetry that dramatized the plight of women held captive in Eastern harems.[2] An object of sexual and economic desire to Esther Lyon, Transome has not yet been weighed as a disruption or subversion in the novel now considered solely as Eliot's affirmation of the stability and benign "prosperity" of English culture. By the novel's end, Harold Transome wishes that "he had never come back to this pale English sunshine," and the problem of dual captivities under an Orientalism that is defined as strictly British critiques both the project of empire and the position of women at home (582).

A Byronic "Giaour" and a political opportunist, Harold Transome wages two campaigns in the novel, one to win Esther Lyon and one to win a seat in the House of Commons (541). As the political alter ego and romantic rival of Eliot's retiring, Arnoldian radical, Felix Holt, Transome shifts the gendering of Otherness in Eliot's canon. Anticipating the problem of miscegenation, which is to become a central focus in *The Spanish Gypsy* and in the following two novels, *Middlemarch* and *Daniel Deronda,* Transome and his cloak of Orientalism is less an interruption of *The Spanish Gypsy* than a logical step toward that text's Other figure. Like Fedalma, he too possesses multiple allegiances to race, class, and culture. Indeed, it may be that Eliot's Gypsy is absent only in name from *Felix Holt.* All the dangers inherent in writing her story—the Other's overt sensuality, her rejection of European values, her political ambition—are substantially present in this novel of the Midlands where Otherness rears its intricately threatening head. Ultimately, the excoriation and final redemption of Harold Transome might say as much about the difficulties of escaping the prescribed plots of English domestic fiction as about radicalism, Toryism, or Whiggery.

As in Eliot's earlier works, which create characters with allegiances to two races or cultures, in *Felix Holt* the Other is a half-caste. Harold Transome is an illegitimate Englishman who has come of age in the East at Smyrna. He returns, like the Byronic Childe Harold, skilled in business, pleasure, the slave trade, and radicalism, from the East to his ancestral home. Like Eliot's half-blooded Gypsies, the mysterious Will Ladislaw, and the half-Jewish, half-English gentleman, Daniel Deronda, Harold Transome complicates the question of national allegiance. In again focusing on an "Other" who is neither fully English nor authentically Eastern, Eliot complicates racist perceptions of the white self in provocative, although not unproblematic, ways. Making the object of desire an "Oriental" or a "Giaour," the novel studies not just the English self's connection to a provincial community but also to the wider, multicultural world. The heroine's attraction to her exotic suitor and to the socially constructed mythology of exoticism then becomes a metaphor for the narrative drive toward the breaking of bonds with self and community as well as toward their reinvention. Often literally or metaphorically "savage," the cultural Other becomes a repository of the violent energy involved in tearing down, and then "making up," society.[3] Eliot's introduction of a *Giaour* in the English Midlands setting seems to follow convention, "displac[ing] the source of patriarchal oppression onto an 'Oriental,' 'Mahometan,' society, enabling British readers to contemplate local problems without questioning their own self-definition as Westerners and Christians."[4]

However, the convention is immediately subverted, because unlike *Jane Eyre*'s "sultan," Mr. Rochester, Harold Transome truly has been to the East where he actually owned a slave woman himself.[5] The vehicle of the metaphor comes home quite effectively.

*Felix Holt's* Orientalism and its connection between racial darkness or Otherness and class have been ignored in favor of neat definitions of Eliot's political ideas in regard to the process of reform. Focusing exclusively on Eliot's conservative, Arnoldian view of a politics of culture and a legislation of human kindness, critical studies have failed to see that, like the two plots of *Daniel Deronda,* the miscegenational romance plot of *Felix Holt* connects the problems of blood and race, and their metaphoric content of the self's conflict with community, to the plots of vocation and reform. As in Eliot's last great novel, her clean conservatism, or the "high mountain air" of her idea of reform, possesses a correspondent depravity, a "Red Deeps" of moral uncertainty.[6] In *Felix Holt,* those depths are reached through Harold Transome's moral position as a slave-owner and empire builder, his illegitimacy and that of his "savage" child, Harry. In contrast to the "Gothic" or Northern European superiority of Felix Holt and Esther Lyon's French-English aristocratic delicacy of feature and frame, Transome, Matthew Jermyn, Mrs. Transome's bourgeois solicitor, and the child Harry are all posited as "savage" or of a lower order. As the products both of Otherness and Englishness, the stereotypes in *Felix Holt* undermine rather than stabilize the English community. The "Oriental" here is as tainted by his identity as an imperialist Englishman is by his participation in "barbaric" Oriental custom.

Some readers have noted that the issue of reform in *Felix Holt* connects an individual's moral to his or her political awareness to such an extent that "family politics" reflect national politics.[7] But in *Felix Holt* Eliot's notion of "family" extends beyond the national family of England, encompassing "the Oriental" within the colonial Englishman, and issues of race within the "family" of the English class system itself. The politics of race and class infiltrate the politics of Victorian national reform in the novel, much as they did through the career of Benjamin Disraeli in actual Victorian politics.[8] Through its melange of historical and literary "Oriental" figures, racial stereotypes, and reform politics, Eliot's novel deliberately calls into play questions about the moral axioms of Englishness in both the political and domestic spheres. As many critics have noticed, she does not satisfactorily answer them in the "conservative" *Felix Holt* in which the willful heroine ends up married, chastened, and "punished" at novel's end. However, Eliot's questions themselves probe deeply into notions of national identity, deconstructing appearances of English-ness and Otherness, deliberately confusing and subverting those values which other Victorian novelists, like Dickens or Thackeray, hold sacred. The questions about Otherness which the "Oriental" Harold raises do not start from Edward Said's clean slate, where "positive ideas of home, of a nation and its language of proper order, good be-havior, moral values" set a national standard by which Others are measured.[9] Instead, the moral values of Eliot's England are them-selves apparently absent from all but the narrator's supertext. That narrator, a voice for an author who is herself an outsider in a compli-cated, often paradoxical sense, is itself in conflict about the moral axioms of the English world.

Eliot's ideal England, her bright, organic, utopian community, then, has an underside that is often drawn in terms of race and class. Energized by sexual and political desire, like the "brown, determined lizard," Harold Transome, like Caterina Sarti, Fedalma, Maggie Tul-liver, Will Ladislaw, or Daniel Deronda, initiates the processes of re-form and narrative progression in Eliot's canon (*FH*, 98). Torn herself between "disgust" and desire, Eliot's narrator depicts the lower realm such figures inhabit in paradoxical terms of repugnance and attraction. The lower realm in *Felix Holt*, of which Harold Tran-some is prince, is also the seat of sexual attraction, sensual pleasure, and temptation. Like Satan, Harold Transome is "far more interest-ing" than the rather hapless English Felix, whose angelic asceticism is partnered with a "belligerent pedantry" and a profound antisensual-ism, signaled mainly through his disapproval of Esther's taste for Byron.[10] Eliot is clearly intrigued by Transome's presence and by that of his heir, the incomprehensible polyglot child, Harry. These forces, intruding roughly, savagely into the novel's Arnoldian scheme, are ones to be reckoned with, not tossed aside in the desire to create a "moral" George Eliot with a narrative voice devoid of any troubling paradoxes. Indeed, casting her candidate Harold Transome in the shape of Disraeli, who casts himself in the shape of the Orientalist Byron, Eliot's process of reform in her "political" novel, her "making up society," displaces our concept of her morality and brings new moral questions to the study of her canon.

Ascetic, pedagogic, and severe, the morals of Felix Holt himself have in the past been perceived as those of George Eliot. This is particularly crucial in the novel's play on a key moral article of faith, the reading of Byron. Recently, readers of George Eliot have begun to argue that the narrative voice does not necessarily "identif[y] with Felix Holt." As Robin Sheets suggests, Eliot's identification with her protagonist ought not to be such a given. Eliot's "radical" is, after all, boorish, pedantic, and rigid. His naive, homespun speeches and gestures take place in a novel where "honest, direct discourse seems to have no place" and where "words themselves have become difficult to decipher." Ultimately, Felix is unable to master language, to "recover" it for his own and his party's uses. As a way of judging Felix critically, Eliot compares him with Joseph, "a sensitive, well-spoken, and politically acute figure from the Old Testament." The result, as Sheets convincingly argues, is that Eliot did not identify with her male protagonist, and "his failings [cannot] be ascribed to her ambivalence regarding reform movements."[11] Certainly, the political cynicism of Eliot's letters suggests that her ideas for reform live less in Matthew Arnold's utopia than in Disraeli's empire, and, correspondently, less in Felix Holt's political vision than in Harold Transome's.

IN THE PAST, Eliot's narrator has been linked to Felix Holt's belief that, as a representative of moral depravity, Byron can only corrupt. The reading of Byron and the development of Byronic characteristics become an important test of moral correctness in the novel, and linking Eliot's voice with Felix has contributed to the critical construction of an earnest, morally conservative, politically idealistic George Eliot. Throughout, the young Esther Lyon is seen reading Byron with pleasure and is severely condemned for doing so by the pedantic Felix. Echoing Carlyle, he insists that she put down her edition of Byron and replace it with a more instructive text. The conflict is a significant one throughout the novel. Esther sacrifices her Byronic text, particularly its tales of "Oriental love" and its acute "invective," when she marries Felix.[12] Again, hearing George Eliot in Felix Holt, critics have seen this rejection as firmly based in the biographical record. The mature George Eliot's distaste for Byron is plain for all to see in her letters. Equally plain, however, is the fact that the young Mary Ann Evans was herself a devotee of Byron and that, indeed, he was as much a favorite as Carlyle or Wordsworth. It was only after the 1869 exposure of Byron's incestuous relationship with his sister that Eliot began to deplore him. Written in 1866, Eliot's novel predates that shift. In her letters, the record of her attachment to Byron, indeed her identification with his poetry, suggests an entirely different reading of *Felix Holt*. Deeply interwoven in the makeup of Harold Transome as a Byronic Childe Harold or a *Giaour* himself, Eliot's treatment of Byron becomes an important element in the novel and necessitates the critical rereading of his poetry in Eliot's life as a writer and reader.

Clearly, the Byron who is discussed in *Felix Holt* is a familiar figure to Mary Ann Evans. In her adolescence, Evans formed close friendships at school with two girls, Martha Jackson and Maria Lewis. Addressing each other as Clematis, Ivy, and Veronica in the fashion of the sentimental "Language of Flowers," the girls often took, at Evans's suggestion, "assigned subjects for their letters, bones 'to pick together without contention.'" (*GEL*, 1:48). Usually severely Evangelical and didactic in tone, the letters are an apt illustration of adolescent religious fervor. Written during the "Holy War" period, as Mary Ann Evans defied her father's wishes and refused to attend a church she found theologically moribund, the letters' most significant, and most poignant, resonance is their depiction of a bright young woman living in "a *walled-in world*" that comes vibrantly alive only through books (*GEL*, 1:71). Allusions to Carlyle, Byron, and Shakespeare break through the formal constraints of the "Language of Flowers," coloring the girls' provincial Evangelical piety with the beginnings of an incisive literary sensibility. Clearly identifying with Byron's roving and satanic impulses, Mary Ann Evans alludes to him frequently. Like Esther Lyons, she read Byron for pleasure and for affirmation of her own desire to wander, to leave home and its "walled-in" confines and limitations. Her rage often found its voice through the yearning and the anger expressed in Byron's poetry.

Lonely and depressed, in May 1840 George Eliot wrote to Maria Lewis of her dissatisfaction with her "lot" in life:

> [To] tell you the truth I begin to feel involuntarily isolated, and without being humble, to have such a consciousness that I am a negation of all that finds love and esteem as makes me anticipate for myself—no matter what; I shall have countless undeserved enemies if my life be prolonged, wherever my lot may be cast, and I need rigid discipline, which I have never yet had. Byron in his *Childe Harold* (which I have just begun the second time) checks reflections on individual and personal sorrows by reminding himself of the revolutions and woes beneath which

the shores of the Mediterranean have groaned. We may with more effectual comparison think of the dangers of the Great Ark of the Church in these latter times of the deluge of sin. (*GEL*, 1:51–52)

The remarkable irony here is that Evans, for the moment, finds Byron a source of the "rigid discipline" which she both craves and chafes against. More pious than her letters to Martha Jackson, this letter to Maria Lewis nonetheless marks the special significance that Byron held for her. Thrown into relief against the background of the letter's weak allusion to the "dangers" now facing the "Great Ark of the Church," Eliot's allusion to the opening stanza of *Childe Harold*'s fourth canto has the special ring of personal identification. The allusion to Byron, part self-affirmation, part self-derision, reflects not just the tenor of *Childe Harold* itself, but also Evans's attempts to "check" her own desires, which strongly resist containment. If in the opening of canto 4 Childe Harold assuages his personal sorrows by comparing them with those of the city of Venice, he also expresses his wanderlust. "I've taught me other tongues—and in strange eyes have made me not a stranger. . . . I leave behind the inviolate island of the sage and free, and seek me out a home by a remoter sea." Although the young Mary Ann Evans could not yet actually leave England, as had Byron's Harold, clearly she had the desire to escape her "involuntary isolation" and the imprisoning quality of her domestic routine. Seeking escape, Evans found in Byron the ability to brighten "dull life" with "the beings of the mind . . . essentially immortal."[13]

The allusions to Byron, and particularly to *Childe Harold*, continue to mark Evans's "flower" correspondence, especially during the crucial period of the "Holy War," the standoff between Mary Ann and Robert Evans over churchgoing. At this time she inscribed the flyleaf of her copy of Petrarch with four stanzas from *Childe Harold*'s fourth canto (those referring to Petrarch's tomb). She recorded her reading and rereading of Byron in her journal and letters. Even more significantly, the satanic-Byronic attitude is named and assumed in one of her angriest, most personally revealing, and, paradoxically, most "political" letters from this period. The letter clearly reveals that Byron had become an ally in Mary Ann Evans's personal rebellion or private war of independence. Moreover, its political metaphors have direct significance for Esther Lyon's own internal holy war in *Felix Holt* which also mixes politics, desire, fathers and daughters, and churchgoing. Indeed, Evans's letters find politics an apt metaphor for this domestic dispute just as *Felix Holt* finds it a metaphor for the disputes within the larger family of humanity. As father and daughter attempt to redraw the boundaries of authority and obedience, the daughter's eloquent arguments are illustrated by images culled not from the language of Victorian family values but from an analogous political issue, Chartism. Apparently, Evans felt her role as a daughter to be similar to that of an unchartered artisan: "Carlyle says that to the artisans of Glasgow the world is not one of blue skies and a green carpet, but a world of coperas-fumes, low cellars, hard wages, 'striking,' and gin; and if the recollection of this picture did not remind me that gratitude should be my reservoir of feeling, that into which all that comes from above or around should be received as a source of fertilization for my soul, I should give a lachrymose parody of the said description and tell you all seriously what I now tell you playfully, that mine is too often a world such as Wilkie can so well paint, a *walled-in* world. But I must check this Byronic invective" (*GEL*, 1:71).

This strikes the keynote of Eliot's identification with Byron. Her enjoyment of him is clear. He is irresistible, read and reread. But the pleasure is a guilty one. His "invective," so identifiable with her own rage and her own desire to break free of the rules of her father, must be "checked" and controlled. Like Esther Lyons, she indulges her desire to read but always with the knowledge that the identification is less a communion with God than with a fallen angel. Reading Byron represents, to Mary Ann Evans, leaving home, a risky endeavor, much dreamed of in her adolescent letters in which she often quotes Byron: "both my heart and my limbs would leap to behold the 'great and wide sea,' that old Ocean on which man can leave no trace" (Byron, qtd. in *GEL*, 1:101). Leaving "no trace," leaving identity, girlhood, family, and English society behind, sailing off, like Childe Harold, on the great ocean of independence and self-discovery, is at once terrifying and exhilarating.

After the publication of "The True Story of Lady Byron's Life" in August 1869, two years after the writing of *Felix Holt*, Eliot joined the English readership, scandalized by the revelation of Byron's incest, in a conventional and spasmodic reaction against his poetry. She wrote to her friend Cara Bray in August 1869 that "Byron and his poetry have become more and more repugnant to me of late years (I read a good deal of him a little while ago, in order to form a fresh judgment). As to this story, I cannot help being sorry that it seemed necessary to publish what is only worthy to die and rot. After all Byron remains deeply pitiable, like all of us sinners" (*GEL*, 5:54).

It is clear from Eliot's journal that the "fresh judgment" of which she speaks was formed in January 1869, when she recorded reading the first four cantos of *Don Juan*. But earlier letters reveal a different appreciation of Byron and one that should be considered in light of the adolescent Esther Lyon's reading in *Felix Holt*. Eliot critics may well assume that her mature assessment of Byron is that he was "repugnant," but it is necessary to examine exactly what fears and concerns went into that judgment. Esther Lyon's furtive, pleasurable reading and ultimate rejection of Byron is not likely to be merely attributable to the development of "good" moral taste. Esther Lyon, like Eliot, has a clear but troubled attraction to Byron's sensualism and to his Orientalist fancies, and reexamining Esther's reading and Eliot's recasting of her political radical in the shape of a Byronic Childe Harold challenges the conservatism of the novel and leaves us far less certain that Felix Holt *is* in fact George Eliot. In a novel written by a novelist determined both by temperament and political inclination to show both the overt and covert elements within an organically interwoven community, we cannot assume that the rejection of political radicalism is as clear-cut as it once seemed to Eliot scholars. As in Mary Ann Evans's perception of Byron's poetry itself, in her novel the repugnant and the irresistible are often one and the same. As they are aligned, so is the "moral" choice, here embodied by Felix Holt, often deeply resistible and as unappealing as the distasteful Casaubon himself in *Middlemarch*. As in that later novel, it is necessary in *Felix Holt* to distinguish true morality from ignorant asceticism.

Like Eliot's own reading of Byron, the novel's progress to Esther's ultimate rejection of Byronic ideology is morally and intellectually complicated. Infiltrating the weblike narrative on several different levels and acting as a controversial article of faith, Esther's appreciation for Byron initiates a violent "holy war" of sorts between herself and Felix. In this sense, Byron's Orientalism and his accompanying sensuality inform those two characters' struggle with the experience of sexual desire. Anticipating and literalizing their struggle, the heavily Byronic "Giaour," Harold Transome, serves as a medium through which the pleasures and dangers of desire are acted out. Indeed, the resonances of Byron's *Childe Harold's Pilgrimage* and his *Oriental Tales* help to shape the moral and political universe of *Felix Holt*.

As in *Childe Harold,* the setting of the physical, cultural, and moral universe in *Felix Holt* is a ruin. A metaphor of cultural ruination, Transome Court stands derelict at the novel's opening, ravaged by time. Transome's ancestral home recalls Childe Harold's "good hall" whose "hearth is desolate" and where "wild weeds are gathering on the wall." This pervasive sense of ruination extends, in Eliot's novel as in Byron's poem, beyond setting to modern man himself. "The wreck of modern man" is clearly symbolized in the half-witted "old" Mr. Transome, the embittered, wasted Mrs. Transome, and her corrupt lover. Eventually, ruin of a sort will be visited also upon the young Transome heir Harold when he learns of his illegitimacy. But Eliot's allusions to Byron are marked by important deviations from his text. The middle-class Eliot introduces a class-consciousness which the aristocratic Lord Byron ignores. Here ruination is the pragmatic effect of poverty, class, or race, rather than the result of Romantic *ennui*. Similarly, Eliot's pilgrim is not endowed with the fine cultural sense of Childe Harold. He does not mourn the loss of classical values represented in Byron's poem by his displeasure in the British alliance with the Ottoman Turks over Greece. Significantly, Harold Transome is one of the "barbarous hands" exploiting Greek culture.[14]

Clearly, Harold Transome's sojourn in the East and his self-identification as "an Oriental" seems to complicate the very potent cultural forces that insist on the moral corruption of the cultural Other. The usually "liberal" Eliot, wrestling with the composition of *The Spanish Gypsy,* in some ways her most progressive female narrative, now looks through the mirror of English culture and affirms stereotypical cultural anxieties about Otherness; then, she brings them home. Eliot's abrupt switch from the composition of *The Spanish Gypsy* to *Felix Holt* marks an equally abrupt shift in representing a home culture that seems to have incorporated Oriental despotism itself. Like Fedalma, Transome exudes an intense eroticism that here proves as unmanageable as it is seductive even perhaps to the writer; Transome remains a much richer psychological representation than the novel's hero, Holt, who has no history at all, particularly with women.

Especially as suitor to the Byron-reading Esther Lyons, Harold Transome evokes, as Will Ladislaw will later evoke through both Byron and Shelley, the satanic-Byronic hero as well as Byron's pilgrim Harold. Uniting her own creative vision with this element of allusion, Eliot seems to engage in a moral dialogue with Byron. Like Childe Harold, Transome is a figure of less than moral properties who, as an illegitimate child, has already "run" through "Sin's long labyrinth."[15] The novel's opening, like *Childe Harold,* evokes the tradition of the *romaunt.* Eliot's protagonist has also been "sent upon a mission, the fulfillment of which will prove his courage and other qualities needed for moral survival."[16] Eliot's Harold shares with Byron's antihero his sense of "a crowded, pressing past—not only the fullness of immediate pleasures but also those dense and obsessive memories which will always haunt such heroes."[17] The medieval tradition, as it is filtered through Byron's cynicism, fits Harold Transome. He is a strange, alien pilgrim returned to a strange home that is marked with the memory of sexual sin, remorse, and guilt. At Transome Court, first envisioned to the reader as an "enchanted forest in the underworld," the very trees bleed with "human histories" and "unuttered cries" (*FH,* 84). Emissary knight and captain of industry, Harold Transome has one foot in the blood-wet world of Byronic Romanticism and one in Eliot's Victorian world of real sociopolitical concerns. He is a strange hybrid monster of Gothic Romanticism and Victorian efficiency and energy, for "the lizard's egg, that white-rounded passive prettiness, had become a brown, darting, determined lizard" (98). Marking the evolution of literature itself, he is a hero or villain evolved to suit the spirit of his own age, a study in ruthless energy, a dangerous inversion of Childe Harold's Romantic *ennui* and *welschriften.* If the East represented spiritual revivification and sensual fascination to Byron and Goethe, it represented another opportunity altogether to the pragmatic nineteenth-century industrialist—the opportunity to make a fortune. This Harold's mission was economic. At the opening of the novel, his moral nature is as bankrupt as his coffers are full.

Indeed, Eliot's Harold may share the experiences of Byron's Childe Harold, but, like Disraeli, whose travels to the East in Byron's footsteps involved more the acquisition of the poet's old servants than his cultural understanding, he shares in the luxury of the East without even the usual Western absorption in its perceived mysticism.[18] For Harold Transome also "the East is a career."[19] Much like public perceptions of Childe Harold and the protagonists of Byron's *Oriental Tales,* Harold Transome's sexuality is marked by his Oriental travels. He poses a political and moral threat to the England to which he returns, and the novel regularly relates politics and morality, beginning with Harold's announcement of himself as a Radical candidate, which strikes his mother "as if her son had said that he had been converted to Mahomentanism at Smyrna, and had four wives" (*FH*, 92). Harold signals exactly what Eliot may seek to discipline in the characters of Fedalma, Caterina Sarti, Maggie Tulliver, or Daniel Deronda—a tainted, dark, almost savage, sexual and political desire, unmitigated and uncontrolled by English perceptions of morality and vocation. When Eliot comes to represent those desires, she exoticizes, here Orientalizes, them in order to voice them. In the novel, a literary genre which "was becoming increasingly committed to depicting only the normative 'bourgeois' values of industry, sobriety, and chastity," Orientalizing the rebellious figure "permitted the representation of . . . 'transgressive' moral values." Like Victorian Orientalists who translated *The Thousand and One Nights* into English, Eliot too is breaking the "Victorian taboo of masking sexuality" but is doing so by speaking only of sexuality "in a removed setting—the East."[20]

In this literary exploitation of the East, however, Eliot engages less in redrawing the axioms of imperialism than in challenging them. Harold Transome is not the cheerily unexamined rubber-plantation owner of *Mansfield Park*. He is a lizard, a conscious representation of the fact that "desire and moral scruple merge in fascination with oriental luxury and its commodification in trade and literature." But he is also an Englishman. Because his empire building involved slave owning and union with the Ottoman Empire, he is made an immoral figure. His past and future are part of the English absorption in an East "ripe for moral and economic appropriation."[21] Just as Byron casts *Giaour* and *Hassan* "in the same mold," so too Eliot's narrative stance toward Harold conflates identities.[22]

The fact of Harold's violation of the East is immediately apparent in the presence of his son, Harry. Waiting for Harold's return from Smyrna, his mother is full of anxiety: "If Mrs. Transome had expected only her son, she would have trembled less; she expected a little grandson also: and there were reasons why she had not been enraptured when her son had written to her only when he was on the eve of returning that he had already had an heir born to him" (*FH*, 89). The thinly veiled fact alluded to here will be confirmed by the child Harry's appearance and character and will make another woman "tremble." The shocked and affronted Esther Lyons learns that "Harry's mother had been a slave—was bought, in fact" (541). Here

Eliot suggests that "the *Giaour* concerned" is not a Romantic figure of "Oriental love," as Esther knew it "chiefly from Byronic poems," but a trafficker in women (541). Harry's mother had been Greek. Buying a Greek wife in Smyrna, Harold Transome participates in the modern desecration of Greek civilization that so infuriated Byron. But the image, made so popular and controversial by Hiram Powers's exhibition of *The Greek Slave* at the Crystal Palace exhibition in 1851, had even more resonance for the Victorians (plate 1). Exhibited in America or England, the iconography of Powers's statue spoke to feminists who identified with slaves; to supporters of Greek independence; to abolitionists such as Frederick Douglass; or to feminist poets such as Elizabeth Barrett Browning, who condemned the statue's passivity in her poem "Hiram Powers' *Greek Slave*." The "subjectivity and intensity" of responses to the statue, however, all share one element.[23] That is a deep "hatred of the cruel TURK who does thus violate the sacred rights of human nature . . . our sister with all her affections, aspirations, and high capacities, *sold* to the bestial TURK, whoever he may be, and he designs to cast her down from her god-given estate, into the dominion of *things*."[24]

This is the company Harold Transome keeps in buying a Greek wife. Aligning himself with the "bestial" Turk, he is, of course, more closely associated with a grasping, ugly, dangerously vulgar acquisitiveness and cultural barbarism. But if Powers turns the image of slavery white, Eliot reverses the image of the slave-owner, who here is not authentically a Turk, but an Englishman tainted and colored by his associations with the practices of a "bestial" people. As the dead odalisque of Transome's past never appears, Eliot seems less interested in penetrating the harem and its veil than in revealing the slave-owner master.

As a Radical candidate, Harold Transome's decadent and corrupt history is always with him. He is less Byron's Childe Harold than Disraeli's. The fictional politician arrives in Britain just when the historical politician did, returning from Smyrna, where he had enjoyed the same life as had Harold Transome, learning to "repose on voluptuous ottomans and smoke superb pipes, daily to indulge in the luxuries of a bath which requires half-a-dozen attendants for its perfection; to court the air in a carved caique, by shores which are a perpetual scene, and to find no exertion greater than a canter on a barb."[25]

By creating a similarly luxurious political candidate of equally "voluptuous" morality and strongly imperialist tendencies, Eliot seems to be referring to the problematic morality of Disraeli's imperialist policies. She is indicting, as Byron did, Victorian Englishness itself. Peeling the layers away from the multilayered character of Harold Transome reveals that his Byronic "Oriental" trappings are mere affectation. He is a bastardization of Byron, not the book of poems that Esther is reading against Felix Holt's advice, but merely its cover. Here Eliot seems to be challenging Felix Holt's moral perception of Byron, differentiating between the genuine article and its usurpation.

The threat to Eliot's sense of country posed by this false Childe Harold is evident in the new generation of Transomes. With the creation of the heir, Harry, Eliot seems again to be stressing the generational contamination of English culture and English family values from within English culture itself. As the Victorian Harold is no improvement on the Romantic, so the Victorian heir is no improvement on the father; he is a further bastardization of the Transome morality. The dangers of the post-1832, postreform political world are embodied in him. Darkly "savage," gibbering his own incomprehensible polyglot language, the baby Harry literally consumes and is consumed by the forces that created him. He first appears as "a black-maned little boy" who is driving old, feeble-minded Mr. Transome as if his grandfather were a horse and himself the master. The "little savage," whose speech is "a broken lisping polyglot of hazardous interpretation," cannot understand his grandmother's warning that he let her dog "alone—he'll bite" if Harry pulls his tail. But the advice is misconstrued. Harry is like an animal himself, unable to control his appetite or understand the difference between people and animals. In front of the aristocratic Sir Maximus and Lady De Barry, who have come to learn of his father's candidacy, Harry bites his grandmother. They immediately conclude of "that savage boy" that "he doesn't look like a lady's child" (*FH,* 179). "After living in the East so long [the Transomes] may have become the sort of people one would not care to be intimate with" (119). Later, Harry, still unable to understand English, names his grandmother "Bite" (492). As the plot of *Felix Holt* thickens with the mixed blood of racial and class difference, it clearly expresses an almost overdetermined anxiety over the "dilution" of blood and fusion of races.

Characteristic of Eliot's narrative technique in fiction, Harry's name for his grandmother makes the agency of attack unclear; it does not identify who has bitten whom. The child Harry has, in a sense, been bitten or marked by his grandmother. It is to her, in the scheme of Victorian racial and classist stereotypes, that he owes his father's immoral influence. If he is not "a lady's child," his father is not a gentleman's child. Jermyn possesses, like his son and grandson, "latent savage elements" (115). Once unleashed amidst the gentry and chartered with political power, those elements have teeth. Baby Harry is then a metaphor for his father's "low" heritage and political radicalism. The visiting Sir Maximus and Lady De Barry never get to the question of "Harold's politics" and rush away only to have their suspicions confirmed. Harold "has become a regular beast among those Mahometans—he's got neither religion nor morals left. He can't know anything about English politics." The savage Oriental, a very "licentious man" (182), is both personally and politically suspect.

De Barry's condemnation is ironic. Although the English gentry perceive Harold as an Oriental usurper, Eliot's narrator critically identifies his character with English imperialism and an empty, economic Orientalism. Not truly of the East in the sense that Fedalma or Daniel Deronda will be, not truly different in the sense that Will Ladislaw, Dorothea Brooke, or Maggie Tulliver are, Harold Transome is a purely English entity. His illegitimate, biting child, confused in the very direction of his attack, represents the illegitimacy of his Oriental trappings.

Although Eliot condemns Harold Transome's imperialist exploits, his exotic sexuality still clings to him like the scent of "atta of roses" (601). Esther's *Giaour* becomes the object of her desire; her reading of Byron, which sensitizes her to the "Oriental love" she thinks Transome represents, becomes the stuff of her resistance to the ascetic, pleasure-denying Felix Holt. Indeed, the English lovers' standoff over Esther's reading of Byron is explosive and violent. So intense is Holt's reaction to the poet that, ironically, this pacifist "should like to come and scold [Esther] every day, and make her cry and cut her fine hair off" (154). Willing to "live on raw turnips to subdue [his] flesh," Felix perceives Esther and her Byron as a sensual, luxurious trap meant to keep him from his "fine" political "purpose." Quite literally, he hates her: "'I could grind my teeth at such self-satisfied minxes, who think they can tell everybody what is the correct thing, and the utmost stretch of their ideas will not place them in a level with the intelligent fleas. I should like to see if she could be made ashamed of herself'" (*FH*, 156). Felix's sadistic desires to punish, scold, and injure Esther are returned, like Dorothea's to Casaubon's or Romola's to Savonorala's, with something approaching love. Although she thinks "she could never love anyone who was so much of a pedagogue and a master," she also experiences "a strange contradiction of impulses"; sexual desire and sexual repugnance are clearly at issue in the flare-up over Byron (*FH*, 213).

For Felix Holt and Esther Lyon, the exiled Byron becomes an emblem of the sexuality which Esther must conceal or distance herself from as a lady and which Felix Holt labels "debauchery" and a distraction from his "fine purpose" (156). Discovering Esther's reading, Felix discovers her sexuality, and in the act of that discovery, Esther notes Felix's virility, his "massive" build and his "large clear grey eyes and full lips." Discovering Byron in Esther's workbasket takes on the quality of violent sexual exposure when the large, rough Felix accidentally knocks over the basket, revealing her reading and her private thoughts: "[D]own went the blue-frilled work basket, flying open, and dispersing on the floor reels, thimble, muslin work, a small, sealed bottle of atta of rose, and something heavier than these—a duodecimo volume which fell close to him. . . . 'Byron's *Poems!*' he said, in a tone of disgust, while Esther was recovering all the other articles. 'The Dream'—he'd better have been asleep and snoring. What! do you stuff your memory with Byron, Miss Lyon?'" (150). The basket, dressed in blue like Esther herself, goes down and spills its "small, sealed" feminine secrets, the "heavier" of which is the hidden volume.

Blundering and invasive, disapproving and pedagogic, Felix now acts the role of moral arbiter. As his voice has been assumed to be Eliot's own, traditional readings find this "first determining confrontation" with Felix central to the novel. "The theme of Esther's 'dreaming' consciousness, stuffed as it is with illusion, and her progressive awakening, is central to *Felix Holt.*"[26] Esther's "illusions," symbolized by her admiration for "The Dream," impede her moral progress. This reading is underscored by strict interpretations of George Eliot's aestheticism. How could the admirer of the Dutch realists also admire the literary tinsel of Byron's poetry? But such wholesale generic distinctions break down in the face of the novel's complexity. The rejection of Byron, consistently placed in aesthetic terms, is less a question of ways of writing than of ways of experiencing desire. Better to examine what so repulses in "The Dream" and exactly what Felix Holt would like to see left "asleep" (150).

In "The Dream," Esther is reading the narrative of what is later to "disgust" Mary Ann Evans, the story of a forbidden, perhaps incestuous love. Already repulsed by the sexual nature of the poem, Felix Holt is reacting not just to Esther's penchant for what he thinks is inferior poetry but also to sex. Overtly misogynistic, he cannot bear the poetry of seduction. Byron is an especially acute representation here because his poetry so often explores the male self under siege from predatory women. Ironically, Byron's male heroes express "what it might be like to be a heroine, compelled to negotiate and often to feign compliance in a world made by and for those who hold power."[27] This type of threat is clear in "The Dream," in which the young male narrator is in love with a compelling woman who seduces him and then leaves him grieving and in "misery."[28] Felix's crude protests against women reflect the promise of Byron's "Dream" in which exactly what Felix fears from women happens to the protagonist:

> He had no breath, no being, but in hers:
> She was his voice; he did not speak but to her,
> But trembled on her words: she was his sight,
> For his eye follow'd hers, and saw with hers,
> Which coloured all his objects: — he had ceased
> To live within himself: she was his life,
> The ocean to the river of his thoughts,
> Which terminated all.[29]

When Esther's frilled workbasket falls down and her private desires are made public, it is, for Felix, as if Pandora's box has been opened. That opening strikes a deep-seated fear that Esther's femininity is dangerously encompassing, capable of sapping the powerful man's strength, canceling his intellectual power. Like the lover in Byron's poem, the "clear, grey eyes" will have no sight, "the full lips" no voice, and the massive body no life "within himself." His fear speaks in his misogyny: "Women," he tells Esther, are "a curse; all life is stunted to suit their littleness. That's why I'll never love, if I can help it; and if I love, I'll bear it, and never marry" (212). Felix is afraid that his mouth will become "stuffed" with love and that his political voice will be stopped.

That Felix will eventually accept Esther as his wife and that Esther will reject her Byron and pseudo-Byronic Oriental lover, Harold Transome, suggests that the novel is less interested in Esther's "moral" progress than in focusing on an explosive, nearly violent sexual negotiation which is mediated through Byron's poetry and through the Byronic resonances in Eliot's Harold Transome. After Felix makes his feelings about women known, Esther trembles and actually "pinch[es] her own hand to overcome her tremor" in a "desperate effort" not to reveal the emotional wound inflicted by his words (212). At this moment, when physical self-punishment seeks to squelch sexual interest or desire, the novel's paramount concern with the denial of sexual pleasure rather than with "moral progress" and aesthetics becomes clear. Indeed, those elements are integrated here. It is no wonder that the text must bring Byron to life, calling upon an outsider, Harold Transome, to mediate desire between Esther and Felix. In their moral standoff, similar to that between Maggie Tulliver and Stephen Guest, Esther and Felix are in an antiprogressive, static position. If anyone is to move toward marriage rather than death, "moral progress" of the type that motivates Maggie Tulliver or the young Dorothea Brooke must be replaced with the ability to experience and act upon sexual desire. Felix Holt must learn to dream.

INDEED, FROM THE opening of *Felix Holt*, we are asked to value dreams. In the concluding paragraph of her preface to the novel, Eliot makes an analogy between Transome Court and "a dolorous enchanted forest in the underworld. The thornbushes there, and thick-barked stems, have human histories hidden in them; the power of unuttered cries dwells in the passionless-seeming branches, and the red warm blood is darkly feeding the quivering nerves of a sleepless memory that watches through all dreams. These things are a parable" (84). The prince of this "enchanted forest in the underworld" is the errant pilgrim, Harold Transome. He is the "someone expected," returning from the East to his mother and ancestral home at the novel's opening (85). Harold, the illegitimate child of the well-born Mrs. Transome and Mr. Jermyn, carries within his body a mixture of blood that "darkly feeds" his mother's omnipresent memory of her adultery with a member of the bourgeoisie. The violation of that taboo, strong enough to be termed miscegenation, is reinforced by Eliot's constant references to Jermyn's brownness. Jermyn may also, like Maggie Tulliver or Daniel Deronda, be a Gypsy, a mulatto, or a Moor. His ambitions and sexual desire, like those of Maggie, Daniel, and Will Ladislaw, literally blacken him. His is an unchecked immorality that guilt and asceticism will never wash white. Harold Transome, his son, also literally marked by the "black seal," his father's darkness of skin, low birth, and immoral behavior, has naturally gravitated to the Orient (583). In Smyrna he becomes a merchant king much as little Maggie envisions herself as a Gypsy queen. He returns a captain of industry, literally "plump" with Turkish money, rose satin cushions, and a round brown baby.

Indeed, as an "Oriental" British imperialist and a political radical, a member of the bourgeoisie and the gentry, Harold Transome is an ingenious fashioning of what much of Victorian England feared and desired in 1832 and in 1867. Created in 1866, when the country was focused on the Reform Bill of 1867, this fictional alliance with the East, and particularly with Turkey, resonates with the idea of political despotism. Harold's Turkish fortune alone has important ramifications for the novel's feminism and its reform politics. In fact, in the early nineteenth century, in part due to Byron's poetry, which detailed the treatment of women and the underclass in Eastern cultures, "Turkey was a byword for tyranny," particularly "in Whiggish political jargon."[30] Byron's speech in the House of Lords on the twenty-seventh of February, 1812, was in keeping with earlier tendencies to align Western political conservatism or Toryism with Turkish "despotism." Comparing "barbaric" abuses in Turkey with the treatment of his own working countrymen, Byron said: "I have been in some of the most oppressed provinces of Turkey; but never under the most despotic of infidel governments did I behold such squalid wretchedness as I have seen since my return in the very heart of a Christian country."[31]

In addition to criticizing the treatment of the male underclass in Turkey, Byron's Oriental tales often focused on Turkish sexual politics, the tyranny special to the Turkish harem. Often, in the last days of the Ottoman Empire, the harem was populated by enslaved Greek women. As did the American sculptor Hiram Powers later in the century, Byron used the image of the Greek slave woman to dramatize the crisis of slavery, the usurpation of the classical ideals of democracy, and the universal sexual exploitation of women. Using the image of "barbaric" imperialist Turks to critique their own politics, Byron and George Eliot follow a Western tradition established in the eighteenth century. Mary Wollstonecraft and Montesquieu both found the sexual politics of the harem an appropriate analogy for their own political discontents. In her *Vindication of the Rights of*

*Woman,* Wollstonecraft used the harem as a "constant referent."[32]
Earlier, Montesquieu's *Persian Letters* were a "sustained and profound
meditation on the interrelationships of familial and political life."
There, he "ironically parallels control of the seraglio with strategies
of monarchical tyranny—comparing France with Turkey."[33] Montesquieu's protagonist, Usbek, is a sultan visiting the West and corresponding all the while with his wife and eunuchs in the harem. In
Montesquieu's treatment, "oriental love" becomes a metaphor for
despotism and sexual tyranny. "Under Usbek's rhetoric of love lies an
absolutism based on mutual fear: he is both husband and prince; the
eunuchs are both harem guards and political ministers. The denoue-
ment is shocking: his favorite wife writes defiantly that she has taken
poison, her lover having been executed, and that she dies proclaiming
her joy at release through death from Usbek's tyranny."[34] Caroline
Franklin suggests that Byron begins his Oriental tales at this point in
the Western tradition of the representation of the Eastern harem,
with the death or mistreatment of a heroine at the hands of a *Hassan.*
George Eliot is indeed concerned with the same Oriental narrative
pattern in the positioning of Harold Transome as half-*Hassan,* half-
"Giaour" to the vulnerable Esther Lyon and the adulterous Mrs.
Transome.

The resonances of Montesquieu, Byron, and Wollstonecraft are
clear in *Felix Holt.* Using the harem captive to represent the liminal
position of girlhood itself persisted as a theme in high-Victorian culture where paintings like Henriette Browne's 1863 *A Greek Captive*
represented a girl whose gaze directly confronts her audience (plate
2). Eliot's particular recasting of the harem also allows her to critique
both domestic and sexual politics in an innovative way. In Byron's
poem, or in any of his Eastern tales, the Western expatriate *Giaour* is
in sympathy with the adulterous slave girl, not the *Hassan,* her Eastern captor. The *Giaour* is a tragic hero, a thwarted rescuer. This order
is obscured in *Felix Holt* in which Harold Transome, "the *Giaour* concerned," is a slave-owner himself. Here Eliot appears to be criticizing
her own society as much as that of the "barbaric Turks." As Said has
argued, the nineteenth-century Western writer's world vision is
defined by "positive ideas of home, of a nation and its language, of
proper order, good behavior, moral values," and that vision necessarily validates the Western world and devalues other worlds. The vision
of empire in Jane Austen's *Mansfield Park,* for instance, does not "in-
hibit or give resistance to horrendously unattractive imperialist prac-

tices."[35] However, in *Felix Holt*, empire works both ways. The "barbaric" Turks are in league with the equally barbaric English. Moreover, Eliot's narrative is further complicated by the issue of gender and sexual politics. For George Eliot is an outsider to an extent that Austen never was. Maggie Tulliver, for example, would not head out for the Gypsies' camp had she a "positive idea of home"; traditional Christian values become the Inquisition which Fedalma flees in *The Spanish Gypsy*; Dorothea leaves Middlemarch with the object of her desire; and Daniel Deronda departs from the philistinism of England "to the East" at the end of Eliot's last novel. In Eliot's novels, it is often the familiar, white face that is barbaric, the "cruel Turk"; the dark face looks as if it could be mother to Maggie Tulliver. Here, in *Felix Holt*, the Westerner, who calls himself, paradoxically, an "Oriental," represents the white British male's potential for tyranny. In an English society dominated by cultural philistinism, it is the English man who is a barbarian. By having owned a Greek slave himself, Harold signals his corruption of classical political values and the corruption of the British imperialist.

But, despite her criticism of Harold Transome's sexual politics, Eliot, ultimately in *Felix Holt*, seems to return to more hegemonic standards. Her anxiety about her radical candidate's political and sexual desires is written not in the Victorian terms of race and empire but in the Victorian terms of race and class. As in the seventeenth-century *Othello*, in *Felix Holt*, race, immorality, miscegenation, and untempered and unregulated sexual desire are represented through color. Like his scheming father, Jermyn, Harold is "brown" rather than white (90). Indeed, the racial dimensions of this, perhaps Eliot's least sophisticated narrative, are almost cartoonlike. Thoroughly English, he is also thoroughly dark, somehow of a less-white breed than the "Gothic" Felix Holt. His secret "low" birth, his sexual transgressions in Turkey, his radicalism, have all washed him dark. Here, as in the rest of Eliot's canon, darkness of hair and eye signal sexual receptivity. Always dangerous elements, they are even more so in *Felix Holt*. Placed so explicitly within the context of reform, the dark threat of Harold Transome and Matthew Jermyn represents Eliot's anxieties about the reinvention of English society itself. Transome, a study in paradoxes, represents political ambition and sexual desire; his alter ego, Felix Holt, opposes those desires. The ultrawhite, ultra-Anglo, remarkably politically passive and misogynist radical Felix Holt is as much the bogeyman of English culture here as is Harold Transome.

Esther's choice between the two reflects less the "positive ideas" of home and more Eliot's attempt to contain the threatening energy of reform.

A "white" dove, fettered to the nineteenth-century female narrative, Esther knows that "after all, she [is] a woman, and [can]not make her own lot." That, she acknowledges, "is made for her by the love she accepts" (525). The practical problem of Esther's future clearly informs her decision to marry either hero. It is telling that the above realization is a memory. Esther first describes her predicament to Felix, then remembers it when she thinks of marrying Harold. Contrasting the antisensual Felix Holt with the luxurious Harold Transome, Eliot resists romanticizing Esther's difficult "final choice"; "on each side there was renunciation." Like the dark Maggie's death embrace of the blue-eyed Tom Tulliver, Esther chooses in Felix a disapproving, stern pedagogue and a nearly chaste brotherly love rather than Harold Transome's "passion" (590). That elusive element remains a danger to Esther Lyon, threatening the "supreme," "sublime" love that the didactic moral figure Felix Holt represents. To conquer passion, Esther must thwart her own "will" or desire. The higher moral love "is not to be had where and how she wills: to know that high initiation, she must often tread where it is hard to tread, and feel the chill air, and watch through darkness. It is not true that love makes all things easy: it makes us choose what is difficult" (590). "What is difficult," in the moral universe of George Eliot, is all too often what is chaste. Conquering desire rather than indulging it is the force that creates society in the image of heaven. Hence, "the presence and the love of Felix Holt" make the "vulgarity" and "privation" of their married life "as if it were heaven" (591).

In contrast to that heaven is the "Utopia" of Transome Court, which is consistently described as an Eastern harem. Kept at the manor, Mrs. Transome ruminates about her secret adultery and her suicidal despair over its revelation, recalling the adulterous wives of Montesquieu and Byron's Eastern poems. Harold constructs "pleasure grounds," significantly built on the eastern side of the manor, to amuse his mother and early on tells her that she's had to do far too much in managing the household and worrying "about things that don't properly belong to a woman—We'll set all that right. You shall have nothing to do now but to be grandmamma on satin cushions" (95). This entrapment in static luxury becomes explicitly named later as part and parcel of the "Oriental love" that tempts Esther Lyon.

This representation of the harem and of "Oriental love" is indebted to those of Byron, Montesquieu, and, especially, Mary Wollstonecraft. In the *Vindication of the Rights of Woman,* Wollstonecraft associates the harem with female sexual pleasure as well as with female enslavement. Like opium, the harem entices through its sheer immersion in sensibility. In Enlightenment or Rousseauist political philosophy of exactly the type that Felix Holt espouses, abandoning the self to sensibility promises the death of reason. Like Wollstonecraft's polemic, Eliot's novel uses the harem, a metaphor for the experience of female desire itself, to link "woman's pleasure" to her "dependent and deferential status."[36] The chains on Powers's *Greek Slave* after all "virtually guarantee" her sexual violation, and the statue itself "was the subject of erotic Victorian fantasies."[37] The frivolous, Byron-reading Esther is already, as Felix Holt has noted, an antimodel of Wollstonecraftian feminism, having begun "an early and corrupt initiation in the sensual."[38] The misogynistic Felix's asceticism warns that desire itself is counterrevolutionary.

The heroine in *Felix Holt* is faced then with a difficult choice, and Eliot accents the difficulty by lingering extensively over the pleasures of the enclosed harem that is Transome Court. She emphasizes its luxuries and its "small dignities" along with its vaguely "repugnant" air of moral laxity (547). It is described as Esther's "Utopia," and the longer she stays there as its possible mistress, the more she comes under its influence. Indeed, her visit becomes a metaphor for her capacity to experience pleasure. Quite unlike Maggie Tulliver or Dorothea Brooke, Esther Lyon feels "an exquisite kind of shame" at knowing that she is interested in two men at once. She is "susceptible" to her own desires (522): "It comes in so many forms in this life of ours—the knowledge that there is something sweetest and noblest of which we despair, and the sense of something present that solicits us with an immediate and easy indulgence. And there is a pernicious falsity in the pretense that a woman's love lies above the range of such temptations. . . . Esther began to think that her lot was being made for her by the love that was surrounding her with the influence of a garden on a summer morning" (524–25).

In the luxury of the manor, Esther is not above temptation. Eliot decries the Victorian belief that women are not tempted because "woman's love" lies above the erotic by referring back to the radical political theorists of the novel's pre-Victorian setting. Indeed, perhaps as much in Mary Wollstonecraft's antisensual *Vindication of the*

*Rights of Woman,* as in Eastern sexual mythology, it is just that near-phobia of female sensuality that necessitates the enclosure of women in the harem. Esther responds to Harold's "gradual wooing" and finds him "alluring" in a way that Felix Holt is not (524).

Like Wollstonecraft, Eliot had great difficulty voicing female desire in the face of its role as an antirational, disruptive force. The need for the containment of that force causes the pleasures of the harem to be quickly displaced by the image of enslavement. During a crucial discussion, Harold draws Esther "down the eastern steps into the pleasure-ground" of Transome Court. His maneuver reflects his own move from West to East and his troubling identification as both *Hassan* and *Giaour,* sultan and rescuer. Indeed, Esther has difficulty placing him in any *"genre."* He is not "a tragic hero," "not a romantic figure," not "languishing enough," "not in danger of committing suicide" (540). Instead, Esther says, he is simply a widower. As his Byronic literary veils fall away and the talk becomes serious, Esther literally trembles. At the mention of his marital status, Harold says that his first wife never held the place Esther might. She asks, "How so?" "'Harry's mother had been a slave—was bought, in fact.' It was impossible for Harold to preconceive the effect this had on Esther. . . . Hitherto Esther's acquaintance with Oriental love was derived chiefly from Byronic poems, and this had not sufficed to adjust her mind to a new story, where the *Giaour* concerned was giving her his arm. She was unable to speak" (541).

Eliot's heroine enacts Wollstonecraft's comparisons of English women with harem slaves as Esther makes the connection between herself and Harold's first wife, between his love and "degradation." Eliot pulls apart the "frisson of the white odalisque," unmasking its villain as white and English.[39] The threat to Esther posed by Harold's sexual attention becomes immediately apparent. Like many of the other scenes of "love-talk" between Harold and Esther, this one too is immediately followed by a vision of little Harry's undisciplined play. "Like a barbaric prince," Harry is a "tyrant" who treats others as if they were animals, biting, hitting, and turning family hierarchy upside down in a chaotic swirl. Looking at Harry, who bears the mark of the harem and, paradoxically, that of the empire, "it is inevitable that she should think of his mother." It is also inevitable that the child Harry should represent all the forces of untrammeled sensuous pleasure, the death of reason and the "degradation of culture" in his own genesis. As in Henriette Browne's *A Greek Captive,* here a child's face reifies the practice of human trafficking, effectively putting a face on slavery. Sensitive to the delicacy of his position as suitor to the newly endowed Esther, Harold asks for her sympathy: "I am necessarily in a painful position for a man who has any feeling." "At last Harold had stirred the right fibre" (541). "Feeling" is, as in Wollstonecraft's text, strongly tied to dependency and passivity. The more emotionally solicitous and beseeching Harold becomes toward Esther, "the more passive" she becomes "to his attentions." "A compromise with things repugnant to the moral taste" seems possible, even likely (547). Finally, Esther does not voice her rejection of Harold; he rejects her, out of honor, when he learns of his low birth. And indeed, in accepting a legacy from Transome, Esther, although she marries Felix Holt, participates in those "things repugnant" which his Turkish fortune can buy. Her refusal to be the object of her *Giaour's* campaign is less clearly motivated than the novel's simply crafted ending, the marriage of Esther and Felix.

That marriage is marked, finally, more by renunciation than by any embrace of the passion that distances Esther from Transome. It is complicated by the fact that Harold Transome himself has made moral progress. Facing "the most serious moment" in his life—the failure of his political campaign, the possible failure of his personal attempt to win Esther, and the acknowledgment of his illegitimacy—Transome rises to the occasion. "For the first time the iron had entered into his soul, and he felt the hard pressure of our common lot, the yoke of that mighty resistless destiny laid upon us by the acts of other men as well as our own" (587). Transome has, moreover, "acted so that he could defy anyone to say he was not a gentleman" (590). His passion and tenderness are real; in recognizing their authenticity, Esther rejects him. "Harold Transome's love, no longer a hovering fancy with which she played, but become a serious fact, seemed to threaten her with a stifling oppression." Indeed, despite Harold's reformation, marriage to him continues to fall into the harem paradigm. It is "silken bondage," "a fall and a degradation," "to be languid among all the appliances for pleasure" (592). Consequently, Esther tells him that she loves Felix, and that she "resigned all claim to the Transome estates. She wished to go back to her father" (599). Esther, like Maggie Tulliver, curtails her own ability to experience pleasure or freedom with an exotic outsider. Rejecting her *Giaour,* embracing the very English Felix Holt, she also marries his values and those of her ascetic preacher-father's. When, "not reading, but stitching," she meets Felix again, she tells him that she is there now ready to marry him and "needing to be scolded" (600). "Have you considered well what it would be?—that it will be a very bare and simple life?" he asks. "Yes," she replies, "without atta of roses," and without the sensuous pleasure which distinguishes her attraction to Harold Transome (601).

Like other Victorian writers, Eliot wrote most readily of desire when she dramatized it as the property of other cultures, other classes, or other races. But, unlike Dickens, Thackeray, or the Brontës, Eliot's "long and assured development" of an interest in foreignness results in a conflicted interrogation of that category.[40] That interrogation, to continue in *The Spanish Gypsy, Daniel Deronda,* and *Middlemarch,* makes a remarkable representation of relations between the English and Others. For Harold Transome, the "Oriental," is a kind of fake, an English creation, a strange *Giaour* wrought by inverting the Byronic model. At once a Byronic sensualist and an anti-Byronic Ottoman or *Hassan,* Transome washes Otherness over with Englishness until he is overdetermined as a character. Representing the "sultanic habits" of the East, he nonetheless remains a criticism of British imperialism notwithstanding that his Oriental association with sensuality is defeated by Esther's choice of Felix. A strange melange of the East and West, Transome ultimately represents the desire Eliot struggles to contain and control in her "English story."[41]

Indeed, Esther's choice of Felix Holt over Harold Transome only partially restores the novel's own ideals regarding moral compromise as it only partially restores the Victorian novel's generic conventions regarding race and class. Certainly, Esther's legacy and Felix's release from prison through Transome's intervention have over the years left Eliot's readers dissatisfied. The novel's moral high road is obscured, as is identity itself. Esther finally settles down with Felix to produce, it seems, nothing. "There is a young Felix," who comes of their marriage, and "who has a great deal more science than his father, but not much more money." North Loamshire "does not yet return a radical candidate," and, to thwart that possibility further, Eliot will not reveal where Felix Holt and Esther live: "As to the town in which Felix Holt now resides, I will keep that a secret, lest he should be troubled by any visitor having the insufferable motive of curiosity" (606).

Bent on protecting Felix Holt and, perhaps, her novel, from those who would ask too many questions in regard to his political or domestic future, Eliot's narrator reveals the pressures by which the novel itself is molded. Even the economics of the novel's end are strangely static, as if Esther's stipend, a cut of the huge fortune Harold made in Smyrna, will never multiply and increase, as if Felix Holt's son will not earn an income proportionate to his acquisition of "more science." The stifling of increase and political change, which marks the end of *Felix Holt*—so inconsistent with the social realities of a novel in which we feel from its inception the steam of the Victorian locomotive at our backs—is even more effectively consistent with its attempt to contain, keep secret, and control both political and sexual desire. A view of both Englishness and Otherness, *Felix Holt* leaves the "Oriental" Other, Harold Transome, an outcast at the novel's end, wishing he'd "never come back to this pale English sunshine" (582). The strangely foreign English man foreshadows the arrival in Eliot's canon of another outcast of mixed heritage, Will Ladislaw. His presence in *Middlemarch,* to be written after she had completed her portrait of Fedalma in *The Spanish Gypsy,* continues Eliot's dialogue between Otherness and political and sexual desire. Finally, the marriage of Will Ladislaw and Dorothea Brooke as the consummate accomplishment of *Middlemarch* will release what is still so carefully and problematically contained in *Felix Holt: The Radical.*

## FOUR

# *"A Queer Genealogy"*

## Ethnicity and Sexuality in *Middlemarch*

IN *MIDDLEMARCH* (1871) the "dead hand" of provincial English culture is disrupted by an ethnic outsider. Rumored to be of some "cursed alien blood, Jew, Corsican, or Gypsy," Will Ladislaw threatens to "cross" Middlemarch's Anglocentric "breed" through an act of comparative miscegenation, his marriage to Dorothea Brooke. Intruding on the provincial "Middlemarch tribes," the half-exotic, half-"girl[ish]" Ladislaw acts as a figure whose ethnic Otherness represents the problem of female desire and the desire for political and cultural change. So clear is Eliot's narrative attraction to the figure of the exotic intruder that she creates one where he may not, in fact, exist. In *Middlemarch,* the "story" or rumor that Ladislaw is Jewish becomes "the fact about Will Ladislaw,"[1] literally embodying J. Hillis Miller's realization that in the novel "no fact is in itself single, and no fact is explicable by a single relationship to a single cause."[2] In the novel's development and revelation of the rumor about Ladislaw's background, the "fact" of ethnicity is critiqued as a potentially unstable cultural construction.

That achievement, thought to happen much later in the history of the English novel,[3] contrasts sharply with D. A. Miller's critique of *Middlemarch* as "no substantial challenge to the way things are."[4] As the child of an exiled Polish refugee, Ladislaw makes an unconventional object of attraction for the alienated heroine, Dorothea Brooke, allying the imprisoned heroine's subjectivity and the victimized exotic self in a fairly typical repetition of imperialist "sympathy" for the

Other.[5] However, the gendering of Ladislaw's Otherness complicates patterns established in Eliot's other works. In the early poetry, short stories, and novels, the Other is expropriated, doubling as the English self until the Other's face is expunged and replaced by what remains, a representation of disenfranchised white captivity. That paradigm is supported by the presence of the slave-owning "Giaour," Harold Transome, in *Felix Holt: The Radical* (1866). Eliot's expropriation of Otherness then follows a certain logic in her earlier works that clearly draws from common gendered Victorian appropriations of Otherness. In *Middlemarch,* however, Dorothea Brooke's identification with, attraction and marriage to a nearly girlish "alien" subverts the conventions of racial desire in the English novel (*MM,* 444).

Discounting women's sexual desires and stressing only Dorothea's vocational desire, D. A. Miller envisions her marriage to Ladislaw as "a surrender of desire or its reductive resealing."[6] In fact, Ladislaw's politics, ethnic identity, and androgynous femininity make him an entirely unconventional object of desirous female subjectivity.[7] Dorothea Brooke's belief in Ladislaw's Jewish ancestry and her linking of herself to him marks *Middlemarch* as a potentially subversive text. In *Middlemarch,* the insidious rumor of Ladislaw's "queer genealogy" and then its disappearance into the text is remarkable. Such "marks of race" are almost always made quite clear in Victorian fiction which depends so much upon binary contrasts. Harold Transome would perhaps never declare so confidently, "I'm an Oriental, you know," if, in fact, he really were. It is possible that Dorothea Brooke's discovery of Ladislaw's ethnicity may re-gender an old story, like Rebecca's story in Scott's *Ivanhoe.* In such revivals of "medieval chivalry," the Other's "rescue" worked in "concert with the 'civilizing mission.' Her degradation provided the Englishman with an object to lavish pity on, as well as to educate and enlighten."[8] But Ladislaw's rumored, obscured ethnicity is an innovation in the representation of race in Victorian fiction, which so often strives to see "white as 'white' and black as 'black'–driv[ing] the division of the world according to absolute correspondences between colors, characters, and categories."[9]

Because society excludes Will Ladislaw in *Middlemarch,* he creates his own families, first with the rebellious Lydgate and his wife, Rosamund, who even acts out, for her own entertainment, a sham adultery with Ladislaw. Next, Ladislaw is identified as a father figure to a "troop of droll children" in Middlemarch. Both activities, along with his "dangerous" politics, become a particular "matter of remark" in town.[10]

> He had a fondness, half-artistic, half-affectionate, for little children—the smaller they were on tolerably active legs, and the funnier their clothing, the better Will liked to surprise and please them. We know that in Rome he was given to ramble about among the poor people, and the taste did not quit him in Middlemarch. He had somehow picked up a troop of droll children, little hatless boys with their galligaskins much worn and scant shirting to hang out, little girls who tossed their hair out of their eyes to look at him, and guardian brothers at the mature age of seven. This troop he had led out on gypsy excursions . . . where he drew out a small feast of gingerbread for them, and improvised a Punch-and-Judy drama with some private home-made puppets. Here was one oddity. Another was that in houses where he got friendly he was given to stretch himself at full length on the rug while he talked and was apt to be discovered in this attitude by occasional callers for whom such an irregularity was likely to confirm the notions of his dangerously mixed blood and general laxity. (*MM*, 287)

Addressing multiple imaginary readers, Eliot's narrative voice mocks Middlemarch and urges us to do the same. We hear that Ladislaw's generosity, epitomized by his sweet, playful excursions at "nutting-time" with village children, is read by Middlemarchers as "odd." We understand that Ladislaw is being observed or watched by an absurdly suspicious community whose coldness makes his warmth an "oddity." The second suspicious activity Ladislaw is accused of is informality, marked by "stretch[ing] himself at full length on the rug while he talked." The average native reads this as a sign of "his dangerously mixed blood and general laxity." His spontaneity is an "irregularity" in town (287). The narrative eye of *Middlemarch* exposes the community's absurd conservatism; the Middlemarchers watch Ladislaw almost as a freak, an "oddity" at which they "gape" and then "return home in wonder at the oddities of the 'Other,'" thus reaffirming the enduring normality of their own world," miming Victorian visitors to a sideshow or carnival.[11]

 The community's response to Ladislaw indicts the categorizing, abstracting discourses of the Middlemarch rumor mill which ever return to the binary categories of insider and outsider, self and Other, innocent and suspect, male and female. In his play with children in town and in his flirtations with the Lydgates, Ladislaw seems to deviate "from the purity and order of traditional familial arrangements" and "verg[e] on forms of sexuality that both Victorian and contemporary champions of those arrangements apprehend as enemy number one." But the provincial suspicions surrounding Ladislaw generate Dorothea's defense of his behavior. She admires his jumbling of rank, his playacting, and his arrogance. Always in the process of "metamorphosis," the feminine Ladislaw, with his "girlish complexion" and his close resemblance to his grandmother, offers Dorothea sanctuary from that "'normal' socialization" which deprives her of the intellectual, spiritual, and sexual life she desires. Indeed, where Eliot's depiction of the deviant male body in *Silas Marner* once created a "'pallid, undersized' man isolated amongst full bodied strangers," now in *Middlemarch,* the deviant Ladislaw is at once feminine and a vital embodied man.[12]

As Eliot's Orientalizing of Fedalma, the Spanish Gypsy, permits that character's eroticism, so does Will Ladislaw's liminal ethnic identity influence the representation of his sexuality. The belief that ethnicity influenced sexuality is consistent with the unsubtle controlling idea of most Victorian texts on race which bear the definitive mark of narrative subjectivity, Walter Benjamin's "tasteless seed of time," which flavors all historical narrative with the storyteller's own agenda.[13] Edward Said, Gayatri Chakravorty Spivak, and Patrick Brantlinger have studied the ways in which literary texts invent culture and the constructs of Englishness and Otherness. Their analyses have focused particularly on the English novel's tendency to uphold English culture's value system, to be "the axioms of imperialism" on the global or domestic frontiers.[14] There, paradigms of Victorian Otherness contrast sharply with white virtue, Fagin to Oliver Twist, Bertha Rochester to Jane Eyre. But in *Middlemarch,* these paradigms shift dramatically; difference is martyred and in its abjection, it attracts rather than repels. Conversely, it is no accident that the novel's chief representation of monstrosity, Rosamund Vincy, is also a vision of pink, white, and gold English femininity. Omnivorous and morally corrupt, she plays the role of Bertha Rochester; her desires keep getting out from under the lock and key of Lydgate's good taste and morality. Indeed, in *Middlemarch* the critique of English culture is the hidden assumption, the "tasteless seed of time" whose flavor permeates narrative. Within that narrative of ethnic value, the Other is

seductive and attractive, because he questions the nature of social relationships, of the personal and the familial. The subtext of the novel
is that if "here is one oddity," Others, even more "dangerous" and unmentionable, may be at hand. The absurdity of the English community's demonizing of Ladislaw becomes clear as they feed the rumor
that Will Ladislaw is Jewish.

Despite the recent advent of the study of race and ethnicity in Victorian fiction, no one in the past forty years has examined the rumor,
begun halfway through *Middlemarch,* that Will Ladislaw is of Jewish
ancestry. In the late 1950s and early 1960s the issue of Ladislaw's ethnic heritage was raised and debated by several Eliot scholars. Twice,
argues Jerome Beaty in his 1958 article "The Forgotten Past of Will
Ladislaw," Ladislaw is rumored to be "the grandson of a thieving Jew
pawnbroker."[15] The rumor becomes the "fact about Will Ladislaw"
and gains momentum when even the generous and kind Mr. Farebrother repeats it as gospel: "'So our mercurial Ladislaw has a queer
genealogy! A high-spirited young lady and a musical Polish patriot
make a likely enough stock for him to spring from, but I should
never have suspected a grafting of the Jew pawnbroker. However,
there is no knowing what a mixture will turn out before hand. Some
sorts of dirt serve to clarify'" (*MM,* 444).

The ugliness of Farebrother's remark exemplifies Middlemarch's
narrow vision as it exemplifies the narrative power of rumor. Truth,
like ethnicity, becomes a social construct, malleable, and morally am-
bivalent. It is not surprising that Middlemarch's rumor of Ladislaw's
Jewish heritage once sparked controversy in Eliot scholarship. It is
more surprising that in the past forty years, no one has pursued the
rumor. In his article, Beaty argues that Eliot may have made an error
in introducing the idea of a Jewish heritage into Ladislaw's already
extraordinarily complex family tree. Or, he notes: "Eliot may simply
be indicating the kind of error which gets introduced into such gossip as it spreads." Beaty also suggests the possibility of the "casual
grafting of 'Jew' and 'pawnbroker'" into one derogatory racist slur.
Ultimately, Beaty is interested in Ladislaw's heritage only insofar as
the character may be a precursor to Daniel Deronda. He suggests
that the rumor about Ladislaw's ethnicity is an error arising from
Eliot's conflation of the *Middlemarch* notebooks with her separate
plans for the novel begun as "Miss Brooke." There, Beaty argues, Will
Ladislaw "was to have been at least partly Jewish." Ladislaw's past, he
argues, was, like that of Daniel Deronda, to have been kept mysteri-

ous: "Except for her abandoning 'Miss Brooke' as a separate work and hitching it instead to the becalmed beginning of 'Middlemarch,' George Eliot would have introduced her longtime interest in the Jewish people into her fiction several years earlier than is now the case, and Will Ladislaw may have served in 'Miss Brooke' in much the same way that Daniel Deronda serves in the novel named after him."[16] Beaty's reading continued to provoke debate from Eliot scholars in the early 1960s. Interesting and significant as his logical conjecture is for *Daniel Deronda* (1876), however, it does not explain the significance of the rumor in *Middlemarch*. Robert A. Greenberg offered a counterpoint to Beaty's logical guesswork with his own reading. Concerned only with the "truth" of the rumor rather than with its narrative power, he argues against Beaty's thesis by again referring to *Daniel Deronda*: "The moderately frivolous young man with curly locks that we first meet in *Middlemarch* does seem an unlikely model for the image of the Jew we might expect of George Eliot, if we can use as a measure her portrayal not only of Daniel but of Mirah and other Jews in *Daniel Deronda*."[17] But Deronda's mother, the Alcharisi, also a performer and rebel like Ladislaw and Klesmer, the Jewish musician who marries Catherine Arrowpoint, constitutes the Jewish population of *Daniel Deronda* as well. Deronda, moreover, in his early flirtation with Gwendolen Harleth, mirrors the sensuality or even the frivolity of Will Ladislaw. Indeed, Deronda's sober "image" is itself an icy veneer concealing his own internal discourses of will and desire. And Eliot's other portrayals of Jewish characters, Mirah's father, for instance, represent a potentially explosive sensuality.

Thomas Pinney, in 1962, voiced another objection to Beaty's claims. The tenor of his argument lies in his belief that "whether Ladislaw was originally to have been part Jewish is not in itself an important matter." Despite the "striking resemblance" between Ladislaw and Deronda, moreover, the former "shows merely that frequently noted family resemblance between many of George Eliot's characters." "If Ladislaw was originally to have had Jewish blood, that would be an interesting detail in the biography of George Eliot's novels."[18] In much the same tone, Suzanne Graver and D. A. Miller acknowledge Ladislaw's "outsider" status and that Eliot locates "the desire for reform in characters who are outsiders."[19] But the vehemence of the rumor about Will Ladislaw's Jewish ancestry is particular, and it evokes a chain of events that moves narrative forward.

The community of Middlemarch and the novel itself thrive on the passage of rumor and misinformation. Its "famous web" is also "an information network." That network feeds on the "universal propensity for misinterpretation which infects all the characters in *Middlemarch*."[20] There, as J. Hillis Miller argues, "the concepts of origin, end, and continuity are replaced by the categories of repetition, of difference, of discontinuity, of openness and of the free and contradictory struggle of individual human energies, each seen as a center of interpretation, which means misinterpretation of the whole."[21] It is this web and its propensity for rumor and misinterpretation that jealously guards the secret "fact," the truth of the complicated matter of Ladislaw's heritage. But in the novel, Eliot refuses to let that secret out. Rather, the novel develops Ladislaw's heritage through the passage of rumor, through individual and, finally, communal sanctions of the rumor. Within the "everywhere" of Middlemarch, where community defines self, any deviation becomes a significant force that matters. As a microcosm of a universe whose sun never sets on the British Empire, the rumors of Middlemarch make the "ugly secret" of the English process of Othering, of recategorization, visible. In doing so, the novel erodes the standard of Englishness itself, charting the ethnic standards of "Middlemarch tribes" through their often hysterical or outrageous exaggerations such as Mr. Hawley's equation of the Polish Will Ladislaw with any other non-English person: "Jew, Corsican, or Gypsy" (527).

In this sense, Eliot's novel of the Midlands, what she called, after writing *The Spanish Gypsy,* her "English novel," is remarkably subversive of what critics like Edward Said or Gayatri Spivak have come to term the stable or traditional values of the English novel. Instead of validating the pattern of English superiority and colonialism that Said sees as beginning with Austen's *Mansfield Park* (1814), Eliot devalues the world of Englishness and engages with the outsider, here Will Ladislaw, and, to a lesser extent, Tertius Lydgate. Eliot's *Middlemarch* refuses to banish Other characters or avoid miscegenation to preserve and affirm a paradigm of Englishness that finds its expression in the uneasy domesticity and expulsions of erotic desire that mark the endings of *Jane Eyre, Wuthering Heights,* or *Oliver Twist.*

MIDDLEMARCH, AS ALEXANDER Welsh has noted, is a "novel about opinion" which focuses on a community's ability to define reality through its own network of talk, gossip, and slander. The novel's most inclusive theme is "knowledge . . . and the theme keeps resolving . . . into statements of the limitations of knowledge." The methods of communicating that knowledge are imperfect and random. Eliot's "wariness" of the human web of communication extends "both to the grounds for knowing anything and to the social implications of the theme."[22] Like Dorothea Brooke, we are never quite sure if we as readers ought to believe what we hear, and it is only by engaging in the novel's process of affirmation, denial, and revelation through talk, letters, and narration that we are able to construct a truth about any of the problems that the novel presents.

The process, then, by which Will Ladislaw's Jewish heritage is gradually revealed and sanctioned by Dorothea Brooke is intriguing on many different levels. Each ripple in the slow spread of rumor, innuendo, and "fact" furthers the impression of Ladislaw's exoticism that ultimately is neither denied nor confirmed. In *Middlemarch,* as in *The Mill on the Floss, Felix Holt, The Spanish Gypsy,* or *Daniel Deronda,* the alliance between English and Other selves forges an alliance between the cultural objects of racism and sexism. As the rumor of Will's heritage grows, it becomes powerful indeed, raising more and more empathy in Dorothea, and stirring more and more attraction despite Will's alliance with representations of women rather than men. Dorothea meets him first through the portrait of his grandmother, Julia, which hangs in the woman's space of Dorothea's boudoir. Julia's "peculiar face" does not resemble those of her "own" family. Dorothea tells Casuabon: "'Those deep grey eyes rather near together—and the delicate irregular nose with a sort of ripple in it—and all the powdered curls hanging backward. Altogether it seems to me peculiar rather than pretty. There is not even a family likeness between her and your mother'" (48). The narrator will later adopt Dorothea's words to describe Ladislaw, whose curls also hang backward, and whose nose shares the same sensuous "ripple." Linking Ladislaw's features to those of his grandmother, the viewing of the portrait also comprises Dorothea's discovery of his intriguing and unmentionable heritage which at once becomes the topic of discussion and an antitopic. "You did not mention her to me," Dorothea tells Casaubon. He replies: "'My aunt made an unfortunate marriage. I never saw her.' Dorothea wondered a little, but felt that it would be indelicate just then to ask for any information which Mr. Casaubon did not proffer, and she turned to the window to admire the view. The sun had lately pierced the grey, and the avenue of limes cast shadows" (48). At this very early moment in the novel, the web

surrounding Ladislaw's heritage has already begun. The information
of some *mésalliance,* coupled with Aunt Julia's peculiar face, does not
clarify Will's background but opens it as a mystery. Like the sun
piercing the grey, that information does not illumine but "casts
shadows" about Ladislaw's heritage. Joking a little later about what is
unsaid but understood in the rhetoric of kings to their peoples,
Casaubon asserts that words often "[drop] out of the text, or perhaps
[are] *subauditum;* that is present in the king's mind, but not uttered"
(50). It is clear that Ladislaw's heritage, the fact of his grandmother's
unmentionable sexual rebellion and "peculiarity," are also present in
the reader's and the narrator's mind *subauditum.* What made Julia's
marriage "unfortunate" is never exactly specified—it is some *mésalliance* of class, culture, or race, or of all three. But difference is central
to Dorothea's "wondering."

Always mobile, Ladislaw's features have the power to "change their
form; his jaw looked sometimes large and sometimes small," while
his face seems "a preparation for metamorphosis" (133). At the
novel's crisis of "disenchantment," when Dorothea returns from her
Roman honeymoon, and all else is "deadened as an unlit trans-
parency," Will's face, interchangeable with Julia's portrait, is imbued
with vitality, overtly linking "pictures with nature" (173). In her
boudoir, Dorothea contemplates Julia's portrait along with the "gen-
tlewoman's oppressive liberty" and identifies with the portrait's
"headstrong look, a peculiarity difficult to interpret" (173). Once recognized as the face of woman's rebellion, the portrait metamor-
phoses to represent Ladislaw: "[T]he colours deepened, the lips and
chin seemed to get larger, the hair and eyes seemed to be sending out
light, the face was masculine and beamed on her with that full gaze
which tells her on whom it falls that she is too interesting for the
slightest movement of her eyelid to pass unnoticed and uninter-
preted. The vivid presentation came like a pleasant glow to Dorothea:
she felt herself smiling, and turning from the miniature sat down
and looked up as if she were again talking to a figure in front of her"
(174).

Clearly, in the separate "world" of the boudoir, the sanctuary of
Dorothea's married life, the slippage between fact and imagination which *Middlemarch* encourages extends its range to a subtle
transmutation of gender. Sitting in "a room where one might
fancy the ghost of a tight-laced lady revisiting the scene of her em-
broidery," Dorothea shares that lady's desire to "upset" her lot (48).

Ladislaw elides strict categories of masculinity as he elides categories of ethnicity and class, cementing Eliot's alliance between the imprisoned sexual self and the victimized ethnic self.

Far from having made an "error" of consistency in the creation of Will Ladislaw's ethnic heritage, Eliot seems to keep his origin deliberately vague, establishing and embellishing an air of mystery that makes Ladislaw's character ripe for narrative invention. Indeed, Eliot seems to link the problem of origin to literary creativity and the development of narrative itself, as she does in all her works which develop narrative through the search for ethnic origin. As in *The Spanish Gypsy, Felix Holt, Daniel Deronda,* and even *The Mill on the Floss,* in *Middlemarch* Will Ladislaw's mysterious origin and strangely foreign air necessitate that he seek a vocation undetermined by heritage. Ladislaw "prefer[s] not to know the sources of the Nile" because "some unknown regions [should be] preserved as hunting-grounds for the poetic imagination" (52). Similarly, the mystery of Ladislaw's origin in the text of *Middlemarch* acts as Eliot's own creative "hunting-ground." Ladislaw's "cold vagueness" toward his past is paired with his deliberate internationalism which is used to criticize Middlemarch's interiority and xenophobia. Highly critical of the provinciality of "much English scholarship," Ladislaw identifies the flaw in Casaubon's *Key to All Mythologies* (132). It is that Casaubon is "not an Orientalist. . . . He does not profess to have more than second-hand knowledge there" (141). Much of the work that Casaubon is conducting might as well be "thrown away. . . . If Mr. Casaubon read German he would save himself a great deal of trouble" (132). Ladislaw refers to nineteenth-century German Orientalists whom Casaubon will not read out of prejudice. Flaunting his own lack of a national identity and "caste" in his critique of Casaubon, Ladislaw intensifies his sense of Otherness and becomes more and more attractive to Dorothea.

What Dorothea cannot say about Will Ladislaw's heritage, the rumormongers of Middlemarch have no difficulty saying. Outrageous, exorbitant, a feat of narrative invention, the rumors about his background and ethnicity begin with his public visibility as secretary to the reform candidate, Mr. Brooke. Ladislaw is "said to be of foreign extraction," and "that half-fact" immediately makes him "a revolutionary sort." An "emissary . . . he'll begin with flourishing about the Rights of Man and end with murdering a wench" (223). The rumors that he is the child of a *"mésalliance"* begin and proliferate in part because it may be true, in part because Ladislaw will not refute it (228). His reticence is attributed to his shame at having the "dirt" of ethnic difference thrown at him. Like Fedalma or Daniel Deronda, he is the more vulnerable for not knowing the full story of his own origin. Ladislaw's information does not clarify his origin but mystifies and opens venues for further aspersion. He says: "'My mother, too, ran away from her family, but not for the sake of her husband. She would never tell me anything about her family, except that she forsook them to get her own living—went on the stage, in fact. She was a dark-eyed creature, with crisp ringlets, and never seemed to be getting old. You see, I come of rebellious blood on both sides'" (229). The story of Ladislaw's origin and his self-mythologization as the descendent of "rebellious blood" is intensified by the narrator's indirect discourse and the community's gossip. Both use the analogies of ethnic difference in the language of Victorian racial stereotypes. Affirming that "his nature warmed easily" and, like his rebellion, is "easily stirred," the narrator agrees with Lydgate that Ladislaw "was a sort of gypsy, rather enjoying the sense of belonging to no class; he had a feeling of romance in his position, and a pleasant consciousness of creating a little surprise wherever he went" (286).

With the groundwork of difference already laid, Will Ladislaw's Jewish heritage is constructed out of loose talk begun late in the novel by Raffles. The irony here is that the despicable, loose-tongued Raffles, as immoral a purveyor of information as might be, is the medium through which Ladislaw learns the truth of the past which his mother would not share with him. The drunken Raffles tells Ladislaw that his grandfather's line of business was pawnbrokering or "what you may call the respectable thieving line" (378). The knowledge of his ancestor's business, considered unfit for a gentleman or a Christian, is strangely "confirmed" by Ladislaw's own ignorance of his mother's heritage. The doubt and fear instilled by her silence, that she never would tell him the reason why she had run away from her family, leaves him free to "wonder," like Dorothea, about the nature of his heritage. Information, like the "starlit darkness" in which Ladislaw and Raffles walk, does not illumine but instead creates a shadowy anxiety. "Supposing the truth about the family to be the ugliest," Ladislaw "felt as if he had had dirt thrown on him amidst shouts of scorn" (378). Ultimately, the novel does not attempt to wash Ladislaw of that "dirt," as the information is termed by Farebrother. The rumor, like the source of the Nile, continues as a central intrigue. What is made clear is the corruption of the Middle-march community itself, a corruption that is signaled through its weakness for ethnic prejudice.

Indeed, Raffles, the originator of the "story" about Ladislaw, rep-resents the ugly underside of Eliot's much-celebrated organic web. Like a spider at its center, he is connected to the entire cast of charac-ters. They all contribute to his story until it becomes "the fact about Will Ladislaw with some local colour and circumstance added" (443). The narrative voice, which once played metaphorically with the no-tions of Ladislaw's gypsylike, quick blood, is careful never to distin-guish "local colour" from "fact," and, while it uses the very word and concept of "fact" ironically, it also validates the idea that there is, in-deed, an "ugly secret" in Ladislaw's genealogy. The "ugly secret" is taken up by all segments of the community as gospel truth: "Now with the disclosures about Bulstrode came another fact affecting Will's social position. . . . 'Young Ladislaw the grandson of a thieving Jew pawnbroker' was a phrase which had entered emphatically into the dialogues about the Bulstrode business" (476). "Dialogues" is here a euphemism for Middlemarch gossip. The web, community it-self, then becomes suspect and devalued. When the eminently re-spectable Mr. Farebrother sanctions that gossip with his belief, and his prejudice, the community has undermined its own ostensible moral values, paving the way for Dorothea and Will's rejection of Middlemarch morality and values.

Defying the authority of community in their marriage, Dorothea and Ladislaw have provoked the "intense disappointment" of the contemporary community of literary critics and scholars who read George Eliot.[23] Dorothea's life, Sandra Gilbert and Susan Gubar sug-gest, is "absorbed in another's"; she will never be satisfied through any "great work" of her own. "Still the most subversive act available to" Dorothea, marriage is not subversive enough.[24] D. A. Miller also finds that the novel's "traditional settlement (marriage, family, career) is not an adequate solution . . . the problem has been to find a settle-ment transcending those conventional arrangements." Dorothea's epic vision has "shrunk to the dimensions of mere monogamy." Her "desire for Will is a reduction of her original desire, and, in the end, perhaps even a destruction of what its original value had been."[25]

In addition to seeing marriage as "the site and source of women's op-pression" and to a general disappointment in Dorothea's choice,[26] crit-ics have objected to Ladislaw's "frivolity." Implicit in those arguments is an undercurrent of hostility toward his androgyny. If Dorothea Barrett argues that "Stephen Guest in *The Mill on the Floss* is, at least sexually, a man to complement Maggie's womanhood, Will is consistently characterized as childish and effeminate." Eliot's "recurrent images of him 'shaking his curls,' his frequent blushes, and his transparent girlish complexion" all "create a figure who cannot be seriously contemplated as the appropriate partner for a heroine of Dorothea's scope."[27] Along with a "queer genealogy," Ladislaw possesses a queer sexuality. He is deliberately invested with feminine qualities that may repulse some critics but which clearly attract Dorothea Brooke. Wishing for the much straighter, and much less complex, Stephen Guest, Dorothea Barrett sidesteps the issue of Dorothea's formidable desire for Will, a desire so strong that it leads her to sleep on the floor to subdue her pain at the loss of him.

Daniel Deronda, too, becomes a character represented in the "language of heroines" and is described as "a soft, lovely creature whose clothes enhance his attractiveness." It is a combination that Dorothea Brooke, like Gwendolen Harleth, finds as attractive as light itself. Indeed, the lightning bolt which startles Ladislaw and Dorothea into their first embrace, like the clear rays of light Ladislaw seems to shake from his head of curly hair, serves to awaken Dorothea, who sleeps as Ariadne does in a state of suspended sexual desire. Embodying "the Jew and the Woman's marginality" in his persona, Ladislaw attracts in part because Dorothea identifies with him.[28] Taking the portrait of Julia down from the wall, Dorothea

> lik[es] to blend the woman who had been too hardly judged with the grandson whom her own heart and judgment defended.... She took the little oval picture in her palm and made a bed for it there, and leaned her cheek upon it, as if that would soothe the creatures who had suffered unjust condemnation.... There was something irrevocably amiss and lost in her own lot, and her thoughts about the future were the more readily shapened into resolve. Ardent souls, ready to construct their coming lives are apt to commit themselves to the fulfillment of their own visions. (339)

Dorothea, identifying with Julia and Will, can sense what is "amiss and lost in her own lot." Their Otherness, a trope for her own marginalization, attracts her.

Indeed, when Dorothea learns of "this ugly bit of Ladislaw's ge-

nealogy" and confronts the contempt of Middlemarch, the knowledge "only [gives] more of enthusiasm to [her] clinging thought"
(477). As when she first saw his grandmother's portrait and "wondered" about his heritage, the subject remains too "indelicate" to be
spoken of; but it is nonetheless becoming the center of their conversation. In their final meeting, when the two agree to marry and make
their own "world" an "everywhere," Will is sure that Dorothea has
heard "a painful story about my parentage." He seems to own the
rumor of a Jewish heritage: "I did not believe that you would let any
circumstance of my birth create a prejudice in you against me,
though it was sure to do so in others" (497). "The disagreeable story"
is never denied; it remains "a fact in his destiny" that is "altogether
painful" (497). Dorothea, however, embraces Will and his heritage as
"a new hardship" and thus a "new reason to cling" to him (498). Near
the end of the novel, the ironic Mrs. Cadwallader remarks that "it is
difficult to say what Mr. Ladislaw is, his blood is a frightful mixture"
(504). Ladislaw and Dorothea's marriage affirms, in a remarkably un-
traditional way, the desire to leave the sameness of Middlemarch
Englishness behind, to dilute through new blood that of "the Middlemarch tribes" who cherish their Englishness and despise Ladislaw's foreignness though "they were themselves of a breed very much
in need of crossing" (374).

The dual progressions of reform and sexual desire, which had been
so difficult to articulate in *Felix Holt: The Radical*, unfold more explicitly in *Middlemarch*, Eliot's great English novel whose Englishness has,
in this context, obviously ironic overtones. Constantly using the
image of Otherness, the novel's keynote is the idea of release, the escape from the "dead hand" of an Englishness typified by the ignorant
internationalism of the world-traveled Mr. Brooke, the dim intellectual and sexual "gropings" of the aged bridegroom Casaubon, and
the provincial narrowness of Sir James Chettam and his pack. Leaving Middlemarch for London, Dorothea Brooke and Will Ladislaw
enact the myth of Persephone leaving the underworld for an over-
world of "warm activity and fellowship" (295). Their marriage and
their dual missions of reform are a comment upon their intention to
create their own "world" and to reinvent culture with, quite literally,
"new blood."

In Eliot's first novel, *Adam Bede* (1859), such a progression is impossible. Eve Kosofsky Sedgwick describes the impasse as follows:
"The main locus in the novel for the reproduction and conservation

of gender roles and of male ascendancy is the question of female sexuality. Female sexuality itself, however, is meaningful in the novel chiefly within the context of the exchange of power and of symbolic goods between men; and the scene of female sexuality, whether it be that of the virgin or the whore, seems regularly and fittingly to end, with the banishment of the woman, in an 'affair of honor' between men."[29]

In *Middlemarch*, Eliot fuses the virgin and the whore, the abstinent and the desirous woman, into one much more complex desirous subject. There is no "affair of honor," but a breach of honor, Dorothea's marriage to Ladislaw in defiance of her dead husband and the Middlemarch community, a defiance of other would-be, but powerless male figures, Sir James Chettam and Mr. Brooke. Equally remarkable, Eliot's violation of gender roles acts to erode the heavily conventional masculinity of the early Adam Bede and Arthur Donnithorne who are the male versions of the virgin, Dinah Morris, and the whore, Hetty Sorrel. By the time she wrote *Middlemarch*, Eliot, who in her earlier work seemed so careful to always keep "a lookout for three feet on the floor,[30] seems able to express desire.[31] Making the strangely foreign, "girl[ish]" Ladislaw the object of Dorothea's desire (377), and thus aligning the marginalization of Otherness with that of woman's sexual desire, Eliot, finally, comments in her most sophisticated way on the ability of culture to invent itself. Revealing less the "fact" of ethnicity and more the power of culture to create it, she uses the concepts of exoticism and alterity to expand and reenvision the sexual and political confines of provincial English life.

# FIVE

# Arabian Nights

## "Make-Believe," Exoticism, and Desire in Daniel Deronda

DEPENDENT UPON "the make-believe of a beginning," the discovery of
the hero's ethnic origin in order to light his way "to the East" and vocation, *Daniel Deronda* (1876) is infiltrated by a make-believe exoticism.[1] Like Goethe's "Hegire" (1819), Eliot's last novel alludes to a
powerfully regenerative East that can "disintegrate" the thrones and
empires of North, West, and South.[2] In the East, Deronda, like the
poet, might "fly away" from the dross of the West; as a pilgrim he
may achieve "the Romantic idea of restorative reconstruction (natural supernaturalism)."[3] The rejuvenating effect of this "reverse Orientalism" on Daniel Deronda is well known.[4] It is less well known that
as Deronda's past identity "trembles" before the powers of the East
and exoticism, so does the "empire" of domesticity.[5] Using allusions
to a host of Orientalist images and to Shakespeare's African hero,
Othello, Eliot includes the troubled position of women in the novel's
process of "restorative reconstruction." Consequently, the novel's act
of natural supernaturalism, of self-invention through several narratives of vocation and desire, is disrupted or even haunted by a host of
Others whose presence disturbs the calm of Deronda's vocational re-
solve and Gwendolen Harleth's permanent, virtuous widowhood. Indeed, in a novel which fragments into two plots while attempting to
speak of a woman's "lot" and a man's vocation, the presence and absence of exoticism is another link between both. In contrast to the
Jewish Deronda's pursuit of the East, Gwendolen Harleth's English,
Christian life with her white-handed husband indicts her absence of

agency. Interrupting and fragmenting the novel of vocation, Eliot's persistent, often erotic, allusions to Other stories challenges that absence.

Eliot's allusions to nineteenth-century popular culture's representations of the East and Africa in *Daniel Deronda* flicker uneasily alongside the novel's central figures, the sober, earnest young reformer and the unhappy, spoiled young English girl. Into both of their plots, Eliot inserts references to popular Victorian literary and visual exotica, stories of enchanted captivity and release, illustrations of androgynous twin lovers, and operatic productions of interracial love and murder; each of these allusions is to a text that would have been recognizable as either erotic or sensational to the Victorian reader. Indeed, the positioning of many of these textual intrusions is provocative, seeming to speak to the rigid control, the absence of sexual "make-believe," in English life as it is represented in the novel. The materiality of the Victorian exotica to which Eliot refers, Rossini's opera *Otello* (1819), *The Thousand and One Nights* (1838), amateur Orientalist paintings, and Persian cats, moreover, vexes the novel's attempt to separate out the "best self" from the "anarchy" of modern British culture.[6]

While our own televisions blare highly defined images of Arabs and Jews in conflict in the Middle East, nineteenth-century texts and images envisioned Jewish and Muslim culture as remarkably similar. Both the Jew and the Muslim were perceived as essentially Eastern and exotic in the popular imagination. Eliot's comparison of a Jewish protagonist with a Muslim Arabian prince is far stranger to us than to her. Walter Scott's *Ivanhoe,* one of George Eliot's central resources, Orientalizes the Jewish Rebecca through a collection of visual stereotypes: her "turban," her "Eastern dress," and "Persian silk" are less Jewish than an essentially Eastern fantasy.[7] Rebecca is pure "make-believe," the type that Eliot, like Dickens or Shakespeare, was to use in her depictions of cultural Others. Scott's portrayal of Rebecca clearly reflects how easily such stereotypes could be interchangeably transferred from the Arab to the Jew. Arab or Jewish, exotic Orientalism is traditionally used to contrast with the cool chastity and sexual virtue of white heroines and heroes, such as Rowena and Ivanhoe. Ultimately, value is placed on their chastity and on the absence of sexual desire from their lives. It is these ideals that Eliot resists, disrupts, and subverts in her novel, which blends characteristics of Englishness and Otherness into one character and engages the Victorian controversy over "Jewish traditionalism" and "modernity's universalizing assimilationism."[8]

As Deronda leaves England at the novel's end, Gwendolen Harleth survives what Katherine Bailey Linehan has so aptly called the "bestializing effects of female anger and willfullness"—but just barely. The properly wed Deronda and Mirah seem, like their counterparts from *The Thousand and One Nights,* a compromise out of place in Eliot's realist novel. Indeed, Eliot's refusal to unite Harleth and Deronda decries the limitations imposed by the triple oppressions of race, gender, and class. Linehan, in her insightful essay on the novel's "mixed politics," discusses its disjointed quality, its "phobic tinge of sexism and, ironically, embryonically imperialist racism lurking in the novel alongside Eliot's critique of empire."[9] As the 1990s drew to a close, criticism began to abandon binary readings of the novel's gender or race politics for an examination of the discourses shaped by those categories themselves.

For example, the juxtaposition of the novel's dual plots and agendas is seen to problematize the representation of heterosexual desire itself. As Jacob Press has very convincingly argued, the novel's performances of gender and race overwhelm its plot of empire; although the novel is "famous for its imagination of a proto-Zionism, the actual articulation of this politics is utterly marginalized. There are only three passages in nine hundred pages of text that address themselves explicitly to the question of Jewish nationalism." Instead, Press argues, the novel is devoted to constructing Deronda's masculinity as particularly Jewish, presenting the problem of his "alienated impotence" that is racialized by his unspeakable circumcision. Through that sign, the "mark of (sexual difference) within him—[Deronda] is saved by his marriage to Mordecai," the dying brother of the foundling woman-child Mirah Cohen whom Deronda rescues from drowning. Although Deronda marries Mirah, the novel's language of erotic love is reserved for his intimacy with her religious brother, Mordecai: "Mordecai initiates Deronda into a homosocial brotherhood that reconciles the identity categories of 'Jew' and 'man.'"[10] Deronda's Judaism then is narrated in the domestic realm through other imaginative categories that constantly displace the novel's attempt to keep gender and nation separate. Eliot's continual allusions to exotic and sensual "Other" texts intrude upon the novel's erotics of spirituality and its logic of female self-sacrifice to indict and reveal the compulsory sexual silence upon which each of those constructs rests.

ALLUDING TO THE STORY of Shakespeare's *Othello,* Eliot associates
the gentle Daniel Deronda, his flirtation with Gwendolen Harleth,
and his courtship of Mirah Cohen with a far more menacing sexuality. In Shakespeare's play, the "dark" cultural Other embodies an
overtly dangerous sexuality that is contrasted with the sexual virtue
of a white woman. *Othello* reflects the link in Western culture "between blackness and the monstrous and particularly a monstrous
sexuality." The play, and Rossini's opera *Otello,* from which Deronda
absently hums in the novel, seems to act out stock prejudices, using
white to represent virtue, black to represent a moral "descent into
hell . . . duplicity and lust." But literalizing those moral ideas with
Othello's blackness is only a stepping-off point in the action. Desdemona's attraction to Othello and defiance of her father create a willing link of miscegenation between the threatening, sexual Other and
the white figure. Subverting stock characterizations, the play's "femininity is not opposed to blackness and monstrosity, as white to
black, but identified with the monstrous, an identification that
makes miscegenation doubly fearful."[11]

As Daniel and Gwendolen secretly exchange a handkerchief at the
novel's opening and as he sings from *Otello* shortly before he meets
Mirah Lapidoth, the novel's characters mirror the play of racial desire
from Shakespeare's tragedy. The African Other, who is contrasted
with a white female figure in the play, is also identified with her, as if
both are alien. Like Desdemona's desire for Othello, Gwendolen
Harleth's desire for Deronda subverts the "patriarchal privilege of
disposing daughters" for patrilineal or economic profit. As Gwendolen pawns her father's necklace, creating a secret bond with
Deronda that is symbolized by his returning the necklace wrapped in
his handkerchief, she, too, defies her father. Her link with a cultural
Other is repeated in the unions of Catherine Arrowpoint and Herr
Klesmer, in the broken union between Mirah Cohen and Lapidoth,
and in her union with the partly exotic, partly English Deronda. Reversing and mirroring the traditional role of the exotic in literature,
all these characters employ ethnicity as a way of articulating the
problem of sexual desire. In *Othello,* his ethnicity divides the Moor
from court life and "links him to the play's Other marginality, femininity."[12] In *Daniel Deronda* the problem of ethnicity also speaks to
the position of women.

Indeed, rather than splitting the experience of desire between the
white and the exotic figures, Eliot presents Gwendolen Harleth as a

desirous figure who is ultimately disciplined and, some have said, condemned by her exotic Other. Seeking the "restorative reconstruction" of self through a purified, untainted mission of vocation, Deronda fears his own desire as a process of self-destruction that is linked to the "past effect" of his tainted, sexually suspect origin. Eventually shunning Gwendolen and the prospect of intermarriage, Deronda avoids Othello's rage but at the cost of Gwendolen's desire. Indeed, despite his masculinity, Deronda's actions mirror those of Maggie Tulliver who longs to find a Gypsy self within. But when faced with the opportunity for affirmation of that self by running away with the Gypsies or with Stephen Guest, Maggie becomes mired in sexual fear and guilt. Facing Gwendolen, Deronda, too, perceives marriage and sexual experience less as regeneration than as the vanishing of the self in a strange and suffocating Otherness that is mirrored by the plot of *Othello*.

It is fitting, then, that Eliot's allusions to the exotic, sexually disruptive Moor are interrupted by a striking examination of Deronda's historical sense of sexual guilt. Like many other nineteenth-century novels (*Oliver Twist*, for example), *Daniel Deronda*'s "peculiar plot [is] a systematic disruption of narrative principles and temporal structures" all of which match the novel's disruption of discovery of the self and, ultimately, of the concepts of cause and origin. As Cynthia Chase has noted, the story unfolds "not only as a history of the effects of causes but also as a story of the present causes of past effects."[13] Ultimately, Deronda's discovery of self will be as implausible and as plausible as Oliver Twist's, implausible from the perspective of realism, plausible from the perspective of character. With his fine speech, fair skin, good manners, and good heart, how could Oliver be other than middle class? In subtly evoking Deronda's natural affinities with other Jews (his dark hair and beard, his easy brotherhood with Mordecai), Eliot also indicates Deronda's Other ethnic origin before the plot finally reveals it. But her early indications of Deronda's Judaism are as dark and sexually suspect as Oliver Twist's English is middle class and pure. Thus, it is between the novel's two allusions to *Othello* that the "past effect" of Daniel's actions at the novel's opening is explained. The "present cause" of Daniel's sexual reluctance is, paradoxically, what he perceives as an overabundance of sexual feeling, the original cause of which he thinks is located in his conception.

At the liminal age of thirteen, Daniel Deronda guesses that he is a bastard. The moment of his discovery is described as a fall of Edenic proportions. Seated in a cloistered garden with his tutor, the thirteen-year-old Daniel, while reading Sismondi's *History of the Italian Republics,* enjoys a prelapsarian "moment full of July sunshine and large pink roses shedding their last petals on a grassy court." "In purest boyish tones" he asks his tutor, "How was it that the popes and cardinals had so many nephews?" (*DD,* 203). Upon learning that the nephews were actually illegitimate children, Daniel becomes certain that he too is a bastard, truly the child of his "uncle," Sir Hugo Mallinger. Feeling "the deep blush" of sexual shame, he immediately envisions himself as sexually suspect. "Having read Shakespeare as well as a great deal of history, he could have talked with the wisdom of a bookish child about men who were born out of wedlock" (205). "The ardour which he had given to the imaginary world in his books suddenly rushed towards his own history" (206). Daniel's fall from grace "had been burnt" into him (202). Eliot's language consistently returns to heat and fire, recalling Hotspur, Shakespeare's embodiment of passionate illegitimacy. The shame from "these new thoughts seemed like falling flakes of fire to his imagination" (206). The "purest" moment of childhood is over; the frightening stigma of a sexual sin now marks him.

Deronda's knowledge of his own beauty becomes synonymous with the knowledge that "there was a tinge of dishonor in his lot" (218). Eliot stresses that the secret, internalized shame of his illegitimate origin is a mark, like Byron's "deformed foot doubtfully hidden by the shoe" (215). Deronda seeks early to divorce himself from the sexual taint of his illegitimacy; he becomes curiously "aloof from conspicuous, vulgar triumph, and from other ugly forms of boyish energy" (219). "Burn[ing] his fire" on other, intellectual heights, he successfully manages to avoid women. Doubly displaced by the mother he resents and by Lady Mallinger and her brood of girl children, he remains distant from women throughout the novel. He enjoys a moral purity that contrasts with that of his best friend, the artist Hans Meyrick, who is subject to fits of impish recklessness" and does "things that would have made the worst habits" (221). In contrast, Deronda prefers self-control, "the beauty of the closed lips" (213). Leslie Stephen rightly complained that Deronda is "ethereal. . . . One can't fancy an angel at a London dinner party."[14] What Stephen overlooks is that the content of Deronda's antisensuality is sexual desire, guilt, and anxiety.

As he matures, Deronda grows to hate his own attractiveness as the stamp of his illegitimacy, as the mark of illicit passion and the moral depravity of his parents, particularly of his unknown mother. As much as Oliver Twist's pinkness and fairness are the living proof of his middle-class origin and virtue, Deronda believes that his own physical beauty is the mark of his mother's illicit behavior. Thus, praise of his face or body makes him "angry," for "his own face in the glass had during many years been associated for him with thoughts of some one whom he must be like—one about whose character and lot he continually wondered." In her physical depiction of Deronda, Eliot clearly delineates his virility. Deronda's "lithe, powerful frame," his "long, flexible, firmly-grasping hands . . . show the combination of refinement with force." He is "thoroughly terrestrial and manly," more like a handsome, heterosexual "workman" than an effeminate "tenor." Eliot presents Deronda as an object of desire, and Gwendolen feels his gaze as disturbing, even "dreadful" (226). Further underscoring Deronda's handsome exoticism, Eliot ends chapter 16, the last chapter to precede his introduction to Mirah Lapidoth, with an emphasis on Deronda's physical appearance: the Meyrick girls, having "so thoroughly accepted Deronda as an ideal," set to work "to paint him as Prince Camaralzaman" of *The Thousand and One Nights* (224).

In contrast to Deronda's "pale-brown" beauty (226), Eliot represents Gwendolen, like Scott's Rowena, as almost preternaturally white, an underwater creature or Nereid rather than a human being. As in *Othello,* here whiteness is not necessarily nondesiring nor virtuous. As Gwendolen's eyes meet Daniel Deronda's for the first time, "it did not bring the blood to her cheeks, but sent it away from her lips" (38). Gwendolen's complexion is a "warm paleness" that suggests sensuality and humanity rather than frigidity. Nonetheless, the contrast between Deronda and Gwendolen is exaggerated until Deronda becomes an exotic. Gwendolen must ask if the dark-haired young man is English; he seems "not like" the "young men in general" whom she finds "not in the least" admirable. His "delightfully" exotic name adds to his mysteriousness. Gwendolen "can't at all guess what Mr. Deronda would say. What *does* he say?" (42). Clearly an unknown quantity, Deronda is a challenge, another country which she, on her grand tour, might explore and conquer, an alternative to the relatively tame geography of the Matterhorn. While "every single player differed markedly from every other, there was a certain uniform negativeness" shared by all, "as if they had all eaten of some root that for the time compelled the brains of each" (37). Even ethnicity is diluted in the salon. In a "striking admission of human equality," all are dross (36). Only Deronda amongst these different "species" is authentically exotic and "different," distant and removed from the human dross surrounding Gwendolen. Only Deronda, in his differentness, intrigues her.

Although the novel's contrast between a dark, exotic male and a fair, white woman recalls *Othello,* so does its subtext of a woman thwarting convention. Like Desdemona, the disobedient daughter, Gwendolen asserts her own capacity for desire by gambling, an activity that inevitably exposes her to considerable male conjecture about her sexual virtue and availability. Her actions make her body visually accessible to the male crowd of watchers; she becomes sexually suspect just as Desdemona does by loving a Moor. The latter act alone makes Desdemona's virtue suspect in *Othello.* The beginnings of sexual jealousy are indeed planted by her father who warns, "Look to her, Moor, if thou hast eyes to see. She has deceived her father, may thee."[15] Clearly also a disruptive figure, Gwendolen thwarts the advice of her "friend and chaperon who had wished her not to play" (39). Her "eager experience of gambling" becomes a metaphor for the dangers of sensual pleasure. As Gwendolen adjusts her coins with "taper fingers, delicately gloved in pale grey," she becomes more and more a figure of temptation. For Deronda, sexual desire, "the glow of mingled undefined sensibilities forming admiration," is replaced, like Othello's, with "scrutiny" (38). Deronda senses that Gwendolen is out of control. "She was in that mood of defiance in which the mind loses sight of any end beyond the satisfaction of enraged resistance." Gambling becomes a metaphor for the risk involved in exercising female lust. As lust makes both Othello and Desdemona monstrous, so does it now make Gwendolen a sylph, a sea creature, a serpent, a Lamia or Melusina. Her desire to play ["why should not a woman have a like supremacy" to "male gamblers" and be "followed by a *cortege* who worship her as a goddess of luck?"] suggests her sexual perversity (39). The disapproving Daniel Deronda watching Gwendolen gamble mirrors the jealous Othello as he wonders: "Was the good or the evil genius dominant?" in her (*DD*, 1). Like the Moor, Daniel guards Gwendolen's virtue with a "scrutiny" that can only be described as sexually intimate.

Daniel Deronda's attention and sexual interest in Gwendolen

Harleth also mirror the Moor and Desdemona in that it is markedly disciplinary. Othello denies that his love for Desdemona is "to please the palate of my appetite, not to comply with heat . . . but to be free and bounteous to her mind,"[16] and so does Deronda pretend to be the improver of Gwendolen. Like Othello, Deronda is a powerful and virile male who nonetheless rigorously restrains his own desire even as, during the novel's handkerchief scene, he sends Gwendolen an intimate token suggestive of a sexual liaison. Returning Gwendolen's pawned necklace, Daniel has "taken an unpardonable liberty." He establishes a secret bond between them while at the same moment he defaces, even castrates, the image: "A large corner of the handkerchief seemed to have been recklessly torn off to get rid of a mark; but she at once believed in the first image of 'the stranger' that presented itself to her mind. It was Deronda" (49).

Despite his attempts to preserve his identity, Daniel cannot "get rid" of the mark that makes his action so recognizable to Gwendolen. His return of the necklace is simply "another way of smiling at her ironically" and of indicating his sexual interest, his desire to be intimate with her. Here, as in *Othello,* the handkerchief is a reminder of his masculinity, a substitute for his physical presence. Desdemona who "so loves the token" because Othello "conjured her she should ever keep it," "reserves it evermore about her to kiss and talk to." Thus, "the first remembrance from the Moor"[17] is a transitional object representing him.

Because Deronda is both the Other and the white-handed English gentleman at this early stage in the novel, the message is dual, an invitation to sexual intimacy that reminds a daughter of her responsibility to virtue. With the handkerchief comes a note: "A stranger who has found Miss Harleth's necklace returns it to her with the hope that she will not again risk the loss of it" (49). Establishing himself as an intimate "stranger," Deronda paradoxically reminds Gwendolen of her "virtue" and, in returning her father's necklace in the handkerchief, of her place within patriarchal culture.

In her study of narration in Eliot's novel, Cynthia Chase observes "the distortion of causality" in the novel's plot. "What a reader feels, on the basis of the narrative presentation, is that it is *because* Deronda has developed a strong affinity for Judaism that he turns out to be of Jewish parentage." Thus, "origin, cause, and identity are linked in the plot structure" and the "cause of Deronda's character" seems to be character itself rather than "the myth of origin, the view of origin as having a unique generative power."[18] Yet Eliot's allusions to the myth of "Other" origins and the effects of those origins on sexuality suggest that Deronda's affinities for Otherness have a primal heritage. Hence, from early in the novel, we have a sense that Daniel is genuinely Other, "different," as Gwendolen Harleth perceives him, and "marked," as he perceives himself.

Like Othello, when Daniel sends Gwendolen the token of his handkerchief, he also sends his body, and she responds by feeling "entangled" and "helpless" before his paradoxical attractiveness and rigorous morality. Wrapping her dead father's necklace in his handkerchief, moreover, he underscores his authority as a man and the patrimony of which she wishes to rid herself. Striking a keynote for all the exchanges to come between the two, this exchange is informed by a basic equivocation between the desire to reveal and conceal identity, self, and sexual interest. Neither character is sure that the Other is a suitable object of desire. The confluence of patriarchy, sexual interest, and ethnicity are wrapped in the overdetermined bit of cambric.

The presence of the plot of *Othello* in *Daniel Deronda* suggests the potentially volatile nature of "monstrous difference" and the alliances of both desirous female subjectivity and the dark "imagined monstrous sexual appetite" that is such a potentially destructive force in the novel. Like Deronda, Othello "internalizes alien cultural values, but the Otherness which divides him from that culture and links him to the play's other marginality, femininity, remains in verbal and visual allusion." In introducing Deronda to a member of his own culture, then, Eliot slides back and forth between ethnic sameness and difference, again using allusions to *Othello* to speak to Deronda's profound fear of his own and female sexuality. As "Othello fears Desdemona's desire because it invokes his monstrous difference from the sex/race code he has adopted," so does Daniel Deronda approach Mirah Lapidoth with a simultaneous tension between sexual attraction and the reticence needed to control that disruptive force.[19] The resulting encounter is a series of paradoxes.

Singing the "gondolier's song" from Rossini's *Otello,* as he rows on the Thames and comes upon Mirah, Daniel Deronda is depicted as a rescuer, although his song recalls the crime the play enacts, intensifying the dangerous quality of his combined sexuality and ethnicity. In *Othello,* the "lascivious Moor" is first described as "a knave of common hire, a gondolier," to underscore the sexual virility and strength that Iago envies.[20] While he rows on an English river, Deronda is physically compared with a "workman" (226) to underscore the same qualities. The Moor's body then haunts Deronda as Rossini's opera "haunted his throat all the way up the river." Deronda sings:

> Nessun maggior dolor
> Che ricordarsi del tempo felice
> Nella miseria. (227)

The sorrow that he is unconsciously contemplating is likely Gwendolen Harleth's marriage to Henleigh Grandcourt. Eliot's note glosses Rossini's use of Dante's words in the opera through Tennyson's translation of them in "Locksley Hall": "Dante's words are best rendered by our own poet in the lines at the head of the chapter" (n. 227). The note refers to the chapter's epigraph: "This is the truth the poet sings, That a sorrow's crown of sorrow is remembering happier things" (225). Contemplating his physical appearance, Deronda feels profoundly that he is not, "in Cinthio's words, '*da noi*,' one of us." His belief in his own sexual corruption has led him to hate his exotic appearance. Ultimately, "Othello reveals . . . a complicitous self-loathing for blackness is as loathsome to him as to . . . any male character in the play, or ostensibly, in the audience."[21] Similarly, Deronda, perceiving his own face reflected back by those who sense his differentness, is full of "anger" toward himself and toward the culture that separates him from full inheritance and vocation. Singing of his sorrow, as he rows upon the river, Deronda regretfully ponders his appearance:

> Often the grand meanings of faces as well as of written words may lie chiefly in the impressions of those who look on them. But it is precisely such impressions that happen just now to be of importance in relation to Deronda, rowing on the Thames in a very ordinary equipment for a young Englishman at leisure, and passing under Kew Bridge with no thought of an adventure in which his appearance was likely to play any part. In fact, he objected very strongly to the notion which others had not allowed him to escape, that his appearance was of a kind to draw attention; and hints of this, intended to be complimentary, found an angry resonance in him, coming from mingled experiences, to which a clue has already been given. His own face in the glass had during many years been associated for him with

thoughts of someone whom he must be like—one about whose character and lot he continually wondered and never dared to ask. (226)

Like little Maggie Tulliver, Daniel Deronda is deeply perplexed by "his own face in the glass." Like hers, his appearance "was a kind to draw attention" in its attractiveness and its anomalous darkness, "his uniform pale-brown skin." Although Deronda fears that his appearance links him to the immorality of his mother, his physical exoticism calls visual attention to what he fears. Even rowing on the Thames in "a very ordinary equipment for a young Englishman," he stands out. "Unconsciously" he calls upon Shakespeare's Other to give voice to his alienation (226). Like Maggie, who is called a little "mulatter" amidst the pink-and-white Tullivers, Deronda might as well be a Moor, so different and alienated is he from the English community. "Rowing fast" to avoid the Londoners sauntering over Kew Bridge, heard and understood "only to one ear" (that of the Jewess, Mirah Cohen), Deronda is a vision of alienated, ethnic Otherness. And Mirah's face and body, subtly described as similar to his, "might have been an impersonation of the misery he was unconsciously giving voice to" (227).

The meeting between Daniel and Mirah simultaneously embodies the lure of race to race and Other to Other. Daniel, of course, is both: English by culture, Jewish by ethnicity. Often his Englishness is established by his manners, education, and speech. As often, his physical qualities are stereotypically Jewish—brown skin, penetrating dark eyes, luxurious dark hair, and a beard. Like Maggie, who imagines a Gypsy mother's face to be like her own, or like Fedalma, who instantly perceives her kinship with her unknown father, Deronda experiences a parallel moment of identification with Mirah. That moment may even be described, as it is in the "Sonnets," as "primal," for it returns him to his very origin. "Perhaps my mother was like this one," he thinks as he approaches her (231). Eliot, now with great subtlety, subverts cultural standards of difference and sameness. In the guise of the most "ordinary . . . young Englishman," Daniel collapses endogamous, ethnic prejudice with familiar English manners while he establishes sexual attraction on the basis of an ethnicity that is culturally exogamous and biologically endogamous. Otherness and sameness become strangely one. Othello, the Ethiop, is suddenly "washed white," as Mirah perceives Deronda as a rescuer, not as the "dreadful" sexual figure that Gwendolen Harleth does. "You look good," she says, unable to see him as he sees himself.[22] Deronda's sense of Jewish identity, like the novel's dual exploration of sexuality and desire, origin and vocation, is inseparable from his identity as a sexual figure and as such is established as early as his first meeting with Mirah.

Continuing to reverse the moral color code of *Othello,* Mirah Lapidoth, whose face is "an onyx cameo," is goodness incarnate, a child-woman whose "small, small features and dark long-lashed eyes" wash the darkness of her Otherness with moral virtue (228). With her "small, small features," Eliot intensifies her status as a child-victim as she represents Deronda himself as the child-victim of a fallen mother at this moment. He exclaims, "Great God!" that "exclamation in which both East and West have for ages concentrated their awe." Like Zarca, Fedalma's lost father in *The Spanish Gypsy* immediately identifying the adult daughter he has not seen since infancy, Daniel's intense identification with Mirah conflates the cultural boundaries of "East and West" like a prayer (231). The empathic "awe" becomes a universal identification that "makes mankind whole."[23] He feels a profound, immediate familial connection and an intimate relation to Mirah. Like the little English girl encountering the Gypsy in Eliot's "Brother and Sister Sonnets," Daniel's first encounter with Mirah reminds him of his humanity and his very origin. What he suspects as her sexual sin touches him deeply as similar to the one he imagines as his origin. However, what Daniel and Mirah experience, until the very end of the novel, is a moral and spiritual brother-and-sister union that is so cleansed of Otherness as to be devoid of desire. As Deronda sings, so does Eliot's subtext suggest an aching search for both self and a sexual partner. In the terms of Shakespeare's play, a monstrous perversion of desire destroys itself as Othello murders Desdemona. The lines from Rossini mourn that event. But it is significant that a similar perversion of desire has destroyed Mirah Cohen's desirous subjectivity, leaving her a child-victim rather than an adult agent. Thus as Mirah with her "little woman's figure" leans toward Deronda, she moves "a step backward" (231). Putting "her tiny hand into his which closed round it," she "draws back," hesitating and timid (231). Mirah echoes the sorrow of Desdemona's murder. Her first words to Deronda repeat the gondolier's song: "At last she said in a low sweet voice, with an accent so distinct that it suggested foreignness and yet was not foreign, 'I saw you before' . . . and then added dreamily, after a like pause, *'nella miseria'*" (230). Embodying the words, a small funereal image of female tragedy, Mirah "paused and then went on dreamily,—'Dolore—miseria—I think those words are alive'"(233).

And, indeed, Rossini's words are alive in Mirah. Because of her exploitation and abandonment by her father, Mirah must kill her own appetite as Othello murders Desdemona for hers. When Deronda offers the obviously hungry, suicidal Mirah food, she responds, "No; I cannot eat" (232). She too is an angel at a dinner party. She has no appetite for life itself, no desire: "I cannot see how I shall be glad to live" (233). Her suicidal desire parallels Deronda's self-loathing. In their capacity for misery, Daniel and Mirah are mirror images, brother and sister of a tainted origin. Their relationship is marked by a sexual reticence so guarded by the most rigorous, socially upright morality that it seeks to displace eroticism entirely. As he drifts down the river, for Deronda "thinking and desiring melt together imperceptibly." As a Jew and an English man, he must "habitually shift his centre till his own personality would be no less outside him than the landscape" or risk encountering himself and his own desire (230). In this realization of Deronda's drifting, in his attempt to question and characterize both his Englishness and his Otherness, his moral self and his sexual self, Eliot identifies the problem with the character and her novel.

Eliot's Deronda, like her Gypsy characters, reflects the categorizing habit of Victorian culture. Stereotypically believed to be universally dark of hair and eye, the Jew as a cultural Other was subjected to pariah status and to the sexual stereotyping that accompanied Otherness in the Victorian mind. They all bore "the stamp of identity. None can mistake the aquiline nose, dark eyes, pale forehead, and raven locks; they all bespeak the Jew."[24] Like the Gypsy, the Jew was seen as an economic exploiter of Christians. Gwendolen Harleth, expressing a common Victorian anti-Semitism, states the prejudice quite clearly: "[T]hese Jew dealers were so unscrupulous in taking advantage of Christians unfortunate at play!" (49). And, as with the Gypsy, the leap from economic exploitation to sexual exploitation is quickly made. The Jew as pimp and sexual exploiter of children is a lurid presence in *Daniel Deronda* in which Lapidoth Cohen seeks to sell his childlike daughter to a wealthy gentile as his mistress. The Fagin-like Lapidoth has the capacity to reappear in the most unlikely places. As a stereotyped figure of ethnicized perversion, Lapidoth lurks not just in Mirah's father but also in Deronda himself.

Much as Deronda presents himself as chaste, his identification with the Other's capacity for immorality is omnipresent in the text of the novel. His scrupulous morality toward the abandoned child-woman Mirah resonates with his knowledge that others may think that he is exploiting her. Deronda has "a shuddering sense" of the Mallinger household's reaction to his return home with Mirah. He foresees "chilling suspicious manners from lady's maid and house-keeper." Attracted by Mirah's beauty, "he was full of fears about the issue of the adventure which had brought on him a responsibility all the heavier for the strong and agitating impression this childlike creature had made on him" (235). A protector of Victorian family values and "innocent need," Deronda is nonetheless "full of fears" about his moral responsibility. Deronda's singing from Rossini's *Otello* while he is rescuing Mirah speaks to the difficulty of his managing and controlling his desire for her.

As Deronda's dual sexuality of passion and reticence speaks to the repression of desire, so does his dual attraction to Gwendolen Harleth and Mirah Lapidoth speak to ethnicity's role in the control and regulation of sexual passion in the novel. It is true that *Daniel Deronda* attempts, as many other nineteenth-century texts do not, to show a "prejudicial sympathy" towards the Jew.[25] Beyond Eliot's "sympathy" with racial or ethnic Others, however, lie politically delicate questions of racial and ethnic purity. Although Anne Aresty Naman holds that the novel supports interracial unions through its depiction of Herr Klesmer and Catherine Arrowpoint, the problems of interracial unions are addressed in the subtle, unfulfilled flirtations and sexual tension between Daniel and Gwendolen. Many of Eliot's writings, particularly her letters to Harriet Beecher Stowe, reflect the type of conflicted liberality that Naman sees in Eliot.

Eliot's conflicted allegiances become most clear in her disciplining of the interracial plot line, for her "the great source of romantic interest" as in "*Ivanhoe*."[26] This anxiety manifests itself in the novel's initial scene of the international crowd with its central figure of temptation, Gwendolen, dressed in her *ensemble du serpent* and observed by the unknowingly Jewish, knowingly eroticized Deronda. More subtle than that of Scott's Rebecca or Dickens's Fagin, Daniel Deronda's gaze challenges Gwendolen and then each engages the other in a series of erotic advances and retreats. Their ultimate failure to meet sexually is resonant with the culture's need to eradicate sexual pleasure or play in favor of courtship, domesticity, and nation building. This same power structure constructs Deronda's deep sense of sexual shame as he perceives (wrongly) that his origin did not stem from the sanction of those patterns. Again, Eliot joins this discovery, the make-believe that he is illegitimate, with a heightened erotic Othering of Deronda's body.

Finally, neither Daniel Deronda nor *Daniel Deronda* can be "centered." Both retain an abstract quality that results from their infusion with a duality of selves and repressed desires. Deronda and his story violates our aesthetic expectations because of his desire to displace himself continually. Desire then remains abstracted in the realm of suicidal brooding, of thought rather than action. In an attempt to reconstruct the damaged sexual self and thus to continue the plot's progression, Eliot brings Daniel and Mirah from Othello's murder of Desdemona and Desdemona's desire to a "make-believe beginning" of desire. Becoming Scheherezade, she finds that beginning in the fantasy of the *The Thousand and One Nights*.

DANIEL DERONDA CONTAINS worlds within worlds to a fault. A plot of English county life is interrupted by a man's search for his Jewish self. A story of a woman's search for self-determination becomes a man's story, based on the classic "nineteenth-century plot of the hero's search for his origins." Nancy Pell has suggested that both these "obvious, actual worlds" and their stories function as a continuing metaphor through which Eliot addresses the great contrast between "the separate, conventional virtual worlds of young men and women, regardless of geography."[27] Yet the sexual politics of Eliot's allusions to the perceived exotic, violent, and sensual world of *The Thousand and One Arabian Nights* complicates these claims. If Eliot mourns the repression of desire in the meeting of Daniel Deronda and Mirah Lapidoth, her attempts to awaken that dangerous, disruptive, but regenerative element are troubled by her dual attraction to sexual abandon and productivity, desire and vocation. In her fiction, these issues are consistently represented by dual characters, Dinah Morris and Hetty Sorrel, Arthur Donnithorne and Adam Bede, for instance. In the later, more complex novels, the conflict occurs within characters themselves — in Gwendolen's warm brown hair flowing over the icy chill of her body, in Maggie Tulliver's belief that there is Gypsy blood within her. Similarly, in *Daniel Deronda,* by alluding to a powerfully erotic prince and his consort, Eliot attempts to give sexual life to her iconlike reformers. The experiment is not entirely successful. Eliot's novel ends with the funereal image of Gwendolen Harleth's vocation as an eternal widow, aided and abetted by Deronda's rejection. An irresolvable loose end which has been interpreted as both a political liberation and a tragedy, Gwendolen's presence and her unresolved, unsatisfied desire for Deronda leave the question of his and Mirah's union permanently troubling. Indeed, the novel's ending has eluded critical interpretation as neatly as the vanishing genie of the *Arabian Nights.*

Like another Aladdin's palace, Scheherezade's stories set themselves down anachronistically and anomalously within the "grim-walled slices of space in our foggy London" (*DD*, 237). Eliot's allusions to the East and the *Arabian Nights* begin with Daniel's rescue of Mirah and his sequestering of her within the Meyricks' harem-like house of women. Her epigraph to the first chapter of book three, "Maidens Choosing," evokes the special allure of the East, positing it as a "place of original opportunity."[28] She quotes Lawrence Sterne's *Sentimental Journey,* "I pity the man who can travel from Dan to Beersheba and say, 'Tis all barren; and so it is and so is all the world to him who will not cultivate the fruits it offers" (245). Eliot suggests that the richness of the East, of Dan and Beersheba, is so great that it can only be left uncultivated by those who have no imagination or creativity at all, who see all the world as "barren." But her allusion is especially innovative in that she links the East's intellectual and creative fecundity with human fecundity, with the "fruits" cultivated through courtship and marriage. If exoticism sparks the cultivation of intellectual and cultural riches, it also sparks attraction between Daniel and Mirah and between Daniel and Gwendolen. The Arabian tales, soon to be alluded to again in book three, have a special power to expand the imagination and sharpen sensibility. Eliot's perception of the East's power and its literature's capacity for intellectual and sensual nurture articulates what is usually kept silent in contemporary perceptions of *The Thousand and One Nights.*

As fairy tales for children and travel companions for adults, *The Thousand and One Nights* enjoyed immense popularity during the Victorian age. Translating the *Nights* was a competitive business, dominated by E. W. Lane, the translator of Eliot's personal edition, published in the mid-1850s.[29] Although recognized as fables, the *Nights* were also believed to be representative of Arab people and culture. The translation by Antoine Galland, which Charles Dickens used from childhood, was advertised as a book in which "the customs of Orientals and the ceremonies of their religion were better traced than in the tales of travellers. . . . All Orientals, Persians, Tartars and Indians . . . appear just as they are from sovereigns to people of the lowest condition." Travelers to the East sought to "verify the authenticity of the *Nights*" and wrote home, as did Lady Mary Wortley Montagu, that the tales "(excepting the Enchantments) are a real representation of the manners here." Hence, much of eastern life, its customs and manners, were popularly believed to be "as fabulous as the *Nights*."[30]

The English brought Arabian culture to life through an act of the imagination that invested the tales with a special, creative provenance. Victorian allusions to *The Thousand and One Nights*, then, have a magical quality, a "mingling of the exotic and the actual" which, particularly for the Victorian novelist, celebrates the imaginative power to create through the structure of Scheherezade's narration.[31] Seeing a copy of *The Thousand and One Nights* in a bookstore lights "that wonderful lamp within" and creates "a crowd of phantoms" and "new delight" for Tom Pinch in Dickens's 1843 *Martin Chuzzlewitt* (chapter 6). Similarly, the Meyrick residence in *Daniel Deronda*, full of talented, creative people who paint, sing, and play music, is also full of references to the *Nights*, as are Eliot's and her contemporaries' letters, reviews, and fictions.[32] Amidst the chilly paucity of reduced circumstances, the Eastern tales lend a glow to the small house. Even the Meyricks' domestic cat evokes the literary East. The cat is named for Hafiz, the poet whose work, for European readers like Goethe, envisioned the Orient as "a form of release, a place of original opportunity."[33] "Hafiz the Persian cat" — the "only large thing of its kind" in the house — adds an air of poetry and possibility, as well as grandeur and exotic, sensuous luxury to the otherwise frugal home. In a home that so carefully strives to be a place "spotlessly free from vulgarity" and eschews "all the grand shows of the world" in favor of high artistic culture, the big Persian cat is a promise of imaginative ability and possibility. But the cat is also a signifier of the erotic East. Only Hafiz can express feelings which, for Deronda, are inexpressible and unmentionable. "Hafiz, who had been watching the scene [of Mirah's introduction to the Meyricks] restlessly, came forward with tail erect and rubbed himself against her ankles. Deronda felt it time to take his leave" (*DD*, 242).

Indeed, although Eliot may agree with Dickens in her use of the tales to represent the magic of creativity, one important difference marks her use of the *Nights*. Many Victorian writers shared her sense of the "magical transforming power" of the Arabian tales; however, many, like Dickens, shied away from the tales' eroticism. "The strong erotic element in the *Nights* tends to disappear in Dickens" and other contemporary writers, as do the tales' violence, unconventional sexual liaisons, and misogyny.[34] This is not the case in George Eliot and particularly not in her use of "The History of Prince Camaralzaman and Queen Budoor" in *Daniel Deronda*. Eliot's allusions to this tale, framing Daniel's introduction to Mirah toward the close of book two and the opening of book three, refer to a story of sexual passion and physical attraction between two lovers who are themselves physical paradigms. Sterne's epigraph to book three then has a double entendre to which Prince Camaralzaman's story as a source of both ingenuity and erotic celebration is cleverly suited. Urging the reader to "cultivate the fruits" of an imagined East, to replace barrenness with sensibility, Eliot—also in book three—addresses the problem of desire and sexuality. Her allusions to the tale lend further complexity to the "simplified characters of Daniel, Mirah, and Mordecai."[35] Its erotic subtext is in direct conflict with Eliot's rigorous Victorian supertext of moral virtue and sexual repression. Scheherezade can articulate the desire that the Victorian novelist cannot.

In Lane's translation, "The History of Prince Camaralzaman and Queen Budoor" easily speaks of both the male and female body, of "the violence of passion" and "the flame of desire."[36] As easily, the tale describes frigidity, violence, cross-dressing, polygamy, and both male and female defiance of the father. The tale begins with the long-awaited birth of a boy, Prince Camaralzaman. Sole male heir to King Shah-Zeman's kingdom, the prince is lavished with every attention and exquisitely tutored by the wisest men in the land. Unfortunately, the educated prince emerges from his studies a confirmed misogynist. When urged to marry so that he may carry on Shah-Zeman's ancient lineage, the boy responds, "Oh my father, my soul inclineth not to women; for I have found books with narratives of their fraudulence, and miracles have been occasioned by their cunning." A generous and loving father, Shah-Zeman tolerates his son's obstinance for several years but eventually tires of his son's refusals. The king is shocked at his son's distaste for women, a shock that is exacerbated by the prince's physical beauty. "He became a temptation unto lovers, and as a paradise to the desirous." Finally, enraged, the king locks up his son in a tower.[37]

Meanwhile, in an Oriental kingdom far away, a princess finds herself in much the same situation as Camaralzaman. She worries her father very much because, despite her legendary beauty, she has no interest in marriage. "O my father, I have no wish to marry; for I am a princess, and a queen, ruling over men, and I desire not a man to rule over me." Budoor's father, sadly assuming that she is insane, places her in a harem, to be looked after and guarded by *kahramaneks*, a group of trustworthy and responsible women. Like the prince, however, Budoor is also guarded by a winged genie or an Efreet who is much impressed by her beauty. As he flies through the night sky one evening, the Efreet fortuitously collides with the prince's guardian, an Efreetah, a powerful female genie who is also much taken with her human charge's beauty. The two compare both human paragons and argue over which is more beautiful. Only a direct comparison will settle the argument. The Efreet returns to the Orient for his princess, carrying the sleeping girl to the shah's kingdom. They plan to settle the contest by magically waking first the prince then the princess, one at a time. Each will see the other sleeping. Whoever displays more passion upon waking will win the Efreets' contest. However, upon placing the princess next to the prince, the genies make a startling discovery: despite the difference in gender, the two are identical. "They bore the strongest resemblance to each other, as though they were twins, or an only brother and sister; they were a temptation to the abstinent."[38]

Identical in beauty, the prince and princess are also identical in the passion they feel for each other when each is woken, fleetingly glimpses the other, and is returned to an enchanted sleep. The prince is overcome by the beauty of Budoor's face and "her body softer than butter." He quickly places his ring on her finger to make her his own before he is compelled to sleep. Budoor is equally overcome. "When she beheld him, distraction and ecstasy and desire overcame her, and she said within herself . . . my heart is almost rent by ecstasy of love for him, and by the violence of passion excited by his beauty and loveliness."[39] She too places a ring on his finger before the genies return her to an enchanted sleep.

Having resolved their argument, the genies return Budoor to her kingdom a great distance away. When the royal couple awake, they are separated by deserts and oceans, smitten by each other, and alone. "The slave of love, the victim of passion, persecuted by desire," each appeals to the father only to have his suspicion of insanity sadly confirmed by what is perceived as a new delusion. Each grieving father promises that whoever can cure his child will be rewarded—the prince's father will provide wealth, the princess's will give her hand in marriage. All who try and fail are to be decapitated. Eventually, after many fail, Budoor's brother, Marzawan, travels to Camaralzaman's kingdom and brings the prince back with him to Budoor who is now in chains in her own palace. The two are secretly reunited and begin their journey back to his kingdom. After much travail, during which they are separated and Budoor assumes the identity of a male prince, even marrying a royal princess, Hayat-en-Nufoos, the prince and Budoor are reunited. "Not jealous" of Hayat, Budoor allows Camaralzaman to take her as his second wife. So the prince "resided with his wives in enjoyment and happiness, and fidelity and cheerfulness, behaving towards both of them with impartiality." Finally, the only son of an ancient line "forgot his father, the King Shah-Zeman, and the glory and power that he had enjoyed under him."[40]

"The History of Prince Camaralzaman" has important implications for Eliot's novel. As a frame for the introduction of Daniel and Mirah, the tale brings to the novel a negotiation between sexuality and vocation which has long been thought absent from the liaison between Daniel and Mirah. Moreover, illuminating that supposedly simple marriage of cultural and novelistic convenience, the tale adds a political and psychological dimension to the pairing which is suggestive less of the "clannishness of Jewish endogamy" and more of the cultural management of the experience of desire.[41] The two royal children's resistance to marriage expresses their anxiety at joining their lives with a member of the opposite sex, and their dreamlike enchantments and escape across the desert speak to their desire to enjoy the physical aspects of heterosexual love without the social bargain of marriage and courtship. Indeed, both feel compromised in ways that are startlingly relevant to *Daniel Deronda*, the prince fearing the corruption of his soul by women, the princess fearing the loss of her sovereignty through marriage. Their discovery of sexual passion, which is heightened and exaggerated as part of their enchantment by magical figures, takes place far out of the human reach of either powerful father figure. Indeed, it occurs in the realm of the supernatural, without the sanction of any "real" social figure. Like her allusions to *Othello*, Eliot's evocation of the *Nights* in *Daniel Deronda* speaks to the difficulties in expressing desire within a universe that idealizes the chaste and the moral. The Arabesque tale resists the novel's omnipresent moral whiteness which seeks to wash away the threatening, disruptive desires of the body. The erotic tale of "Prince Camaralzaman and Queen Budoor" is particularly evocative of this battle. Sharing so many aspects of idealized Victorian domesticity and of sexual desire displaced or evolving into conventional, productive domesticity, the whimsical tale frames the introduction of Daniel and Mirah as well as the fragility of desire within a world of real social concerns.

Like Camaralzaman, whose father has previously fathered only girls, Daniel Deronda is, in a sense, the scion of a powerful and wealthy patriarch. Although Deronda is not a son of Sir Hugo's body, he is clearly the spiritual and cultural heir to his legacy of good-hearted gentility. Deronda's cultural and moral legitimacy is contrasted with the absence of either quality in the legal heir, Henleigh Grandcourt, who is, moreover, "the absolute incarnation of the illegitimate father" and heir himself.[42] Like the bookish Camaralzaman, the intellectual Daniel Deronda is a flower of his culture. He is educated in princely style, and that education, including reading Shakespeare on the lawn with his tutor, results in his discovery that he is the product of a fallen woman; he then resents all women and their attention. Although the prince fears that women will prohibit his search for excellence, Deronda knows that a woman's folly has already damaged his future and may have planted a seed of immorality to match her own. Ultimately, Deronda too will reject his known father and country for another inheritance. He will begin life in a new, Eastern state, forgetting the "glory and the power" he enjoyed as a Christian and an English gentleman.

Deronda's journey or vocation begins in tandem with courtship and marriage. Like Budoor and the prince, both Mirah Cohen and Daniel Deronda are shy of the opposite sex, speaking to the same adolescent fears of sexuality addressed in the Oriental tale. As Budoor must be serendipitously placed next to her sleeping twin or other sexual self, so does fortune place Mirah Cohen in Daniel Deronda's path as he is warily drifting and dreaming on the Thames, imagining himself in the role of Othello. The two European lovers evoke the same sense of grieving, punished solitude as do the lovers in the *Nights* tale who are brought together while the multitudes sleep. Amidst the throngs crossing bridges over the Thames in the city of London, Daniel's singing is heard as song "only to one ear," to Mirah's (*DD*, 227). Like the prince, imprisoned for his hatred of women, Deronda himself is imprisoned by "thoughts of some one whom he must be like—one about whose character and lot he continually wondered, and never dared to ask" (226). The Arabian prince's vision of women visualizes the lack of female "character" which Eliot cannot: "with their fingers dyed with henna; with their hair arranged in plaits; with their eyelids painted with kohl," Camaralzaman knows that women's sexuality will hinder him "from attaining perfection in his excellencies" as Deronda knows that one woman has hindered him from attaining his inheritance and has blotted his moral character. This question of his origin, inventing a degrading and damaging "make-believe of a beginning" for himself, has prevented him from starting his adult life. Like Camaralzaman, he is imprisoned still in childhood, abused and victimized. Acting in the role of the Efreetah of the *Nights,* Eliot can only spark her protagonist's sexual desire by interrupting his dreams.

As he drifts on the river, contemplating his anomalous appearance, feeling like Shakespeare's Moor, "thinking and desiring melt together imperceptibly, and what in other hours may have seemed argument takes the quality of passionate vision" (229). Into this abstract vision, Eliot introduces Mirah who speaks and acts "dreamily" herself in a trancelike state of despair (230). Like the unwilling lovers of the *Nights,* the resistant conscious mind must be overcome by appealing to what Eliot terms the "unconscious" (227). Rather than an enchanted sleep, Eliot employs the image of Daniel and Mirah drifting on and into the great Thames as a metaphor for consciousness and unconsciousness, for sexual awakening and the awakening of vocation. Like the two sleepers in the Eastern tales, the two characters drift toward each other on the river. Eliot uses the words "unconscious" and "half conscious" three times as Daniel approaches Mirah (227, 228). She appears to him much like the sleeping Budoor to the prince: "A girl hardly more than eighteen, of low slim figure, with most delicate little face, her dark curls pushed behind her ears. . . . Her hands were hanging down clasped before her, and her eyes were fixed on the river with a look of immovable statue-like despair . . . apparently his voice had entered her inner world without having taken any note of whence it came. . . . It was but a couple of moments, but that seems a long while for two people to look straight at each other. . . . It seemed to Deronda that she was only half-conscious of her surroundings" (227–28). Increasing the sense of childish innocence abused and exploited by the dangers of sexuality, Daniel identifies Mirah as small, tiny, "her little woman's figure" a miniature of adult feminine beauty but vulnerable and innocent as a child (231). Mirah's stance is iconic, suggestive of a "statue" that embodies innocence threatened. Deronda identifies with her; despite her "small, small features," she is "an impersonation of the misery he was unconsciously giving voice to" in his song. The sleep that awaits Mirah, however, is not enchantment but death. This revision of "The History of Prince Camaralzaman" is in keeping with Eliot's realism, an aesthetic vision which places "make-believe" in a harsh, social context (*DD*, 1). As Gwendolen Harleth is a mythical Diana or Melusina, a serpent goddess, standing in the harsh, artificial glare of gaslights at the novel's opening, so Queen Budoor becomes a pretty little Jewish girl who must choose between prostitution or poverty. The Arabian fairy tale, as it is reenvisioned in *Daniel Deronda,* encompasses both the exotic, romantic fantasy and the dark nightmare aspects of human trafficking in Victorian London.

The Arabian tale assists Eliot in further outlining and evaluating "the limitations within which the struggle to achieve personal legitimacy goes on for the fathers' daughters" in late-Victorian England.[43] In defying patriarchal authority, Mirah Lapidoth shares more with Queen Budoor than just her slender feet. Like the Arabian princess, she too resists being traded to a man by her father. Mirah is, like Budoor, an intelligent woman whose "tongue is put in motion by an ample intelligence and a ready reply."[44] Budoor's punishment for refusing to marry her father's choice is to be chained to a window in the palace and declared mad. She can look out and observe the world, but she cannot master it. In Eliot's social-realist novel, so concerned with the daughter's position in patriarchal culture, those romantic elements are realized. Here the father's attempt to partner the errant female child with an aristocrat is an ugly business. Mirah "began to feel a horrible dread of this man" whom her father has chosen for her. "He worried me with his attentions, his eyes were always on me" (258). Neatly fulfilling the promised dangers of Gwendolen's gambling and the game's association with "insatiable desire" and "appetite" (847, 843), Mirah's father is "continually at a gambling-house" where his lust for money erodes and perverts his human relationship to his daughter (258). Her beauty is first made a commodity and soon her body is to follow, twisting the romance plot into sexual slavery. Mirah's father would sell her to a wealthy count who would take her to "his beautiful place, where I might be queen of everything" (259). Like the Queen Budoor, who found herself in a similar situation, Mirah "locked [her]self up" to protect herself from her father. She becomes convinced that she too will be declared insane for going against her father's wishes. "It had sunk into me that my father was in a conspiracy with that man against me" (25). She believes that there "is a plan to take me to a madhouse," a place for "despised women" (260). Mirah resists becoming her father's commodity and seeks to create, through a new marriage and family, an authentic, uncontaminated love affair, far removed from the sins of her father.

Eliot's allusions to the "make-believe" of the *Nights* suggest that she cannot construct new visions of the self, vocation, and family from within her own culture. Her opening injunction that "[m]en can do nothing without the make-believe of a beginning" suggests the need for self-invention which both Daniel and Mirah, like Camaralzaman and Queen Budoor, achieve. But, although they separate themselves, as do so many of Eliot's creations, from the corruption and folly of preceding generations and work toward a vocation of political reform, Eliot's characters remain irrevocably touched, even damaged, by their own earnest denials of folly and vice, of sexual desire and passion. Consequently, the pursuit of sensual pleasure is a fragile and risky endeavor in the world of Eliot's novels. No Eliot character more powerfully manifests this risk than Daniel, who embodies both the sober English gentleman and the Moor, the "beauty of the closed lips" and the beauty of an Arabian night.

As the introductory sentence to book two forewarns, Deronda is not "romantic; but under his calm and somewhat self-repressed exterior there was a fervour which made him easily find poetry and romance among the events of everyday life" (245). Hence, shortly before he meets Mirah, he is susceptible to seeing "the light of the sunset" through the eyes of "some Oriental poet" who makes him feel more intensely the mystical element of "the glory of the sky" (229). As Daniel comes closer to Mirah, he comes closer to the East itself. Just as she does in "The Brother and Sister Sonnets," here Eliot conflates the distance between cultures and races. Soon after he meets Mirah, Daniel is urged by the narrator to embrace "the sense of fellowship which thrills from the near to the distant, and back again from the distant to the near" (245). This will be Deronda's spiritual fellowship with Mordecai, but it will also simultaneously be sexual fellowship and union with Mirah. As he resists his own capacity to find "the poetry and romance among the events of everyday life," so does he resist the temptations of sexuality.

Deronda's hesitance, like Camaralzaman's, is based on his fear of an inappropriate, immoral liaison with Mirah. Her clear position as an exotic sexual temptation is underscored by Mab Meyrick's comparison of her with Queen Budoor, which precedes Mirah's story and the development of her character. The epigraph of the chapter has encouraged us to see virtue in Mirah's body. Eliot uses Alexander Knox to remind us that "even in this frail and corrupted world, we sometimes meet persons who, in their very mien and aspect, as well as in their whole aspect of life, manifest a signature and stamp of virtue" (248). Eliot's sober evangelicalism here acts like her allusions to *Othello* which also seek to wash both Mirah and Daniel clean of sexual desire. The epigraph, from Robert Southey's *Life of Wesley,* precedes a description of Mirah's body that reveals the narrator's difficulty with her as an erotic figure. As Mirah is described waking in the Meyrick home, each accession to her exotic beauty is balanced by an affirmation of her status as a nonsexual virtuous "creature." While her "dark hair curls in fresh fibrils," it is scrupulously clean from its "plenteous bath." The beautiful complexion and dark eyes are not lively erotic signifiers but are marked and ringed by fatigue. Nonetheless, the eroticism which the narrator so carefully suppresses slips through in Eliot's allusion to the *Nights:* "'Oh, if you please, mamma!' cried Mab, clasping her hands and stooping towards Mirah's feet, as she entered the parlor; 'look at the slippers, how beautifully they fit! I declare she is like the Queen Budoor—"two delicate feet, the work of the protecting and all-recompensing Creator, support her; and I wonder how they can sustain what is above them!"'" (249).

Eliot's representation of an attractive Orientalism in conflict with its threatening sexual aspects is remarkable here. If Fagin and Othello lurk within Deronda as images of reckless or perverse sexuality, those images of the Other are now, in the shape of Prince Camaralzaman and Queen Budoor, present in both idealized images. Neither can be divorced from the body or from sexuality. This is particularly true of Queen Budoor's presence in Mirah. In alluding to the Oriental princess, Eliot gestures toward a woman as essentially Other and erotic as Othello is essentially sexually threatening. The phrase Mab quotes directly from Lane's translation discusses one of the few body parts mentionable in the Victorian code of propriety, Mirah's "two delicate feet." As a Victorian common reader would know, Scheherezade's description of Budoor only ends with the queen's feet. It covers the fullness of her body:

> As to her hair, it is like the nights of emigration and separation; and as to her face, it is like the days of union. . . . She hath a

nose like the edge of the polished sword, and cheeks like deep-red wine, or like anemones; her lips resemble coral and carne-lion, and the moisture of her mouth is more delicious than the best wine, and would quench the fire of the inflamed . . . she hath a bosom that is a temptation unto him who beholdeth it . . . by the side of which are two smooth and round arms; and as the poet hath said,—

> She hath hips, connected with a slender waist
> which tyrannize both over me and her:
> They confound me when I think upon them
> and weigh her down when she would rise.[45]

In the *Nights*, this description immediately precedes Eliot's allu-sion. Her audience's knowledge of the *Nights*, testified to by Mab's repetition of the text from memory, allows them to include what for Eliot is unmentionable. Like Daniel Deronda, Mirah Lapidoth has her sexuality and thus her capacity for desire increased and exagger-ated through her comparison to an even more exotic ethnic Other. The novel's subtext dramatically denies the explicit text that strives to infantilize Mirah. Looking at "her own feet in a childish way," Mirah makes it difficult for anyone to "imagine this creature having an evil thought" (249), and the Knox epigraph, suggesting that Mirah's "mien and aspect" reflect her virtue, conflicts with the lush exotic body Eliot recalls through her allusion to Queen Budoor. Here again, the novel attempts to whitewash the exotic, to cleanse the princess of her sexual desire.

As Eliot censors but still implicates the erotic elements of Mirah Cohen's body, indeed as she tries to excise all of Budoor's body but her feet, so does she also attempt to suppress sensuous and erotic ele-ments in the relationship between Daniel and Mirah. Their courtship becomes a series of retreats and evasions, all of which must be care-fully maintained because of what they perceive as their ethnic differ-ences. Rigorously moral, Deronda avoids her because he is sure she will not marry a Christian. Moreover, he is aware that there is a his-tory of compromise in relationships between unmarried Jewish women and Christian men. Yet the revelation of Deronda's Judaism and hence his availability as a suitable lover occur simultaneously with Mirah Cohen's own fears of untrammeled desire. As Daniel meets his mother in book seven, Mirah reports that she has "more reason for being anxious. . . . I am quite sure I saw my father" (713). The return of the errant father is conjoined with her increasing "anxiety" over her shameful experience of desire, her own attraction to Deronda. Her pain "must remain as exclusively her own, and hidden . . . it was something that she felt to be a misfortune of her nature—a discovery that what should have been pure gratitude and reverence had sunk into selfish pain, that the feeling she had hitherto delighted to pour out in words was degraded into something she was ashamed to betray. . . . It was as if her soul had been steeped in poisonous passion by forgotten dreams of deep sleep, and now flamed out in this unaccountable misery. For with her waking reason she had never entertained what seemed the wildly unfitting thought that Deronda could love her" (801). Here Eliot's language reflects Lane's translation of the *Nights*. The evocation of poison, burning flames, and "pincers in her flesh" all describe the torments of passion represented in Queen Budoor's experience of the absence of her prince. Moreover, the experience of awakening from deep sleep by a tormenting glimpse of a passionate lover is evoked from Lane's translation, investing the tiny, gentle Mirah Cohen with a quality of "wild," uncontrolled, unregulated passion. Like Budoor and Camaralzaman, the once sexually unmoved Mirah "had been used to a strong repugnance towards certain objects that surround her, and to walk inwardly aloof from them while they touched her sense." Now experiencing adult passion, "the poor child," is tortured, like the Arabian princess. "I used not to have horrible feelings!" cries Mirah (802).

While Deronda is never quite the English gentleman he appears to be, Mirah Lapidoth, because she is an Other, a Jewish woman, is also invested with exotic properties that complicate her virtue and childish innocence. Indeed, the Jewish woman served as a target for English fears, allowed a seductive beauty in literature where it is always qualified by exoticism. As such, her sexuality contains deeply threatening, disruptive, even violent forces. Charles Lamb voices this fear explicitly in his anti-Semitic essay, "Imperfect Sympathies": "Some admire the Jewish female-physiognomy. I admire it—but with trembling."[46] Like little Oliver Twist, who "felt that his pale face and trembling limbs were neither unnoticed, nor unrelished by" the Jewish Fagin, Lamb himself senses the threat of an unregulated and dangerous sexuality in the Jewess's gaze. Otherness, as in *The Mill on the Floss,* where the anomalously dark Maggie Tulliver is likened to Jael, signals a destructive, potentially contaminating or castrating sexuality.

When applied to the gentle Mirah, this exotic sexual stereotype has a paradoxical effect. While she is figured as tiny and childlike,

Mirah is also compared with the voluptuous Queen Budoor of *The Thousand and One Nights,* whose lush body and capacity for desire are described at length in the tale to which Eliot alludes. If many critics have found her a virtuous bore, that is because they have not asked why it is necessary that Mirah be so good: she has inherited an erotic history well established in English literature. Sartre summarized that history when he wrote: "There is in the words 'a beautiful Jewess' a very special signification. . . . This phrase carries an aura of rape and massacre. . . . [The Jewish woman] has a well-defined function in even the most serious of novels. Frequently violated . . . those who keep their virtue are docile servants or humiliated women in love with indifferent Christians who marry Aryan women."[47] Eliot's Mirah fits Sartre's specifications exactly. Deronda's future wife is a paradox of inviting and reticent sexuality who has only recently escaped rape and defilement through the agency of her own father. Although her body is tiny and childlike, it is also voluptuous and regal, as if she embodies both the stereotyped Victorian Jewess and Queen Victoria at once. Gifted with a passionately beautiful singing voice, Mirah remembers never to voice her attraction to Daniel. Like Scott in his depiction of the virtuous-erotic Rebecca, Eliot speaks to Mirah's exotic, threatening sexuality in the sheer force she exerts to obliterate Mirah's will and cloak her sexuality with moral virtue. Indeed, the strict regulation of Mirah's will, the inflation and idealization of her virtue to the exclusion of her sexuality, speaks volumes to how desire must be reckoned with and controlled in the world of the Victorian novel.

The "horrible feelings" of sexual desire are never fully resolved in the novel. As Daniel and Mirah meet in the novel's last book, "Fruit and Seed," Eliot is careful to stress fecundity, filial love, and patrimony over desire. Approaching Mirah, who appears, like Budoor to Camaralzaman, "a just-wakened child," Daniel Deronda "imagined that the feeling of which he was conscious, had entered too much into his eyes, and had been repugnant to her. He was ready enough to believe that any unexpected manifestation might spoil her feeling towards him and then his precious relation to brother and sister would be marred" (815, 818). As Mordecai sanctions Deronda's Judaism, he locates Deronda not as a lover but as one "performing the duties of brotherhood to my sister" (819). Eliot stresses the brother-sister connection, "the marriage of our [Mordecai's, Daniel's, and Mirah's] souls," over the desires of the body (820). Indeed, Daniel and Mirah's wedding scene is quickly followed by Mordecai's death. "With Mirah's and Deronda's arms around him," he dies, the ephemeral quality of the life of the body marking the only embrace Mirah and Daniel share in the novel.

Shortly before that embrace, Daniel receives Gwendolen's letter, which reveals that she "does not yet see how" to take as her vocation being "one of the best of women, who make others glad that they were born" (882). Her letter, like the embrace between Daniel and Mirah, signifies the presence of duty and the absence of desire. The latter remains a force to be managed, cultivated, turned to "fruit and seed" by the novel's end. In the union of Daniel and Mirah, a fragile memory of desire, of "just-awakened" glimpses of the body and dreams of passion, exists. But it is clear that for Gwendolen no "sort of Moslem paradise would quiet the terrible fury of moral repulsion and cowed resistance" which courtship, marriage, and sexuality have become for her (733). With her icy white skin and her "poisoned diamonds," she is beyond the repair, beyond the touch, of the warm, regenerative East and certainly beyond the touch of the novel's Eastern figure, Daniel Deronda. The erotic dreams of *The Thousand and One Nights* cannot figure in the nightmare of her experience. The final representation of Gwendolen, as she writes to Daniel Deronda of their shared "grief," is funereal.

# *Epilogue*

BETWEEN 1839 AND 1840, William Harvey illustrated Edward William Lane's translation of *The Thousand and One Nights,* an edition that was to become extremely popular in England, where it competed with Richard Burton's translation of the same work. Harvey's wood-cuts for "Prince Camaralzaman" include a typically Orientalist illustration of Queen Budoor, chained to her window (plate 4). Like Hiram Powers's Orientalist statue of white captivity, *The Greek Slave* (plate 1), William Harvey's illustration epitomizes the position of the woman subject in nineteenth-century Orientalism. The queen's eyes are downcast in dejection, and the luxury of her surroundings contrasts sharply with the heavy chain draped over her arm and connected to the collar around her neck. Looking not unlike contemporary depictions of Queen Victoria, William's Arabian queen has small features and rounded limbs. The draped costume and veil that cling to her suggest the curves of her body, creating an erotic tension that contrasts with the chaste stillness of her cross-legged pose. Dramatizing the cruelty of her imprisonment, the fretted screened window upon which the queen leans suggests her isolation and the nearness of the world outside. Budoor's captivity is doubly ironic in that her queenliness is no protection from subjugation. She is imprisoned, after all, for refusing to marry, "for I am a princess, and a queen, ruling over men, and I desire not a man to rule over me."[1]

Harvey's Budoor is conventional in many respects. Her regal status and beauty engage the reader's sympathy as Powers's *Greek Slave* did. With downcast eyes and sweet expression, she epitomizes feminine modesty—despite her rebellious role in Scheherezade's tale. Her veil hangs back over her hair and away from her face, its half-presence suggesting to the Western viewer that we are seeing what should otherwise be covered. The illustration invades the privacy of the harem in the usual Orientalist ways, representing the space as the epicenter of female captivity. In this, as in many Orientalist paintings, the irony of the displacement of that captivity to the East is lost on the artist. The image is a powerful depiction of impotent queenliness, representing Budoor's helplessness and vulnerability before the powerful despotic father who has imprisoned her. In contrast, Henriette Browne's *Greek Captive* (plate 2), painted thirty years later, lifts the gaze of the imprisoned odalisque to confront the viewer. Still eroticized, dressed in elaborate Turkish costume, Browne's captive with her erect posture and preternaturally large dark eyes seems to begin to write in what Harvey conceals, the female self as a subject that is coming to consciousness.

It is no wonder that George Eliot admired the work of Henriette Browne.[2] Her contemplative women of both the convent and the harem were beginning to confront contemporary limitations to the representation of female subjectivity. A frequenter of galleries and museums, Eliot's penchant for reconstructing conventions of the visual arts is well known, although the political import of her interest is rarely discussed. At the opening of *Daniel Deronda*, Gwendolen Harleth too is dressed in costume, an *ensemble du serpent*. And, despite the fact that her gambling takes place in modern Europe and "not in the open air under a southern sky, tossing coppers on a ruined wall, with rags about her limbs," she is inspected by a variety of men who watch her. Gwendolen Harleth's body, face, hair, skin, costume, lips, and mouth are critiqued as if she were an illustration of an odalisque herself. But her "long, narrow eyes" do not drop down when she is watched, and, in the bazaar of the gambling casino, "measured" by Daniel Deronda's gaze. Rather, she watches Deronda herself. Surely, after "contriv[ing] a secret" and intimacy between the two, Eliot, in a sense, backs down. But Gwendolen Harleth, the "lioness," pays a heavy price for her immodesty (43).[3]

However, Harvey's captive Queen Budoor epitomizes a discourse of subjugation that Eliot clearly critiques in her last novel as well. In Eliot's "Brother and Sister Sonnets," *The Mill on the Floss, The Spanish Gypsy, Felix Holt,* or *Middlemarch,* the juxtaposition of whiteness and darkness both relies on and critiques the sexist-racist constructs of art, literature, science, and popular culture that block the desirous subjectivity of women in particular. Pleasure, it seems, needs to "infiltrate" the plots of English provincial life through Otherness. Once there, racial or ethnic difference does not always deliver what postcolonial criticism has suggested. Even as Maggie Tulliver, Esther Lyon, Dorothea Brooke, Daniel Deronda, and Gwendolen Harleth participate in a Victorian epistemology of racial difference, they indict our current critical insistence upon the unexamined Victorian acceptance of the British constructs of "home" and "home rule."

Moreover, in their fusion of gender and Otherness through the problem of miscegenation, Eliot's Others offer a new way of examining gender roles in her fiction. Her representations of runaway Gypsy girls, for example, record a protest to the fierce limitations of Victorian girlhood and to the gendered tradition of such masculinist escapes as Arnold's "The Scholar Gipsy." If Dorothea Brooke's embrace of Will Ladislaw at the end of *Middlemarch* was once seen as a compromise, it can now be seen as a problematic embrace of both Otherness and the erotic, and, necessarily, a rejection of British provincialism. In eroticizing the "Oriental" Harold Transome while condemning his imperialist politics, Eliot creates a figure of temptation that forever throws off balance the neat marriage of Esther and Felix in *Felix Holt: The Radical*. In her novel of vocation, *Daniel Deronda*, Eliot's allusions to exotic difference permanently disrupt the narrative's chaste reconciliation of marriage and vocation.

Recently, in her *Rule Britannia: Women, Empire, and Victorian Writing*, Deirdre David discussed Joseph Conrad's fiction as the traditional boundary marking the beginning of the end of the imperialist narrative in British literary history. His creation of "ambiguous" anti-imperialism still contrasts with "Kipling's robust flag-waving" to constitute our own postcolonial vision of the Victorians and their consuming enterprise of empire.[4] But, as David notes, between both visions of empire lies a world of subtle and problematic categorizing constituted by the writing of Victorian women. As the Orientalist category of "the captive" then problematically contains the separately gendered and raced visions of Power's statue, Harvey's illustration, and Browne's painting, so do binary visions of imperialist energies fail to encompass the subtleties of Eliot's racing and gendering of narratives of female vagrancy and captivity, desire and courtship, embodied and figuritive maternity, nationalist and local vocations. The "robust flag-waving" of Victorian imperialism, then, in Eliot's fiction and other writings, is rejected as a category through which the novelist of the midlands pursues her own agenda, a pronounced critique of "home."

# *Notes*

NOTES TO INTRODUCTION

1. bell hooks, *Black Looks: Race and Representation* (Boston: Southend Press, 1990), 159.

2. For the text of Frederick Douglass's letter to *The North Star* and for the social history of Hiram Powers's *The Greek Slave,* I am indebted to Jean Fagan Yellin's discussion of the statue, "Woman and Emblem in Stone and Story," in *Women and Sisters: The Antislavery Feminists in American Culture* (New Haven: Yale University Press, 1989), 99–124.

3. Frederick Douglass, qtd. in Yellin, 110.

4. The importance of all forms of culture in creating powerful perceptions of race and sexuality is now becoming more and more a topic of study as literary scholars expand the boundaries of the field. Although we have long recognized Mary Ann Evans's interest in landscape, portraiture, and architecture, we should as well consider the extent to which representations of power and race informed such arts and her perception of them. Juxtaposing painting and literature as equally potent forms of cultural representation, Reina Lewis's *Gendering Orientalism: Race, Femininity, and Representation* (New York: Routledge, 1996), studies George Eliot and the painter Harriet Browne separately. Lewis's book is not interdisciplinary in that it avoids discussing a visual legacy of Orientalism in Eliot's work.

5. Joy Kasson, *Marble Queens and Captives: Women in Nineteenth-Century American Sculpture* (New Haven: Yale University Press, 1990), 55.

6. On the sexual politics of Powers's *The Greek Slave,* see Joy S. Kasson's "Narratives of the Female Body: The Greek Slave," in *Reading American Art,* ed. Marianne Doezema and Elizabeth Milroy, (New Haven: Yale University Press, 1998) 163-189; and Jennifer DeVere Brody's *Impossible Purities: Blackness, Femininity, and Victorian Culture* (Durham: Duke University Press, 1998).

7. Meyda Yeğenoğlu, *Colonial Fantasies: Towards a Feminist Reading of Orientalism* (New York: Cambridge University Press, 1998), 98. On the politics of such visual representations as the odalisque, see Rosemary Betterton, *Looking On: Images of Femininity in the Visual Arts and Media* (London: Pandora, 1987); Susan P. Casteras, *Images of Victorian Womanhood in English Art* (London: Associated University Press, 1987); Sander L. Gilman, "Black Bodies,

White Bodies: Toward an Iconography of Female Sexuality in Late Nineteenth-Century Art, Medicine, and Literature," in *"Race," Writing and Difference,* ed. Henry Louis Gates Jr. (Chicago: University of Chicago Press, 1986), 223–61; Hatem Mervat, "Through Each Other's Eyes: The Impact on the Colonial Encounter of the Images of Egyptian, Levantine-Egyptian, and European Women, 1862–1920," in *Western Women and Imperialism: Complicity and Resistance,* ed. Nupur Chaudhuri and Margaret Strobel (Bloomington: Indiana University Press, 1992), 35–60; Linda Nochlin, *The Politics of Vision: Essays on Nineteenth-Century Art and Society* (New York: Harper Collins, 1989).

8. Kasson, 55.

9. Ibid. In the absence of authentic Other voices in Eliot's texts, we can read what African American feminists like Valerie Smith have long recognized as the phenomenon in literature where "black women operate in oppositional discourse as a sign for the author's awareness of materialist concerns . . . they seem to be fetishized." See Valerie Smith, "Black Feminist Theory and the Representation of the 'Other,'" in *Feminisms: An Anthology of Literary Theory and Criticism,* ed. Robyn R. Warhol and Diane Price Herndl (New Brunswick: Rutgers University Press, 1997), 311–25. If, as Smith argues, in contemporary U.S. films "black women are employed, if not sacrificed, to humanize their white superordinates, to teach them something about the content of their own subject positions," this phenomenon also has a history in the Victorian novel, where racial and ethnic Others are employed to point to an absence within the white heroine's subject position (Smith, 317).

10. For a discussion of the liaison between Chapman and Evans, see Gordon Haight's *George Eliot: A Biography* (New York: Penguin Books, 1986), 82–88, and his *George Eliot and John Chapman; with John Chapman's Diaries* (New Haven: Yale University Press, 1940).

11. See Brody, *Impossible Purities,* 12. Brody's discussion of Powers's *Greek Slave* notes its celebrity and the parodies that followed it. However, it is important to note that the "overwhelming reverence the statue evoked in both America and England" was not shared by all, particularly by the intellectual *avant-garde* (69). Yellin notes that the image of the white female supplicant had been appropriated by Powers from the abolitionist's emblem of a black female captive above whom appeared the words: "Am I not a woman and a sister?" The irony of the statue's whiteness then was not lost on many abolitionists who decried the image of slavery wrought in white marble (99–124).

12. Gordon Haight, *George Eliot,* 84, and *George Eliot and John Chapman with Chapman's Diaries,* 94.

13. Ann Rosalind Jones, "Writing the Body: *L'Ecriture féminine,*" in *The New Feminist Criticism: Essays on Women, Literature, and Theory,* ed. Elaine Showalter (New York: Pantheon Books, 1985), 367–68.

14. Nancy Armstrong is stating this theory "according to Foucault." With Foucault, she rejects the idea that any "specific form of sexuality is natural" or that a "prior and essential form of sexuality" exists "prior to its written representation." Thus Armstrong argues "sexuality," including the representation of physiological "desire" or erotic longing is "the cultural dimension of sex, which . . . includes as its most essential and powerful component the form of representation we take to be nature itself," *Desire and Domestic Fiction: A Political History of the Novel* (New York: Oxford University Press, 1987), 11.

15. See, most significantly, Sandra Gilbert's and Susan Gubar's "Captivity and Consciousness in George Eliot's Fiction," in *The Madwoman in the Attic: The Woman Writer and the Nineteenth-Century Literary Imagination* (New Haven: Yale University Press, 1979), 443–538.

16. Susan Meyer, *Imperialism at Home: Race and Victorian Women's Fiction* (Ithaca: Cornell University Press, 1996), 194.

17. George Eliot, *The Mill on the Floss* (New York: Penguin, 1989), 155.

18. Jenny Sharpe, *Allegories of Empire: The Figure of Woman in the Colonial Text* (Minneapolis: University of Minnesota Press, 1993), 29.

NOTES TO CHAPTER 1

1. See Mary Jacobus, "The Question of Language: Men of Maxims and *The Mill on the Floss*," *Critical Inquiry* 8(winter 1981): 207–22. Jacobus writes eloquently of the floodwaters of *The Mill on the Floss* as "merg[ing] the literal with a figural flow" and moving the novel "into the unbounded realm of desire" (221). Robert Polhemus discusses the erotic nature of landscape in Eliot's novels, in particular the sexual valency of the "Red Deeps" setting in *The Mill on the Floss* in his *Erotic Faith: Being in Love from Jane Austen to D. H. Lawrence* (Chicago: University of Chicago Press, 1990). In *George Eliot and the Landscape of Time*, (Chapel Hill: University of North Carolina Press, 1986), Mary Wilson Carpenter interprets the "'text' of the [Eliot] landscape," which holds a fluidity of meaning in its ability to signify "remembered joy" and the "hidden dread" of sexual experience (42–43). On Eliot's sexually compelling silences, William A. Cohen eloquently reads *The Mill on the Floss* as "as fully perverse a work as one could desire . . . [Eliot's narrative] voice is so commanding that it can aver the ethics of relegating sexuality to the status of unspeakability at the same moment that it cultivates places of refuge for the sexual alienation in which it shares." See his *Sex Scandal: The Private Parts of Victorian Fiction* (Durham: Duke University Press, 1996).

2. The word "Oriental" is from George Eliot's *Felix Holt: The Radical* (New York: Penguin, 1989), 79 (hereafter cited in the text as *FH*). The historical and economic dimensions of the discourses of Victorian repression are important to note here. Writing to conceal was a political and economic fact of life. Publishers shrank from frankness. The Victorian publisher John

Chapman held an "utter contempt for monogamy" in his private life (see Gordon Haight, *George Eliot and John Chapman with Chapman's Diaries* (New Haven: Yale University Press, 1940), 16. He nonetheless refused to publish anything like Eliza Lynn's *Realities* because of the "warm description of a love scene. 'I said that such passages were addressed to and excited the sensual nature and were therefore injurious; and that as I am the publisher of works notable for their intellectual freedom, it behoves me to be exceedingly careful of the *moral* tendency of all I issue'" (Chapman's diary, qtd., 18). Chapman stresses that the ability to speak freely about some things is purchased at the cost of silencing others. Like Chapman, Eliot seems particularly aware that she too is an especially notable practitioner of intellectual and sexual freedom in her private life and in her religious writings, and she also must be exceedingly careful of moral "tendencies" in her literature. Her personal transgressions, and their effect on her position as a professional writer hover like a specter over Eliot's early career, but are never directly mentioned in her letters to her publishers which are doubly guised by her pseudonym and by their mediation through George Henry Lewes.

3. Michael Ragussis, *Figures of Conversion: The "Jewish Question" and English National Identity* (Durham: Duke University Press, 1995), 60.

4. Jennifer DeVere Brody discusses the prevalence of the image of blackness in Victorian culture and its importance in constructing Englishness as white, masculine, and pure, and Americanness as black, feminine, and impure in her book, *Impossible Purities: Blackness, Femininity, and Victorian Culture* (Durham: Duke University Press, 1998).

5. The image "backwards and forwards" belongs to Timothy Mitchell, *Colonising Egypt* (Cambridge: Cambridge University Press, 1988). I'm indebted to Meyda Yeğenoğlu's *Colonial Fantasies: Towards a Feminist Reading of Orientalism* (Cambridge: Cambridge University Press, 1998) for finding a way to read the implications for feminist postcolonial studies in Timothy Mitchell's eloquent identification of the Orientalist East as "itself not a place . . . but a further series of representations, each one reannouncing the reality of the Orient but doing no more than referring backwards and forwards to all the others" (31).

6. George Eliot. "Brother and Sister Sonnets" (hereafter cited in the text as "B & S") in *Selected Essays, Poems, and Other Writings* (New York: Penguin Classics, 1990), 426–36, 5.3.

7. Valerie Smith, "Black Feminist Theory and the Representation of the 'Other,'" in *Feminisms: An Anthology of Literary Theory and Criticism,* ed. Robyn R. Warhol and Diane Price Herndl (New Brunswick: Rutgers University Press, 1997), 324.

8. The "us/them" distinction of Victorian colonialism and gender roles is here constructed from Michel Foucault's writings on "binary systems" in *The History of Sexuality,* vol. 1(New York: Vintage Books, 1990). Having bor-

rowed the term from Jacques Derrida, Foucault elucidates how "binary systems" construct "licit and illicit, permitted and forbidden" desires which are policed by language (83). Like other feminist postcolonial critics, Anita Levy or Reina Lewis, for example, I am interested in how the particular "us/them" dichotomies of binary systems appear in the novel and in art to articulate a "construction of the other woman (the feminine and orientalized other)." However, I am also interested in ways in which George Eliot might disrupt that construct with the representation of Other men. See Reina Lewis, *Gendering Orientalism: Race, Femininity, and Representation* (New York: Routledge, 1996), 27.

9. Deirdre David, *Rule Brittania: Women, Empire, and Victorian Writing* (Ithaca: Cornell University Press, 1995), 5.

10. Sander Gilman, "Black Bodies, White Bodies: Toward an Iconography of Female Sexuality in Late Nineteenth-Century Art, Medicine, and Literature " in *"Race," Writing, and Difference,* 248.

11. See Margaret Homans's "Dinah's Blush, Maggie's Arm: Class, Gender, and Sexuality in George Eliot's Early Novels," *Victorian Studies* 36 (winter 1993): 155–78, for an important discussion of the construction of desirous female subjectivity as a "chief signifier of the new economy and the new middle class, a class that seeks to efface the fact that it is a class and strives instead to consolidate its predominance by generalizing its tendencies as human nature" (171). In a note, Homans suggests that Eliot's tendency to universalize the middle class has implications for race because of Eliot's "admiring" essay on Wilhelm von Riehl (177 n. 3). Riehl terms peasants a "race" and Eliot's use of the term "rank" and "race," for Homans, marks her "social conservatism" (177 n. 3). This view is contested by Philip Fisher, Homans notes, who finds Eliot's essay on Riehl as "exposing this stability as coercive" (177 n. 3).

12. The quotation is from Antoinette M. Burton, "The White Woman's Burden: British Feminists and the Indian Woman, 1865–1915," in a special issue of *Women's Studies International Forum* 13 (1990): 296. Yeğenoğlu's *Colonial Fantasies,* in particular, also discusses such voyeurism, in the context of Orientalism, as representative of the masculinist desire to "penetrate" the Other, signified particularly in Western women's narratives of the harem which Yeğenoğlu envisions as a "successful penetration into the closed space and revelation of the Other in its most 'essential' aspects" (90).

13. Nupur Chaudhuri and Margaret Strobel, "Western Women and Imperialism: Introduction," *Women's Studies International Forum* 13 (1990): 289–93.

14. See Nancy Paxton's "Feminism Under the Raj: Complicity and Resistance in the Writings of Flora Annie Steel and Annie Besant," *Women's Studies International Forum* 13 (1990): 336–46. Paxton's article refers to both Adrienne Rich's essay "'Disloyal to Civilization': Feminism, Racism,

Gynephobia" in Rich's *On Lies, Secrets, and Silence: Selected Prose, 1966–78* (New York: W. W. Norton & Co., 1979) 275–310, and to Laura Finke's "The Rhetoric of Marginality: Why I Do Feminist Theory," *Tulsa Studies in Women's Literature* 5 (fall 1986): 251–72, as influencing her own concept of marginality and complicity. The essays by Paxton and Burton have been germinal in my own understanding of the importance of the discourses of race and empire to Victorian constructions of both woman and race.

15. In "George Eliot and the Jewish Question," *Yale Journal of Criticism* 10 (spring 1997): 39–61, Amanda Anderson carefully examines Eliot's study of the Jewish-German historian Leopold Zunz who "undertook a protracted study of Jewish history, literature, and tradition, zealous to convince his nineteenth-century European audience of the importance of Judaism to the history and progress of human culture as a whole." The problematic nature of the framing of the "Jewish Question" as shaped by conflicting visions of the "preservation of Judaism as a culture as well as a desire to incorporate that tradition into a broader, universal project" (40) meets as well "the destructive capabilities of a romantic doctrine of nationalism that influences Eliot's portrayal of Mordecai" (57). Of all the essays on Eliot and Judaism, Anderson's, along with Michael Ragussis's chapter on Daniel Deronda in his *Figures of Conversion,* is perhaps the most "positive." Anderson argues: "In the story of Deronda's return to his cultural heritage, Eliot intervenes in the debate on the Jewish Question, refusing simple oppositions between Jewish tradition and European modernity, and drawing out the ways in which radical Jewish cosmopolitanism might become . . . a 'positive cultural product'"(57). See Susan Meyer's *Imperialism at Home: Race and Victorian Women's Fiction* (Ithaca: Cornell University Press, 1996) for a less enthusiastic reading of Eliot's representation of Judaism and Proto-Zionism. In *Orientalism* (New York: Vintage Books, 1979), Edward Said discusses the problematic assumptions of Daniel Deronda's Zionism (169). For critiques of Eliot's representations of Judaism, see Christina Crosby, *The Ends of History: Victorians and the "Woman Question"* (New York: Routledge, 1991); and Terry Eagleton, *Criticism and Ideology: A Study in Marxist Literary Theory* (London: Verso, 1978) 122–25.

16. Here I refer to Susan Meyer's argument that in Eliot's *Daniel Deronda,* the "strong selves of women, like the aliens within English borders, are at risk of annihilation" (194). Discussing only Deronda's exit from the text in her chapter on *Daniel Deronda,* Meyer does not treat the extraordinary textual ease with which the intelligent heiress Catherine Arrowpoint marries for love to the Jewish musician, Herr Klesmer. I suggest then, that the novel's treatment of the morally problematic Gwendolen Harleth and the "expulsion" of the Jewish Daniel Deronda does not alone account for Eliot's representation of Judaism in the novel. We must ask why Eliot included the Arrowpoint-Klesmer subplot, a seamless example of intermarriage without the conver-

sion of Klesmer to Christianity, in the novel which is so engaged with separating its morally problematic heroine from its Othered protagonist.

17. Ali Behdad, *Belated Travelers: Orientalism in the Age of Colonial Dissolution* (Durham: Duke University Press, 1994), 82–83. I will return to Behdad's characterization of the English women of the "club" later in this chapter.

18. Yeğenoğlu, 91. Montagu is quoted in Yeğenoğlu, 91.

19. Behdad, 84.

20. Christopher Castiglia, *Bound and Determined: Captivity, Culture-Crossing, and White Womanhood from Mary Rowlandson to Patty Hearst* (Chicago: University of Chicago Press, 1996), 158.

21. Elaine Showalter, *Sexual Anarchy: Gender and Culture at the Fin de Siècle* (New York: Viking, 1990) 59.

22. Michel Foucault, *The History of Sexuality*, vol. 1 (New York: Vintage Books, 1990), 48; Gilman, 223.

23. Patrick Brantlinger, "Nations and Novels: Disraeli, George Eliot, and Orientalism," *Victorian Studies* 35 (spring 1992): 255.

24. Ann Laura Stoler, *Race and the Education of Desire: Foucault's "History of Sexuality" and the Colonial Order of Things* (Durham: Duke University Press, 1995), 193.

25. In later chapters I will discuss the androgyny of Will Ladislaw and of the twin lovers from *The Thousand and One Nights,* to whom Daniel Deronda and Mirah Cohen are compared.

26. See Sandra Gilbert and Susan Gubar, *The Madwoman in the Attic: The Woman Writer and the Nineteenth-Century Literary Imagination* (New Haven: Yale University Press, 1984), 443–539.

27. For my understanding of the sexual politics of Victorian anthropology, I am particularly indebted to Anita Levy's book, *Other Women: The Writing of Class, Race, and Gender, 1832–1898* (Princeton: Princeton University Press, 1991).

28. Rosemarie Bodenheimer, *The Real Life of Mary Ann Evans* (Ithaca: Cornell University Press, 1994), 50.

29. Ibid., 38. I refer only in part here to the fiction of a male voice in the pseudonym "George Eliot." The complexity of Eliot's narrative voice that I wish to develop follows Rosemarie Bodenheimer's brilliant reading of the many "shadowy interlocuters" who make up the Eliot narrator. See also 50, 49. In her discussion of "Amos Barton," Bodenheimer aptly proves this point. Here "the reader is addressed affectionately, but as a child," or "as a lesser or narrower being who has entirely missed the point of the narrator's immersion in the story" (50).

30. Gordon Haight, *The George Eliot Letters* (London: Yale University Press), 1:246 (hereafter cited in the text as *GEL*).

31. George Eliot, *The Impressions of Theophrastus Such,* ed. Nancy Henry (Iowa City: University of Iowa Press, 1994), vii, 136 (hereafter cited in the text as *ITS*).

32. Bodenheimer, *Real Life*, 49.

33. Susan Meyer, *Imperialism* (Ithaca: Cornell University Press, 1996), 192, 193.

34. Anderson, 39.

35. I am following Bodenheimer's example here, identifying George Eliot by the names she chose to be called at particular points in her life. Eliot's many names: MaryAnn, Mary Ann, Marian, Polly, Mater, and, of course, her pseudonym, all point to the richness and complexity of her identity.

36. On the Indian Mutiny, see Nancy Paxton's *Writing Under the Raj: Gender, Race, and Rape in the British Colonial Imagination, 1830–1947* (New Jersey: Rutgers University Press, 1999). And on the British *literati*'s partisan critiques of the Jamaican Uprising, see George H. Ford, "The Governor Eyre Case in England," *University of Toronto Quarterly* 17 (1948): 219–33.

37. In "The Governor Eyre Case in England," George H. Ford writes that the group of "leading conservative writers" provided "Eyre with his most valuable support" (226). The group included "Carlyle (as chairman), Ruskin . . . Charles Kingsley" and "received support from Dickens, Tennyson, and later J. A. Froude. Even Matthew Arnold seems to have given his more discreet blessing to it" (226).

38. Said, *Orientalism*, 14.

39. Nancy Henry, "George Eliot's Investments in the Colonies" (paper presented at the Interdisciplinary Nineteenth-Century Studies Annual Conference, Loyola University, April 17, 1998). Henry quotes from George Henry Lewes's journal, 1860, in which he wrote that he "undertook to purchase 95 shares in the Great Indian Peninsular Railway for Polly. For £1825 she gets £1900 worth of stock guaranteed 5%," (see Rosemary Ashton, *George Henry Lewes: A Life* [New York: Oxford University Press, 1991], 210). Henry's work on Eliot's investments is forthcoming in *George Eliot and the British Empire* (Cambridge: Cambridge University Press, 2002).

40. See Eliot, *The Journals of George Eliot* (Cambridge: Cambridge University Press, 1998), 150.

41. Henry, "Investments," 2. Nancy Henry argues that for us to read Eliot's investments as "a straightforward mode of complicity" with "imperialist expansion" and "racist oppression" is "anachronistic because imperialism, as a totalizing term applying to the British colonies, did not exist as a concept which anyone in the mid-Victorian period could recognize or criticize; while Eliot opposed brutality, she did not view the empire *per se* as an evil to be economically undermined. Had Eliot conceptualized British imperialism as a coherent ideology and opposed it on moral grounds she might have been sensitive to her own economic complicity. Her fiction reveals a similar pattern of thinking—the renouncing of commodities based on the knowledge of their production, or even the history of their possession" (2).

42. There were many ways in which Marian Evans and George Henry

Lewes were not "average." However, their possession of some earned wealth and its investment, their need to find suitable, respectable occupations for his children, and their support of a large extended family was certainly not unusual in Victorian England.

43. Henry, 7.

44. See Anderson, 54.

45. Gates, 5.

46. Eliot's Theophrastus is here quoting popular opinion which he undermines with the following: "There is truth in these views. . . . But it is rather too late for liberal pleaders to urge them in a merely vituperative sense" (146). Theophrastus urges the nation of England not "to hinder people of other blood than our own from getting the advantage of dwelling among us" (147).

47. Anderson, 57.

48. Anderson, 39–40.

49. Behdad, 83.

50. George Henry Lewes, "Uncivilised Man," *Blackwood's Edinburgh Magazine* 89 (1861): 28.

51. Said, *Orientalism,* 161.

52. See Eliot, *Selected Essays, Poems, and Other Writings* (New York: Penguin Classics, 1990), 380.

53. Walter Scott, *Ivanhoe* (New York: Penguin Classics, 1986), 83.

54. William Acton, qtd. in Pat Jalland, *Women from Birth to Death: The Female Life Cycle in Britain: 1830–1914* (Atlantic Highlands, N. J.: Humanities Press International, 1986), 216.

55. James Kincaid, *Child-Loving: The Erotic Child in Victorian Culture* (New York: Routledge, 1992), 180, 154.

56. Scott, 44, 45, 60.

57. Behdad, 83.

58. Lewes, 29.

59. The ethnographers Eliot studied in preparation for writing *The Spanish Gypsy* imagined that the Gypsies had originated in Africa.

60. Showalter, *Sexual Anarchy,* 59–60.

61. Gillian Beer, *Darwin's Plots: Evolutionary Narrative in Darwin, George Eliot, and Nineteenth-Century Fiction* (Boston: Routledge & Kegan Paul, 1983), 161.

62. Gayatri Chakravorty Spivak, "Three Women's Texts and a Critique of Imperialism," in *"Race," Writing, and Difference,* 270.

63. Nancy Armstrong, *Desire and Domestic Fiction: A Political History of the Novel* (Oxford: Oxford University Press, 1987), 56.

64. Polhemus, 187.

65. Said, *Orientalism,* 14.

66. Brantlinger, "Nations and Novels," 268.

67. Elaine Showalter, ed., *The New Feminist Criticism: Essays on Women, Literature, and Theory* (New York: Pantheon, 1985), 197.

68. Patrick Brantlinger, *Rule of Darkness: British Literature and Imperialism, 1830–1914* (Ithaca: Cornell University Press, 1988), 44.

69. Herbert Spencer, *The Principles of Sociology* (Westport, Conn.: Greenwood Press, 1975), 1:757

70. Elizabeth Fee, "The Sexual Politics of Victorian Social Anthropology," in *Clio's Consciousness Raised: New Perspectives in the History of Women,* ed. Mary Hartman and Lois W. Banner (New York: Harper Colophon, 1974), 87.

71. Spencer, 1:629.

72. Fee, 100.

73. Fee, 101.

74. Nancy L. Paxton, *George Eliot and Herbert Spencer: Feminism, Evolutionism, and the Reconstruction of Gender* (Princeton: Princeton University Press, 1991), 70, 71, 161.

75. Levy, 109, 111, 109. See Gilman, 245; Levy, 80, 111.

76. Cora Kaplan, "Wild Nights: Pleasure/Sexuality/Feminism," in her *Sea Changes: Essays on Culture and Feminism* (London: Verso, 1986), 62.

77. George Eliot, "Mr. Gilfil's Love Story," in George Eliot's *Scenes of Clerical Life* (New York: Penguin Classics, 1989), 146.

78. Levy, 77.

79. George Eliot, *The Spanish Gypsy* 21, 25 (New York: Belford, Clarke, & Co., 1885), 180.

80. George Eliot, *Middlemarch,* ed. Bert G. Hornback (New York: W. W. Norton & Co., Inc., 2000), 527, 155, 203.

81. Dorothea Barrett, *Vocation and Desire: George Eliot's Heroines* (New York: Routledge, 1989), 134.

82. Adrienne Munich, *Andromeda's Chains: Gender and Interpretation in Victorian Literature and Art* (New York: Columbia University Press, 1989), 23.

83. bell hooks, *Black Looks: Race and Representation* (Boston: Southend Press, 1990), 159–160.

84. George Eliot, *Daniel Deronda* (New York: Penguin Classics, 1989), 758.

85. Spivak, 262.

86. Said, *Culture and Imperialism* (New York: Alfred A. Knopf, 1993), 79.

87. D. A. Miller, *Narrative and Its Discontents: Problems of Closure in the Traditional Novel* (Princeton: Princeton University Press, 1981), 122.

88. Said, *Culture and Imperialism,* 79.

89. Miller, 188.

90. Said, *Culture and Imperialism,* 162.

91. Ibid., 81.

92. Said, *Orientalism,* 169.

93. Karen Newman, "'And Wash the Ethiop White': Femininity and the Monstrous in *Othello*," in *Shakespeare Reproduced: The Text in History and Ideology*, ed. Jean Howard (New York: Methuen, 1987), 145.

NOTES TO CHAPTER 2

1. George Eliot, "The Brother and Sister Sonnets" (hereafter cited in the text as "B & S"), in Eliot, *Selected Essays, Poems, and Other Writings* (New York: Penguin Classics, 1990), 4.9, 4.14, 5.3.

2. Heinrich Moritz Gottlieb Grellmann, *Dissertation on the Gipsies, being an historical enquiry concerning the manner of life, economy, customs and conditions of these people in Europe and their origin* (London: P. Elmsley, 1787), 23. Of the people whom Eliot termed "Gypsies," many now define themselves as "travelers." I use the term "Gypsy" with the understanding that it is Eliot's term, one that implies an ethnic descent from Egypt which many travelers deny.

3. George Eliot, *The Spanish Gypsy* (New York: Belford, Clarke, & Co., 1885), 327 (hereafter cited in the text as *TSG*).

4. Sharon Aronofsky Weltman discusses Victorian representations of the "laying on of hands" in her essay, "'Be No More Housewives but Queens': Queen Victoria and Ruskin's Domestic Mythology," in *Remaking Queen Victoria*, ed. Margaret Homans and Adrienne Munich (Cambridge: Cambridge University Press, 1997), 118–119.

5. George Eliot, *The Mill on the Floss* (New York: Penguin Classics, 1989), 168 (hereafter cited in the text as *TMF*).

6. See Kimberly VanEsveld Adams's *Our Lady of Victorian Feminism: The Madonna in the Work of Anna Jameson, Margaret Fuller, and George Eliot* (Athens: Ohio University Press, 2001), 110–14; Carol Mavor, "To Make Mary: Julia Margaret Cameron's Photographs of Altered Madonnas," in her *Pleasures Taken: Performances of Sexuality and Loss in Victorian Photographs* (Durham: Duke University Press, 1995), 46–69; and Reina Lewis, *Gendering Orientalism: Race, Femininity, and Representation* (New York: Routledge, 1996), 106.

7. See Audrey Carr Shields, *Gypsy Stereotypes in Victorian Literature* (Ph.D. diss., New York University, 1993), 25–26.

8. See Edward Said's discussion of despotism in *Orientalism* (New York: Vintage Books, 1979); and Meyda Yeğenoğlu's discussion of the gendering of despotism and tyranny in her *Colonial Fantasies: Towards a Feminist Reading of Orientalism* (New York: Cambridge University Press, 1998). By "maternalism" I refer to that ideology which espouses the essential nature of women as nurturing through a symbolic or physical process of reproduction. Maternalism is a system of thought that values women first as mothers and promotes a "child-centered" or "dyadic" maternity that may elide or overwhelm the subjectivity of mothers themselves. See Linda M. Blum, *At the Breast: Ideologies of Breastfeeding and Motherhood in the Contemporary United*

*States* (Boston: Beacon Press, 1999), 23. See also Susan Greenfield's discussion of "woman's social purpose . . . defined in terms of the bearing, nurturing, and educating of children" in the early modern period in her introduction to *Inventing Maternity: Politics, Science, and Literature, 1650-1865*, ed. Susan Greenfield and Carol Barash (Lexington: University Press of Kentucky, 1999), 1-33.

9. As I shall demonstrate later, however, the average nonroyal Gypsy rarely displays this idealized loyalty or maternalism. Victorian anthropologists record the "baseness" of untitled Gypsies and their women.

10. Weltman, 105-22; 110. Weltman contrasts Victorian "woman worship" as it was represented in the domestic ideology of Coventry Patmore's "Angel in the House," with Ruskin's potentially radical urging of women to "use their influence in economic and political matters" (113).

11. Ibid.

12. John Ruskin, "Of Queens' Gardens," *Sesame and Lilies*, in *The Complete Works of John Ruskin* (New York: Kelmscott Society Publishers, 1880), 50.

13. Weltman, 119-20.

14. Ruskin, 50.

15. George K. Behlmer, "The Gypsy Problem in Victorian England," *Victorian Studies* 28 (winter 1985): 239.

16. Grellmann, 22-23.

17. Ian Duncan, "Wild England: George Borrow's Nomadology," *Victorian Studies* 41 (spring 1998): 381-401.

18. Ibid., 381.

19. Matthew Arnold, "The Scholar Gipsy," in *The Broadview Anthology of Victorian Poetry and Poetic Theory*, ed. Thomas J. Collins and Vivienne J. Rundle (Orchard Park, N.Y.: Broadview Press, 1999), 727-32, ll. 203-05.

20. Grellmann, 8.

21. Ibid., 34.

22. Deborah Epstein Nord, "'Marks of Race': Gypsy Figures and Eccentric Femininity in Nineteenth-Century Women's Writing," *Victorian Studies* 41 (winter 1998): 189.

23. John Cross, *George Eliot's Life as Related in Her Letters and Journals* (London: Blackwood & Sons, 1885).

24. Shields, 92.

25. Nord, 189, 192.

26. Ibid., 189.

27. *Oxford English Dictionary* (Oxford: Oxford University Press, 1971) 7th ed., s.v. "lore."

28. In her *Writer's Notebook, 1854-1879, and Uncollected Writings* (ed. Joseph Weisenfarth [Charlottesville: University of Virginia Press, 1981]), Eliot twice records the skin color and racial origin of the tribe of Gypsies she has chosen to represent in *The Spanish Gypsy*. These are the Zincali, a tribe de-

scended from Africa which later emigrated to India, Persia, and then Spain. In a rush of excitement and discovery she hastily records "Zíncalo = the black men (of Sind or Ind!)." The next entry in her notebook repeats the observation, underscoring that the name of the tribe Zíncali "signifies 'the black men'" (94). Borrow, her source, is quite clear that the "countenances" of the Spanish Gypsies are "as dark as those of Mulattos . . . and in some few instances of almost Negro blackness" (298). It is evident that when he suggests that these people are "of savage ancestry" he means that they are of African descent (94).

29. Nord, 190.

30. Margaret Homans, "Eliot, Wordsworth, and the Scenes of the Sisters' Instruction," 8 *Critical Inquiry* (winter 1981): 230n, 240.

31. Weltman, 119.

32. George Eliot, *Scenes of Clerical Life* (New York: Penguin Classics, 1989), 147, hereafter cited in the text as *SCL*.

33. Caterina perhaps also begins Eliot's career-long difficulty in articulating embodied maternity. The list to follow is a long one, Hetty Sorrel will commit infanticide, Dorothea Brooke will nearly die in childbirth (an event the novel does not narrate), and Romola improves upon the mothering of her husband's children by her mistress.

34. Shields, 192.

35. See Shields on both novels by William Harrison Ainsworth and Hannah Maria Jones, 192–98, 194.

36. Deirdre David, "Getting Out of the Eel Jar: George Eliot's Literary Appropriations of Abroad," in *Creditable Warriors: 1830–1876*, vol. 3, *English Literature and the Wider World*, ed. Michael Cotsell (London: Ashfield Press, 1990), 266.

37. Mary Jacobus, "The Question of Language: Men of Maxims and *The Mill on the Floss*," *Critical Inquiry* 8 (winter 1981): 213.

38. Catherine Gallagher discusses the importance of this industrial rhetoric to the novel in her *Industrial Reformation of English Fiction: Social Discourse and Narrative Form, 1832–1867* (Chicago: University of Chicago Press, 1985): "[T]he metaphor [of white slavery] enfolded paradigms of freedom that became parts of the complex structure of both industrial social criticism and the fictional narratives that tried to embody that criticism" (5).

39. Nina Auerbach, *Woman and the Demon: The Life of a Victorian Myth* (Cambridge: Harvard University Press, 1982), 382.

40. Nord, 207.

41. See Jennifer DeVere Brody's fascinating discussion of this logic of presence and absence in *Impossible Purities: Blackness, Femininity, and Victorian Culture* (Durham: Duke University Press, 1998). Her discussion of minstrelsy argues the logic of self-constitution through appropriations of Otherness: "The white man becomes a subject through the subjection (as in

ridicule and subjugation) of the black. By giving a face to what is an abstracted, objectified, and actually absent black female, the white male creates and expropriates the black Other, thereby reproducing and supplementing white male identity" (84).

42. Susan Fraiman, "*The Mill on the Floss,* the Critics, and the *Bildungsroman,*" *PMLA* 108 (January 1993): 136–50.

43. Of the family romance, women, and Gypsy plots, Nord writes: "In the fantasy of social superiority, the male child takes revenge on the father in imagination. In the fantasy of social stigmatization, perhaps, the girl child rebels against—or erases—the mother as the model and reproducer of femininity and imagines a bond with an alien or exotic people that enables her to reinvent feminine identity" (4).

44. Susan Meyer, *Imperialism at Home: Race and Victorian Women's Fiction* (Ithaca: Cornell University Press, 1996), 158, 135.

45. Homans, 213.

46. Brody, 85.

47. Jenny Sharpe, *Allegories of Empire: The Figure of Woman in the Colonial Text* (Minneapolis: University of Minnesota Press, 1993), 3.

48. Homer, *The Odyssey* 6.135–141, trans. Albert Cook (New York: W. W. Norton & Co., Inc., 1974).

49. Ibid., 1:103

50. See Jacobus on Maggie's desire for an "incestuous reunion" with her brother, as well as on the chaotic swirl of her desires throughout the novel.

51. Sharpe, 3.

52. See A. S. Byatt's editorial comments on *Leonore* in her notes to *The Mill on the Floss* (675).

53. See Joy Kasson's discussion of Erastus Dow Palmer's *The White Captive* in *Marble Queens and Captives: Women in Nineteenth-Century American Sculpture* (New Haven: Yale University Press, 1990), 73–100.

54. In "Dinah's Blush, Maggie's Arm: Class, Gender, and Sexuality in George Eliot's Early Novels," *Victorian Studies* 36 (winter 1993): 155–78, Margaret Homans argues that Stephen Guest takes advantage of Maggie's poverty and her "low" station in life when he kisses her arm: "It is an important feature of the class meanings of this scene that Maggie protests against the kiss. To accept it uncomplainingly, much less to reciprocate it, would be the act of a lower-class woman such as Hetty [of Adam Bede], and Maggie's feeling of 'humiliation' ('what right have I given you to insult me?') makes it clear that she wishes to be understood as Stephen's equal" (176).

55. Brody, 85.

56. See Gallagher.

57. Weltman, 111, 105.

58. See Adams's discussion of the ending of the poem in *Our Lady of Victorian Feminism,* 200–208.

59. Ibid., 208.

60. Joe Snader, *Caught between Worlds: British Captivity Narratives in Fact and Fiction* (Louisville: University of Kentucky Press, 2000), 288.

61. Henry James, "The Spanish Gypsy," *North American Review* (October 1868).

62. Julia Kristeva, "Stabat Mater," in *The Kristeva Reader,* ed. Toril Moi (New York: Columbia University Press, 1986), 168.

63. Adams, 209.

64. Ludwig Feuerbach, *The Essence of Christianity,* trans. by George Eliot (Amherst, N.Y.: Prometheus Books, 1989), 91, 90.

65. Adams also discusses the Inquisition's representation of the Madonna as "Our Lady of Pain," 209.

66. Ibid.

67. Snader discusses the importance of British capture amongst the Spanish as providing narratives with "many motifs that will later stand as hallmarks of the captivity narrative, whether British or American." In such narratives, prisoners had to "endure the humiliating ritual of an inquisitorial *auto da fe,* and suffer the rigors of forced labor in what Europeans regarded as one of its most terrible instances, rowing a galley" (14).

68. George Eliot, *Daniel Deronda* (New York: Penguin Classics, 1989), 1.

69. See prologue, *The Spanish Gypsy* in *George Eliot's Works: Miscellaneous Essays and Complete Poems* (New York: Hovendon Co., 1885).

70. Mavor, 44–69, 48, 50.

71. See the end of *Middlemarch* and Judith Mitchell's reading of this trope in *The Stone and the Scorpion,* (Westport: Greenwood Press, 1994) 151.

72. Mavor, 56, 57, 59.

73. Behdad, 84.

74. Ibid., 94.

75. Yeğenoğlu, 94.

76. Nord, 205.


NOTES TO CHAPTER 3

1. George Eliot, *Felix Holt: The Radical* (New York: Penguin Classics, 1989), 85 (hereafter cited in the text as *FH).*

2. As Reina Lewis notes, the importance of such stable categories and the "separateness" of East and West in the representations of Orientalist ideology is the linchpin of Orientalist discourse: "The ongoing separation of the West and the East mediates any fundamental challenge to the imperial ideology that informs Orientalism." See Lewis's *Gendering Orientalism: Race, Femininity, and Representation* (New York: Routledge, 1996), 171. The term *Giaour* is one "of reproach applied by the Turks to non-Mussulmans, esp. Christians" (*Oxford English Dictionary* [Oxford: Oxford University Press, seventh edition, 1971], s.v. *Giaour).* The term *Hassan* refers to the Islamic

slaveowner in Byron's poem. It is a European corruption of the term "has-sassin" meaning "hashish eater" or "Moslem fanatic" (*OED*, s.v. "hassassin" and "assassin").

3. Philip Fisher, *Making Up Society: The Novels of George Eliot* (Pittsburgh: University of Pittsburgh Press, 1981), 1.

4. Joyce Zonana, "The Sultan and the Slave: Feminist Orientalism and the Structure of *Jane Eyre*," *Signs* 18 (spring 1993): 593.

5. Charlotte Brontë, *Jane Eyre*, ed. Richard J. Dunn (New York: W. W. Norton & Co., Inc., 1987), 236.

6. See Eliot's essay "Thomas Carlyle," in *Essays of George Eliot*, ed. Thomas Pinney (New York: Routledge & Kegan Paul, 1963), 213, and George Eliot's *The Mill on the Floss* (New York: Penguin Classics, 1989), 391.

7. Catherine Gallagher, *The Industrial Reformation of English Fiction: Social Discourse and Narrative Form, 1832-1867* (Chicago: University of Chicago Press, 1985), 258.

8. Rosemary Bodenheimer's *The Politics of Story in Victorian Fiction* (Ithaca: Cornell University Press, 1988); Gallagher's *Industrial Reformation of English Fiction;* and Suzanne Graver's *George Eliot and Community: A Study in Social Theory and Fictional Form* (Berkeley: University of California Press, 1984) have all studied her alliance of domestic and reform politics.

9. Edward Said, *Culture and Imperialism* (New York: Alfred A. Knopf, 1993), 81.

10. Fred C. Thomson, "The Genesis of *Felix Holt*," *PMLA* 74 (December 1959): 576.

11. Robin Sheets, "*Felix Holt*: Language, the Bible, and the Problematic of Meaning," *Nineteenth-Century Fiction* 37 (1982): 157, 147, 157.

12. George Eliot, *The George Eliot Letters*, ed. Gordon Haight, 9 vols. (New Haven: Yale University Press, 1954-78), 1:71.

13. George Gordon, Lord Byron, *Childe Harold's Pilgrimage*, in *The Poetical Works of Lord Byron* (New York: P. F. Collier, 1885), 4:7, 4:4.

14. Ibid., 1: xciii.

15. Ibid., 1:5.

16. William H. Marshall, *The Structure of Byron's Major Poems* (Philadelphia: University of Pennsylvania Press, 1962), 36.

17. Frederick Garber, *Self, Text, and Romantic Irony: The Example of Byron* (Princeton: Princeton University Press, 1988), 9.

18. In contrast refer to Edward Said's interest in Europeans such as Richard Burton's "sympathetic self-association" with Islam and the Orient as less "individualistic" than "preternaturally knowledgeable about the de-gree to which human life in society was governed by rules and codes," complex systems of power which appeared in social institutions and constructs. See Said's *Orientalism* (New York: Vintage Books, 1979), 195-97.

19. Benjamin Disraeli, *Tancred; or, The New Crusade* (Westport, Conn.: Greenwood Press, 1970).

20. Mitchell Leask, *British Romantic Writers and the East* (New York: Columbia University Press, 1993), 20, 21.

21. Ibid., 21.

22. Patrick Brantlinger, *Rule of Darkness: British Literature and Imperialism, 1830–1914* (Ithaca: Cornell University Press, 1988), 61.

23. Jean Fagan Yellin, *Women and Sisters: The Antislavery Feminists in American Culture* (New Haven: Yale University Press, 1989), 110.

24. Frederick Douglass, qtd. in Yellin, 110.

25. Benjamin Disraeli, *The Benjamin Disraeli Letters,* ed. J. A. W. Gunn (Toronto: University of Toronto Press, 1982), 1:174.

26. Editor's note, *FH,* 655 n. 11.

27. Caroline Franklin, *Byron's Heroines* (New York: Oxford University Press, 1992), 72.

28. Byron, "The Dream," in *The Poetical Works of Lord Byron* (New York: P. F. Collier, 1885), 475, 9:208.

29. Ibid., 474, 11:51–57.

30. Franklin, 34.

31. Byron, George Gordon, Lord, *Selected Prose* (New York: Penguin, 1972), 111.

32. Franklin, 34.

33. Mary Lyndon Shanley and Peter G. Stillman, "Political and Marital Despotism: Montesquieu's *Persian Letters,*" in *The Family in Political Thought,* ed. Jean Bethke Elshtain (Amherst: University of Massachusetts Press, 1982), 66.

34. Franklin, 35.

35. Said, *Culture and Imperialism,* 81.

36. Cora Kaplan, "Wild Nights: Pleasure/Sexuality/Feminism," in *Sea Changes: Essays on Culture and Feminism* (London: Verso, 1986), 32.

37. Yellin, 111.

38. Kaplan, 35.

39. See Reina Lewis's discussion of the gender politics of the "white odalisque" in art. The "frisson" comes "from the projection of the white wife (the licit object) into what amounts to a brothel situation (an illicit site): she is pitied but desired as the fantasy combination of Europe's splitting of female sexuality into both Othered desirousness and home chastity." See her *Gendering Orientalism,* 172.

40. Barbara Hardy, "Rome in *Middlemarch:* A Need for Foreignness," *George Eliot – George Henry Lewes Studies* 24–25 (September 1993): 9.

41. Gordon Haight, *George Eliot: A Biography* (New York: Penguin Books, 1986), 381.

NOTES TO CHAPTER 4

1. George Eliot, *Middlemarch,* ed. Bert G. Hornback (New York: W. W. Norton & Co., Inc., 2000), 444, 374, 373, 377, 444, 443 (hereafter cited in the text as *MM*).

2. J. Hillis Miller, "Optic and Semiotic in *Middlemarch"* in *George Eliot,* ed. Harold Bloom (New York: Chelsea House, 1986), 102.

3. In his *Rule of Darkness: British Literature and Imperialism, 1830–1914* (Ithaca: Cornell University Press, 1988), Patrick Brantlinger dates the beginning of the English novel's ability to critique empire with Conrad's *Heart of Darkness* and other "late Victorian" texts (39).

4. D. A. Miller, *Narrative and Its Discontents: Problems of Closure in the Traditional Novel* (Princeton: Princeton University Press, 1981), 122.

5. Jenny Sharpe, *Allegories of Empire: The Figure of Woman in the Colonial Text* (Minneapolis: University of Minnesota Press, 1993), 30.

6. D. A. Miller, *Narrative and Its Discontents,* 149.

7. U. C. Knoepflmacher, "Unveiling Men: Power and Masculinity in George Eliot's Fiction," in *Men by Women,* ed. Janet Todd (New York: Holmes Meier Publishers, 1981), notes other instances of androgyny in Eliot's fiction, not the least of which is the ambiguous gender of the narrative voice which "blends" conventional "masculine and feminine traits" (136).

8. Brody's discussion of the "maiden mulattaroon" in English fiction is, as she notes, similar to the narrative modeled by Scott's Rebecca. See Jennifer DeVere Brody's *Impossible Purities: Blackness, Femininity, and Victorian Culture* (Durham: Duke University Press, 1998), 22.

9. See Brody's prologue, *Impossible Purities,* 12.

10. Ibid., 598.

11. Yvette Abrahams, "Images of Sara Bartman: Sexuality, Race, and Gender in Early Nineteenth-Century Britain," in *Nation, Empire, Colony: Historicizing Gender and Race,* ed. Ruth Roach Pierson (Bloomington: Indiana University Press, 1998), 225.

12. Jeff Nunokawa, "The Miser's Two Bodies: *Silas Marner* and the Possibilities of the Commodity," *Victorian Studies* 36 (spring 1993): 274.

13. Walter Benjamin, qtd. in J. Hillis Miller, "Narrative and History," *ELH* 41 (fall 1974): 472.

14. Gayatri Chakravorty Spivak, "Three Women's Texts and a Critique of Imperialism," in *"Race," Writing, and Difference,* ed. Henry Louis Gates Jr. (Chicago: University of Chicago Press, 1986), 262.

15. Jerome Beaty, "The Forgotten Past of Will Ladislaw," *Nineteenth-Century Fiction* 13 (September 1958): 159–63.

16. Ibid., 162, 164, 163.

17. See Robert A. Greenberg, "The Heritage of Will Ladislaw," *Nineteenth-Century Fiction* 15 (March 1961): 355–58.

18. Thomas Pinney, "Another Note on the Forgotten Past of Will Ladislaw," *Nineteenth-Century Fiction* 17 (June 1962): 71, 73.

19. See Suzanne Graver, *George Eliot and Community: A Study in Social Theory and Fictional Form* (Berkeley: University of California Press, 1984); and D. A. Miller, *Narrative and Its Discontents*, 122.

20. Alexander Welsh, *George Eliot and Blackmail* (Princeton: Princeton University Press, 1988), 223, 224.

21. J. Hillis Miller, "Optic and Semiotic in *Middlemarch*," in *George Eliot*, ed. Harold Bloom (New York: Chelsea House, 1986), 224.

22. Welsh, 221, 223.

23. Bonnie Zimmerman, "'What Has Never Been': An Overview of Lesbian Feminist Criticism," in *The New Feminist Criticism: Essays on Women, Literature, and Theory*, ed. Elaine Showalter (New York: Pantheon, 1985), 210.

24. Sandra Gilbert and Susan Gubar, *The Madwoman in the Attic: The Woman Writer and the Nineteenth-Century Literary Imagination* (New Haven: Yale University Press, 1979), 530.

25. D. A. Miller, *Narrative and Its Discontents*, 149, 188, 187.

26. Cora Kaplan, "Wild Nights: Pleasure/Sexuality/Feminism," in her *Sea Changes: Essays on Culture and Feminism* (London: Verso, 1986), 52.

27. Dorothea Barrett, *Vocation and Desire: George Eliot's Heroines* (New York: Routledge, 1989), 134.

28. Adrienne Munich, *Andromeda's Chains: Gender and Interpretation in Victorian Literature and Art* (New York: Columbia University Press, 1989), 23.

29. Eve Kosofsky Sedgwick, *Between Men: English Literature and Male Homosocial Desire*, (N.Y.: Columbia University Press, 1985), 146.

30. Jeff Nunokawa, "The Miser's Two Bodies: *Silas Marner* and the Sexual Possibilities of the Commodity," *Victorian Studies* 36 (spring, 1993): 277.

31. Nunokawa, envisioning a more sexually conservative Eliot than I do, stresses that conservatism in his article "The Miser's Two Bodies." He argues that all Dorothea Brooke wants to do is "look" at Will Ladislaw and quotes their early encounters as proof (278). He does not read their final scene in which the two are drawn together and embrace during an erotically charged thunderstorm.

NOTES TO CHAPTER 5

1. George Eliot, *Daniel Deronda* (New York: Penguin Classics, 1989), 1, 882 (hereafter cited in the text as *DD*). See Matthew Arnold, *Culture and Anarchy* (Cambridge: Cambridge University Press, 1993), 99.

2. Goethe, "Hegire," Edward Said's translation, in *Orientalism* (New York: Vintage Books, 1979), 167.

3. Said *Orientalism*, 168.

4. Brantlinger, "Nations and Novels: Disraeli, George Eliot, and Orientalism," *Victorian Studies* 35 (spring 1992): 272.

5. Goethe, 203; by referring to Deronda's "past identity," I mean, of course, the "mistaken identity" of his youth when he believed himself to be a Christian. Deronda's spirituality is remade by Judaism which, after his dis-

covery of Mordecai, speaks to him with compelling and even familiar intensity.

6. Here I am referring to the "best self" as Matthew Arnold defines it in *Culture and Anarchy,* 99.

7. Sir Walter Scott, *Ivanhoe* (New York: Penguin Classics, 1986), 83.

8. Amanda Anderson, "George Eliot and the Jewish Question," *Yale Journal of Criticism* 10 (spring 1997): 40.

9. Katherine Bailey Linehan, "Mixed Politics: The Critique of Imperialism in *Daniel Deronda,*" *Texas Studies in Literature and Language* 34 (fall 1992): 324–25.

10. Jacob Press, "Same Sex Unions in Modern Europe: *Daniel Deronda, Altneuland,* and the Homoerotics of Jewish Nationalism," in *Novel Gazing: Queer Readings in Fiction,* ed. Eve Kosofsky Sedgwick (Durham: Duke University Press, 1997), 310, 306.

11. Karen Newman, "'And wash the Ethiop white': Femininity and the Monstrous in *Othello,*" in *Shakespeare Reproduced: The Text in History and Ideology,* ed. Jean Howard (New York: Methuen, 1987), 148, 152, 145.

12. Ibid., 152, 151.

13. Cynthia Chase, "The Decomposition of the Elephants: Double-Reading *Daniel Deronda,*" *PMLA* 93 (1978): 217, 215.

14. Sir Leslie Stephen, *George Eliot* (London: MacMillan, 1902), 188.

15. William Shakespeare, *Othello: The New Folger Library Edition* (New York: Washington Square Press, 1993), 1.3.333–34.

16. Ibid., 1.3.262–65,

17. Ibid., 3.3.293–96, 291.

18. Chase, 217.

19. Newman, 152, 151.

20. *Othello,* 1.1.124–25.

21. Newman, 153.

22. Patrick Brantlinger, in "Nations and Novels: Disraeli, George Eliot, and Orientalism," has commented on the effect of the "reverse Orientalism" of Eliot's novel (273). He writes that "romantic liberation from provincial confinement comes in the paradoxical form of Judaism and 'Oriental' mystery" (268). These are the elements Brantlinger suggests lure Deronda to the "choir invisible."

23. George Eliot, "The Brother and Sister Sonnets," in her *Selected Essays, Poems, and Other Writings* (New York: Penguin Classics, 1990), 429.

24. John Dunlop, ed. *Memories of Gospel Triumphs among the Jews during the Victorian Era* (London: S.W. Partridge, 1894), 344.

25. Anne Aresty Naman, *The Jew in the Victorian Novel: Some Relationships between Prejudice and Art* (New York: AMS Press, 1980), 161.

26. Eliot, "Dred," in *Selected Essays,* 380.

27. Nancy Pell, "The Fathers' Daughters in *Daniel Deronda,*" *Nineteenth-Century Fiction* 36 (March 1982): 424–45, 427.

28. Said, *Orientalism,*167.

29. Peter L. Caracciolo, ed., *The Arabian Nights in English Literature: Studies in the Reception of the Thousand and One Nights into British Culture* (New York: St. Martins Press, 1988), 22.

30. Fatma Moussa-Mahmoud, "English Travelers and the *Arabian Nights*," in Caracciolo, *Arabian Nights,* 95, Lady Mary Wortley Montagu, qtd. 96, 95.

31. Moussa-Mahmoud, 130.

32. Eliot's letters reflect her easy familiarity with the tales. A first-class train passage "is almost as good as having Prince Hussein's carpet" (*GEL,* 2: 65). While trying to write without distraction, she needs "Princess Parizade's cotton wool in my ears" (8: 239). An English derivation of a tale from the *Arabian Nights* is greatly admired in her 1856 reviews of George Meredith's *The Shaving of Shagput* in the *Leader* and the *Westminster Review.* Charles Dickens, Wilkie Collins, Alfred Lord Tennyson, Elizabeth Gaskell, and the Brontës joined George Eliot in their admiration for the exotic tales. As different from European fairy tales as an Ottoman palace is from a Victorian parlor, the tales provided the Victorian reader with a representation of the social structure, morals, and values of a non-Western, non-Christian society. The family relationships, class stratification, and sexual roles in the tales, for example, were perceived as fact. "Everything was exotic, yet somehow believable too, for the stories and all their trappings came out of a mysterious East where soft fountains and hanging gardens, harems and pleasure domes, sultans and scimitars, did most veritably exist" (Harry Stone, *Dickens and the Invisible World: Fairy Tales, Fantasy, and Novel-Making* [(Bloomington: Indiana University Press, 1979), 25].

33. Said, *Orientalism,* 167.

34. Michael Slater, "Dickens in Wonderland," in Caracciolo, *Arabian Nights,* 132, 133.

35. Nancy Pell, "The Fathers' Daughters in *Daniel Deronda,*" *Nineteenth-Century Fiction* 36 (March 1982): 432.

36. Edward William Lane, *The Thousand and One Nights: A New Translation from Arabic with Copious Notes by Edward William Lane* (London: Charles Knight, 1839–41), 2:73.

37. Ibid., 2:71, 73.

38. Ibid., 2:82, 86.

39. Ibid., 2:87, 90.

40. Ibid., 2:116, 136.

41. Michael Scrivener, "Forum," *PMLA* 108 (May 1993): 540.

42. Pell, 442.

43. Ibid., 451.

44. *Thousand Nights,* 81.

45. Ibid., 86.

46. Charles Lamb, *Selected Prose* (New York: Penguin Classics, 1985), 54.

47. Jean-Paul Sartre, *Anti-Semite and Jew* (New York: Schocken Books, 1965), 48.

NOTES TO EPILOGUE

1. Edward William Lane, *The Thousand and One Nights: A New Translation from Arabic with Copious Notes by Edward William Lane* (London: 1839–41), 2:82.

2. In her diary of 1866, Eliot writes that she "walked with G[eorge Henry Lewes] to the Water Colour and French Exhibitions. The only thing that rejoiced us was Henriette Browne's 'Nun.'" See *Journals of George Eliot*, ed. Margaret Harris and Judith Johnson (Cambridge: Cambridge University Press, 1998), 128.

3. George Eliot, *Daniel Deronda* (New York: Penguin Classics, 1989), 41, 35 41, 42, 43.

4. Deirdre David, *Rule Britannia: Women, Empire, and Victorian Writing* (Ithaca: Cornell University Press, 1995), 206.

# Bibliography

Abrahams, Yvette. "Images of Sara Bartman: Sexuality, Race, and Gender in Early Nineteenth-Century Britain." In *Nation, Empire, Colony: Historicizing Gender and Race,* ed. Ruth Roach Pierson, 220–36. Bloomington: Indiana University Press, 1998.

Adams, Kimberly VanEsveld. *Our Lady of Victorian Feminism: The Madonna in the Work of Anna Jameson, Margaret Fuller, and George Eliot.* Athens: Ohio University Press, 2001.

Anderson, Amanda. "George Eliot and the Jewish Question." *Yale Journal of Criticism* 10 (spring 1997): 39–61.

Arac, Jonathan, and Harriet Ritvo, eds. *Macropolitics of Nineteenth-Century Literature: Nationalism, Exoticism, Imperialism.* Philadelphia: University of Pennsylvania Press, 1991.

Armstrong, Nancy. *Desire and Domestic Fiction: A Political History of the Novel.* Oxford: Oxford University Press, 1987.

Arnold, Matthew. *Culture and Anarchy.* Cambridge: Cambridge University Press, 1993.

———. "The Scholar Gipsy." In *The Broadview Anthology of Victorian Poetry and Poetic Theory,* ed. Thomas J. Collins and Vivienne J. Rundle, 727–32. Orchard Park, N. Y.: Broadview Press, 1999.

Ashton, Rosemary. *George Henry Lewes: A Life.* New York: Oxford University Press, 1991.

Auerbach, Nina. *Communities of Women: An Idea in Fiction.* Cambridge: Harvard University Press, 1978.

———. *Private Theatricals: The Lives of the Victorians.* Cambridge: Harvard University Press, 1990.

———. *Woman and the Demon: The Life of a Victorian Myth.* Cambridge: Harvard University Press, 1982.

Baker, William. *George Eliot and Judaism.* Salzburg: Universität Salzburg, 1975.

Baker, William, ed. *The George Eliot–George Henry Lewes Library: An Annotated Catalogue of Their Books at Dr. Williams' Library.* New York: Garland Publishing, 1977.

Barrett, Dorothea. *Vocation and Desire: George Eliot's Heroines.* New York: Routledge, 1989.

Beaty, Jerome. "The Forgotten Past of Will Ladislaw." *Nineteenth-Century Fiction* 13 (September 1958): 159–63.

Beer, Gillian. *Darwin's Plots: Evolutionary Narrative in Darwin, George Eliot, and Nineteenth-Century Fiction.* Boston: Routledge & Kegan Paul, 1983.

Behdad, Ali. *Belated Travelers: Orientalism in the Age of Colonial Dissolution.* Durham: Duke University Press, 1994.

Behlmer, George K. "The Gypsy Problem in Victorian England." *Victorian Studies* (winter 1985): 221–53.

Betterton, Rosemary. *Looking On: Images of Femininity in the Visual Arts and Media.* London: Pandora, 1987.

Bhabha, Homi K. "Signs Taken for Wonders: Questions of Ambivalence and Authority under a Tree Outside Delhi, May 1817." In *"Race," Writing, and Difference,* ed. Henry Louis Gates Jr., 163–84. Chicago: University of Chicago Press, 1986.

Bivona, Daniel. *Desire and Contradiction: Imperial Visions and Domestic Debates in Victorian Literature.* Manchester: Manchester University Press, 1990.

Bloom, Harold. *George Eliot.* New York: Chelsea House, 1986.

Blum, Linda M. *At the Breast: Ideologies of Breastfeeding and Motherhood in the Contemporary United States.* Boston: Beacon Press, 1999.

Bodenheimer, Rosemary. *The Politics of Story in Victorian Fiction.* Ithaca: Cornell University Press, 1988.

——. *The Real Life of Mary Ann Evans.* Ithaca: Cornell University Press, 1994.

Borrow, George. *The Zíncali, or, An Account of the Gypsies of Spain.* London: J. Murray, 1843.

Brantlinger, Patrick. "Nations and Novels: Disraeli, George Eliot, and Orientalism." *Victorian Studies* 35 (spring 1992): 255–75.

——. *Rule of Darkness: British Literature and Imperialism, 1830–1914.* Ithaca: Cornell University Press, 1988.

Brody, Jennifer DeVere. *Impossible Purities: Blackness, Femininity, and Victorian Culture.* Durham: Duke University Press, 1998.

Brontë, Emily. *Wuthering Heights.* New York: Penguin, 1975.

Brontë, Charlotte. *Jane Eyre.* New York: W. W. Norton & Co., Inc., 1987.

Burton, Antoinette M. "The White Woman's Burden: British Feminists and the Indian Woman, 1865–1915." *Women's Studies International Forum* 13 (1990): 295–308.

Byron, George Gordon, Lord. *The Poetical Works of Lord Byron.* New York: P. F. Collier, 1885.

——. *Selected Prose.* Harmondsworth, England: Penguin Classics, 1972.

Carpenter, Mary Wilson. *George Eliot and the Landscape of Time.* Chapel Hill: University of North Carolina Press, 1986.

Carraciolo, Peter L., ed. *The Arabian Nights in English Literature: Studies in the Reception of the Thousand and One Nights into British Culture.* New York: St. Martin's Press, 1988.

Carroll, David. *George Eliot and the Conflict of Interpretations.* Cambridge: Cambridge University Press, 1992.

Casteras, Susan P. *Images of Victorian Womanhood in English Art*. London: Associated University Press, 1987.

Castiglia, Christopher. *Bound and Determined: Captivity, Culture-Crossing, and White Womanhood from Mary Rowlandson to Patty Hearst*. Chicago: University of Chicago Press, 1996.

Chase, Cynthia. "The Decomposition of the Elephants: Double-Reading *Daniel Deronda.*" *PMLA* 93 (1978): 215–27.

Chaudhuri, Nupur, and Margaret Strobel. "Western Women and Imperialism: Introduction." *Women's Studies International Forum* 13 (1990): 289–93.

——. *Western Women and Imperialism: Complicity and Resistance*. Bloomington: Indiana University Press, 1992.

Cheyette, Bryan. *Constructions of "the Jew" in English Literature and Society: Racial Representations, 1875–1945*. Cambridge: Cambridge University Press, 1995.

Cohen, William A. *Sex Scandal: The Private Parts of Victorian Fiction*. Durham: Duke University Press, 1996.

Cotsell, Michael, ed. *Creditable Warriors: 1830–1876*. Vol. 3. *English Literature and the Wider World*. London: Ashfield Press, 1990.

Crosby, Christina. *The Ends of History: Victorians and "The Woman Question."* New York: Routledge, 1991.

Cross, John. *George Eliot's Life as Related in Her Letters and Journals*. London: Blackwood & Sons, 1885.

David, Deirdre. "Getting Out of the Eel Jar: George Eliot's Literary Appropriation of Abroad." In *Creditable Warriors: 1830–1876*. Vol. 3. *English Literature and the Wider World,* ed. Michael Cotsell, 257–72. London: Ashfield Press, 1990.

——. *Rule Brittania: Women, Empire, and Victorian Writing*. Ithaca: Cornell University Press, 1995.

Dickens, Charles. *Oliver Twist: The Norton Critical Edition,* ed. Fred Kaplan. New York: W. W. Norton & Co., Inc., 1993.

Disraeli, Benjamin. *Tancred; or, The New Crusade*. Westport, Conn.: Greenwood Press, 1970.

——. *The Benjamin Disraeli Letters,* ed. J. A. W. Gunn. Toronto: University of Toronto Press, 1982.

Doezema, Elizabeth. *Reading American Art*. New Haven: Yale University Press, 1998.

Duncan, Ian. "Wild England: George Borrow's Nomadology." *Victorian Studies* 41 (spring 1998): 381–401.

Dunlop, John, ed. *Memories of Gospel Triumphs among the Jews during the Victorian Era*. London: S. W. Partridge, 1894.

Eagleton, Terry. *Criticism and Ideology: A Study in Marxist Literary Theory*. London: Verso, 1978.

Eisenbach, Artur. *The Emancipation of the Jews in Poland, 1780–1870*. Edited by Antony Polonsky; trans. by Janina Dorosz. Cambridge, Mass.: Institute for Polish-Jewish Studies and Basil Blackwell, 1991.

Eliot, George. *Adam Bede*. New York: Penguin Classics, 1989.

———. "The Brother and Sister Sonnets." In George Eliot, *Selected Essays, Poems, and Other Writings*, 426–36. New York: Penguin Classics, 1990.

———. *Daniel Deronda*. New York: Penguin Classics, 1989.

———. *Essays of George Eliot*, ed. Thomas Pinney. New York: Columbia University Press, 1963.

———. *Felix Holt: The Radical*. New York: Penguin Classics, 1989.

———. *The George Eliot Letters*, ed. Gordon Haight. 9 vols. New Haven: Yale University Press, 1954–78.

———. *George Eliot's Works: Miscellaneous Essays and Complete Poems*. New York: Hovendon Co., 1885.

———. *The Journals of George Eliot*, ed. Margaret Harris and Judith Johnson. Cambridge: Cambridge University Press, 1998.

———. *The Impressions of Theophrastus Such*, ed. Nancy Henry. Iowa City: University of Iowa Press, 1994.

———. *Middlemarch*, ed. Bert G. Hornback. New York: W. W. Norton & Co., Inc., 2000.

———. *The Mill on the Floss*. New York: Penguin Classics, 1989.

———. "Prologue," *The Spanish Gypsy*. In George Eliot's Works: Miscellaneous Essays and Complete Poems. New York: The Hovendon Co., 1885.

———. Review of "The Shaving of Shagpat" by George Meredith. *The Leader* 7 (5 Jan. 1856): 15–17.

———. Review of "The Shaving of Shagpat" by George Meredith. *The Westminster Review* 65 (April 1856): 638–39.

———. *Scenes of Clerical Life*. New York: Penguin Classics, 1989.

———. *Selected Essays, Poems, and Other Writings*. New York: Penguin Classics, 1990.

———. *The Spanish Gypsy*. New York: Belford, Clarke, & Co., 1885.

———. *A Writer's Notebook: 1854–1879, and Uncollected Writings*, ed. Joseph Wiesenfarth. Charlottesville: University of Virginia Press, 1981.

Fee, Elizabeth. "The Sexual Politics of Victorian Social Anthropology." In *Clio's Consciousness Raised: New Perspectives in the History of Women*, ed. Mary Hartman and Lois W. Banner. New York: Harper Colophon Books, 1974.

Feverbach, Ludwig. *The Essence of Christianity*, trans. George Eliot. Amherst: Prometheus Books, 1989.

Finke, Laura. "The Rhetoric of Marginality: Why I Do Feminist Theory." *Tulsa Studies in Women's Literature* 5 (fall 1986): 251–72.

Fisher, Philip. *Making Up Society: The Novels of George Eliot*. Pittsburgh: University of Pittsburgh Press, 1981.

Ford, George. "The Governor Eyre Case in England." *University of Toronto Quarterly* 17 (1948): 219–33.

Fraiman, Susan. "*The Mill on the Floss*, the Critics, and the *Bildungsroman*." *PMLA* 108 (January 1993): 136–50.

Franklin, Caroline. *Byron's Heroines.* New York: Oxford University Press, 1992.

Foucault, Michel. *The History of Sexuality.* Vol. 1. Trans. Robert Hurley. New York: Vintage Books, 1990.

Garber, Frederick. *Self, Text, and Romantic Irony: The Example of Byron.* Princeton: Princeton University Press, 1988.

Gallagher, Catherine. "George Eliot and *Daniel Deronda:* The Prostitute and the Jewish Question." In *Sex, Politics, and Science in the Nineteenth-Century,* ed. Ruth Bernard Yeazell. Baltimore: Johns Hopkins University Press, 1986.

——. *The Industrial Reformation of English Fiction: Social Discourse and Narrative Form, 1832–1867.* Chicago: University of Chicago Press, 1985.

Gaskell, Elizabeth. *The Life of Charlotte Bronte.* London: Dutton, 1971.

Gates, Henry Louis Jr., ed. *"Race," Writing, and Difference.* Chicago: University of Chicago Press, 1986.

Gilbert, Sandra, and Susan Gubar. *The Madwoman in the Attic: The Woman Writer and the Nineteenth-Century Literary Imagination.* New Haven: Yale University Press, 1979.

Gilman, Sander L. "Black Bodies, White Bodies: Toward an Iconography of Female Sexuality in Late Nineteenth-Century Art, Medicine, and Literature." In *"Race," Writing, and Difference,* ed. Henry Louis Gates Jr., 223–61. Chicago: University of Chicago Press, 1986.

Girouard, Mark. *Life in the English Countryhouse: A Social and Architectural History.* New Haven: Yale University Press, 1978.

Goethe, Johann Wolfgang von. "Hegire." Translated by Edward Said. In *Orientalism* by Edward Said. New York: Vintage Books, 1979.

Graver, Suzanne. *George Eliot and Community: A Study in Social Theory and Fictional Form.* Berkeley: University of California Press, 1984.

Greenberg, Robert A. "The Heritage of Will Ladislaw." *Nineteenth-Century Fiction* 15 (March 1961): 355–58.

Greenfield, Susan, and Carol Barash, eds. *Inventing Maternity: Politics, Science, and Literature, 1650–1865.* Lexington: University Press of Kentucky, 1999.

Grellmann, Heinrich Moritz Gottlieb. *Dissertation on the Gipsies, being an historical enquiry concerning the manner of life, economy, customs and conditions of these people in Europe and their origin.* London: P. Elmsley, 1787.

Haight, Gordon. *George Eliot and John Chapman; with John Chapman's Diaries.* New Haven: Yale University Press, 1940.

——. *George Eliot: A Biography.* New York: Penguin Books, 1986.

Hancock, Ian. "The Origin and Function of the Gypsy Image in Children's Literature." *The Lion and the Unicorn* 11 (April 1987): 47–59.

Hardy, Barbara. "Rome in *Middlemarch:* The Need for Foreignness." *George Eliot—George Henry Lewes Studies* 24–25 (September 1993): 1–16.

Hartman, Mary, and Lois W. Banner, eds. *Clio's Consciousness Raised: New Perspectives in the History of Women.* New York: Harper Colophon Books, 1974.

Henry, Nancy. "George Eliot's Investments in the Colonies." In *George Eliot and the British Empire*. Cambridge: Cambridge University Press, 2002.

Homans, Margaret. "Dinah's Blush, Maggie's Arm: Class, Gender, and Sexuality in George Eliot's Early Novels." *Victorian Studies* 36 (winter 1993): 155–78.

———. "Eliot, Wordsworth, and the Scenes of the Sisters' Instruction." *Critical Inquiry* 8 (winter 1981): 112–41.

Homans, Margaret, and Adrienne Munich, eds. *Remaking Queen Victoria*. Cambridge: Cambridge University Press, 1997.

Homer. *The Odyssey*. Translated by Albert Cook. New York: W.W. Norton & Co., 1974.

hooks, bell. *Black Looks: Race and Representation*. Boston: Southend Press, 1990.

Howard, Jean. *Shakespeare Reproduced: The Text in History and Ideology*. New York: Methuen, 1987.

Jacobus, Mary, "The Question of Language: Men of Maxims and *The Mill on the Floss*." *Critical Inquiry* 8 (winter 1981): 210–23.

Jalland, Pat. *Women from Birth to Death: The Female Life Cycle in Britain: 1830–1914*. Atlantic Highlands: Humanities Press International, 1986.

James, Henry. "The Spanish Gypsy." *North American Review,* October 1868.

Jones, Ann Rosalind. "Writing the Body: *L'ecriture féminine*." In *The New Feminist Criticism: Essays on Women, Literature, and Theory*, ed. Elaine Showalter, 361–77. New York: Pantheon Books, 1985.

Jordan, John O. "The Purloined Handkerchief." In Charles Dickens, *Oliver Twist: The Norton Critical Edition*, ed. Fred Kaplan, 580–608. New York: W. W. Norton & Co., Inc., 1993.

Kaplan, Cora. "Wild Nights: Pleasure/Sexuality/Feminism." In *Sea Changes: Essays on Culture and Feminism*. London: Verso, 1986.

Kasson, Joy S. *Marble Queens and Captives: Women in Nineteenth-Century American Sculpture*. New Haven: Yale University Press, 1990.

———. "Narratives of the Female Body: The Greek Slave," in Doezema, Marianne. *Reading American Art*. New Haven: Yale University Press, 1998. 163–189.

Kincaid, James. *Child-Loving: The Erotic Child and Victorian Culture*. New York: Routledge, 1992.

Knoepflemacher, U. C. "Unveiling Men: Power and Masculinity in George Eliot's Fiction," in *Men by Women*, ed. Janet Todd, New York: Holmes Meier Publishers, 1981.

Kristeva, Julia. *The Kristeva Reader*. Edited by Toril Moi. New York: Columbia University Press, 1986.

Lamb, Charles. *Selected Prose*. Edited by Adam Phillips. New York: Penguin, 1985.

Lane, Edward William. *The Thousand and One Nights: A New Translation from Arabic with Copious Notes by Edward William Lane*. 3 vols. London: Charles Knight, 1839–1841.

Lassner, Phyllis, Karen Alkalay Gutt, and Anita Goodblatt. "Forum." *PMLA* 10 (October 1992): 1281–82.

Leask, Mitchell. *British Romantic Writers and the East.* New York: Columbia University Press, 1993.

Levy, Anita. *Other Women: The Writing of Class, Race, and Gender, 1832–1898.* Princeton: Princeton University Press, 1991.

Lewes, George Henry. "Uncivilised Man." *Blackwood's Edinburgh Magazine* 89 (1861): 27–41.

Lewis, Reina. *Gendering Orientalism: Race, Femininity, and Representation.* New York: Routledge, 1996.

Linehan, Katherine Bailey. "Mixed Politics: The Critique of Imperialism in *Daniel Deronda.*" *Texas Studies in Literature and Language* 34 (fall 1992): 324–25.

Marcus, Stephen. *Representations: Essays on Literature and Society.* New York: Random House, 1976.

Marks, Sylvia Casey. "A Brief Glance at George Eliot's *The Spanish Gypsy.*" *Victorian Poetry* 21 (summer 1983): 184–90.

Marshall, William H. *The Structure of Byron's Major Poems.* Philadelphia: University of Pennsylvania Press, 1962.

Mavor, Carol. *Pleasures Taken: Performances of Sexuality and Loss in Victorian Photographs.* Durham: Duke University Press, 1995.

Mervat, Hatem. "Through Each Other's Eyes: The Impact on the Colonial Encounter of the Images of Egyptian, Levantine–Egyptian, and European Women, 1862–1920," in Chaudhuri 35–60.

Meyer, Susan. *Imperialism at Home: Race and Victorian Women's Fiction.* Ithaca: Cornell University Press, 1996.

Miller, D. A. *Narrative and Its Discontents: Problems of Closure in the Traditional Novel.* Princeton: Princeton University Press, 1981.

———. *The Novel and the Police.* Berkeley: University of California Press, 1988.

Miller, J. Hillis. "Optic and Semiotic in *Middlemarch.*" In *George Eliot,* ed. Harold Bloom. New York: Chelsea House, 1986.

———. "Narrative and History." *ELH* 41 (fall 1974): 455–73.

Miller, Nancy. "Emphasis Added: Plots and Plausiblities in Women's Fiction." *PMLA* 96 (January 1981): 36–48.

Mitchell, Judith. *The Stone and the Scorpion. The Female Subject of Desire in the Novels of Charlotte Brontë, George Eliot, and Thomas Hardy.* Westport: Greenwood Press, 1994.

Mitchell, Timothy. *Colonising Egypt.* Cambridge: Cambridge University Press, 1988.

Moussa-Mahmoud, Fatma. "English Travellers and the *Arabian Nights.*" In *The Arabian Nights in English Literature: Studies in the Reception of the Thousand and One Nights into British Culture,* ed. Peter L. Carraciolo, 95–110. New York: St. Martin's Press, 1988.

Munich, Adrienne. *Andromeda's Chains: Gender and Interpretation in Victorian Literature and Art.* New York: Columbia University Press, 1989.

Naman, Anne Aresty. *The Jew in the Victorian Novel: Some Relationships between Prejudice and Art.* New York: AMS Press, 1980.

Neufeldt, Victor A. "The Madonna and the Gypsy." *Studies in the Novel* 15 (spring 1983): 44–53.

Newman, Karen. "'And Wash the Ethiop White': Femininity and the Monstrous in *Othello.*" In *Shakespeare Reproduced: The Text in History and Ideology,* ed. Jean Howard. New York: Methuen, 1987.

Nochlin, Linda. *The Politics of Vision: Essays on Nineteenth-Century Art and Society.* New York: Harper Collins, 1989.

Nord, Deborah Epstein. "'Marks of Race': Gypsy Figures and Eccentric Femininity in Nineteenth-Century Women's Writing." *Victorian Studies* 41 (winter 1998): 189–210.

Novy, Marianne. *Engaging with Shakespeare: Responses of George Eliot and Other Women Novelists.* Athens: University of Georgia Press, 1994.

Nunokawa, Jeff. "The Miser's Two Bodies: *Silas Marner* and the Possibilities of the Commodity." *Victorian Studies* 36 (spring 1993).

*Oxford English Dictionary.* Oxford: Oxford University Press, seventh ed., 1971.

Parker, Andrew, et al., eds. *Nationalisms and Sexualities.* New York: Routledge, 1992.

Paxton, Nancy L. "Feminism Under the Raj: Complicity and Resistance in the Writings of Flora Annie Steel and Annie Besant." *Women's Studies International Forum* 13 (1990): 336–46.

———. *George Eliot and Herbert Spencer: Feminism, Evolutionism, and the Reconstruction of Gender.* Princeton: Princeton University Press, 1991.

———. *Writing Under the Raj: Gender, Race, and Rape in the British Colonial Imagination, 1830–1947.* New Brunswick: Rutgers University Press, 1999.

Pell, Nancy. "The Fathers' Daughters in *Daniel Deronda.*" *Nineteenth-Century Fiction* 36 (March 1982): 424–51.

Perera, Suvendrini. *Reaches of Empire: The English Novel from Edgeworth to Dickens.* New York: Columbia University Press, 1991.

Pierson, Ruth Roach. *Nation, Empire, Colony: Historicizing Gender and Race.* Bloomington: Indiana University Press, 1998.

Pinney, Thomas. "Another Note on the Forgotten Past of Will Ladislaw." *Nineteenth- Century Fiction,* 17 (June 1962): 69–73.

Pdhemus, Robert. *Erotic Faith: Being in Love from Jane Austen to D. H. Lawrence.* Chicago: University of Chicago Press, 1990.

Press, Jacob. "Same Sex Unions in Modern Europe: *Daniel Deronda, Altneuland,* and the Homoerotics of Jewish Nationalism. In *Novel Gazing: Queer Readings in Fiction,* ed. Eve Kosofsky Sedgwick, 299–329. Durham: Duke University Press, 1997.

Putzell, Sara M., and David C. Leonard. *Perspectives on Nineteenth-Century Heroism: Essays from the 1981 Conference of the Southeastern Nineteenth-Century Studies Association.* Potomac, Md.: Studia Humanitatis, 1982.

Ragussis, Michael. *Figures of Conversion: The "Jewish Question" and English National Identity*. Durham: Duke University Press, 1995.

Rich, Adrienne. "'Disloyal to Civilization': Feminism, Racism, Gynephobia." In *On Lies, Secrets, and Silence: Selected Prose, 1966–1978*, 275–310. New York: W. W. Norton & Co., Inc., 1979.

Rignall, John, ed. *George Eliot and Europe*. Brookfield, Vt.: Scholar Press, 1997.

Robbins, Bruce. "Death and Vocation: Narrativizing Narrative Theory." *PMLA* 107 (January 1992).

Ruskin, John. "Of Queens Gardens," *Sesame and Lilies* in the *Complete Works of John Ruskin*. New York: Kelmscott Society Publishers, 1880.

Said, Edward. *Culture and Imperialism*. New York: Alfred A. Knopf, 1993.

——. *Orientalism*. New York: Vintage Books, 1979.

Sartre, Jean-Paul. *Anti-Semite and Jew*. New York: Schocken Books, 1965.

Scott, Sir Walter. *Ivanhoe*. New York: Penguin, 1986.

Scrivener, Michael. "Forum." *PMLA* 108 (May 1993): 540–41.

Sedgwick, Eve Kosofsky. *Between Men: English Literature and Male Homosocial Desire*. New York: Columbia University Press, 1985.

——. "Nationalisms and Sexualities in the Age of Wilde." In *Nationalisms and Sexualities*, ed. Andrew Parker, et al., 235–45. New York: Routledge, 1992.

——, ed. *Novel Gazing: Queer Readings in Fiction*. Durham: Duke University Press, 1997.

Semmel, Bernard. *George Eliot and the Politics of National Inheritance*. New York: Oxford University Press, 1994.

Shakespeare, William. *Othello, The New Folger Library Edition*. New York: Washington Square Press, 1993.

Shanley, Mary Lyndon, and Peter G. Stillman. "Political and Marital Despotism: Montesquieu's *Persian Letters*." In *The Family in Political Thought*, ed. Jean Bethke Elshtain, 66–80. Amherst: University of Massachusetts Press, 1982.

Sharpe, Jenny. *Allegories of Empire: The Figure of Woman in the Colonial Text*. Minneapolis: University of Minnesota Press, 1993.

Shaw, Harry E. *Narrating Reality: Austen, Scott, Eliot*. Ithaca: Cornell University Press, 1999.

Sheets, Robin. "*Felix Holt:* Language, the Bible, and the Problematic of Meaning." *Nineteenth-Century Fiction* 37 (1982): 146–69.

Shields, Audrey Carr. *Gypsy Stereotypes in Victorian Literature*. Ph.D. diss., New York University, 1993.

Showalter, Elaine. "The Greening of Sister George." *Nineteenth-Century Fiction* 35 (December 1980): 292–311.

——. *A Literature of Their Own: British Women Novelists from Brontë to Lessing*. Princeton: Princeton University Press, 1977.

——, ed. *The New Feminist Criticism: Essays on Women, Literature, and Theory*. New York: Pantheon, 1985.

———, *Sexual Anarchy: Gender and Culture at the Fin de Siècle*. New York: Viking, 1990.

Slater, Michael. "Dickens in Wonderland." In *The Arabian Nights in English Literature: Studies in the Reception of the Thousand and One Nights into British Culture,* ed. Peter Carraciolo, 132–42. New York: St. Martin's Press, 1988.

Smith, Valerie. "Black Feminist Theory and the Representation of the 'Other.'" In *Feminisms: An Anthology of Literary Theory and Criticism,* ed. Robyn R. Warhol and Diane Price Herndl, 311–25. New Brunswick: Rutgers University Press, 1997.

Snader, Joe. *Caught between Worlds: British Captivity Narratives in Fact and Fiction.* Louisville: University of Kentucky Press, 2000.

Spencer, Herbert. *The Principles of Sociology.* Vol. 1. Westport, Conn.: Greenwood Press, 1975.

Spivak, Gayatri Chakravorty. "Three Women's Texts and a Critique of Imperialism." In *"Race," Writing, and Difference,* ed. Henry Louis Gates Jr., 262–80. Chicago: University of Chicago Press, 1986.

Steiner, George. *On Difficulty and Other Essays.* Oxford: Oxford University Press, 1978.

Stephen, Sir Leslie. *George Eliot.* London: MacMillan, 1902.

Stoler, Ann Laura. *Race and the Education of Desire: Foucault's History of Sexuality and the Colonial Order of Things.* Durham: Duke University Press, 1995.

Stone, Harry. *Dickens and the Invisible World: Fairy Tales, Fantasy, and Novel Making.* Bloomington: Indiana University Press, 1979.

Thomson, Fred C. "The Genesis of *Felix Holt.*" *PMLA* 74 (December 1959): 576–84.

Walkowitz, Judith R. "The Indian Woman, the Flower Girl, and the Jew: Photojournalism in Edwardian London." *Victorian Studies* 42 (autumn 1998).

Warhol, Robyn R., and Diane Price Herndl, eds. *Feminisms: An Anthology of Literary Theory and Criticism.* New Brunswick: Rutgers University Press, 1997.

Waxman, Barbara. "Ethnic Heroism: Matthew Arnold's and George Eliot's Gypsies." In *Perspectives on Nineteenth-Century Heroism: Essays from the 1981 Conference of the Southeastern Nineteenth-Century Studies Association* ed. Sara M. Putzell and David C. Leonard. Potomac, Md.: Studia Humanitatis, 1982.

Welsh, Alexander. *George Eliot and Blackmail.* Princeton: Princeton University Press, 1988.

Weltman, Sharon Aronofsky. "'Be No More Housewives but Queens': Queen Victoria and Ruskin's Domestic Mythology." In *Remaking Queen Victoria,* ed. Margaret Homans and Adrienne Munich, 105–22. Cambridge: Cambridge University Press, 1997.

Wills, Gary. "The Loves of Oliver Twist." In Charles Dickens, *Oliver Twist: The Norton Critical Edition,* ed. Fred Kaplan, 593–608. New York: W. W. Norton & Co., Inc., 1993.

Yeğenoğlu, Meyda. *Colonial Fantasies: Towards a Feminist Reading of Orientalism.* Cambridge: Cambridge University Press, 1998.

Yellin, Jean Fagan. *Women and Sisters: The Antislavery Feminists in American Culture.* New Haven: Yale University Press, 1989.

Zimmerman, Bonnie. "'What Has Never Been': An Overview of Lesbian Feminist Criticism." In *The New Feminist Criticism: Essays on Women, Literature, and Theory,* ed. Elaine Showalter, 200–25. New York: Pantheon, 1985.

Zonana, Joyce. "The Sultan and the Slave: Feminist Orientalism and the Structure of *Jane Eyre.*" *Signs: Journal of Women in Culture and Society* 18 (spring 1993): 592–617.

# *Index*